100 ESSENTIAL *Lincoln* BOOKS

100 ESSENTIAL *Lincoln* BOOKS

MICHAEL BURKHIMER

CUMBERLAND HOUSE

NASHVILLE, TENNESSEE

Published by
CUMBERLAND HOUSE PUBLISHING, INC.
431 Harding Industrial Drive
Nashville, Tennessee 37211

Cover design by Gore Studio, Nashville, Tennessee.

Library of Congress Cataloging-in-Publication Data
Burkhimer, Michael, 1973–
    100 essential Lincoln books / Michael Burkhimer.
        p. cm.
    ISBN 1-58182-369-X (pbk. : alk. paper)
    1. Lincoln, Abraham, 1809–1865—Bibliography. 2. Presidents—United States—Biography—Bibliography. 3. Presidents—United States—Biography—History and criticism. I. Title: One hundred essential Lincoln books. II. Title.
Z8505.B93 2003
[E457]
016.9737'092—dc22
                                                                    2003022181

ISBN 1-58182-369-X

1 2 3 4 5 6 7 8 9 10—08 07 06 05 04 03

To Beth
who not only takes care of our own children
but of many others as principal of a school
named for the Great Emancipator

CONTENTS

INTRODUCTION

HISTORIAN JAMES G. RANDALL famously asked in 1934, "Has the Lincoln theme been exhausted?" The short answer is no. In 1943 Jay Monaghan counted 3,958 books and pamphlets about Lincoln in the hundred-year period of 1839 to1939. Since then thousands more have appeared, and there is no sign of a slowdown. The 1990s witnessed a renaissance in Lincoln scholarship that has continued into the new century.[1]

How does the interested reader or collector identify what is truly important in this mass of material? Lincoln book lists have appeared on the Internet from various people giving their opinion on what are the best books. Of course, there is no scientific way of determining what makes one book more worthwhile than another. There is probably a core of books on almost every list, but total agreement is impossible. Besides, a list does not explain why a book is important; it merely names it.[2]

This present volume is my attempt to present one hundred books I deem "essential" for a Lincoln collection and explain why an individual book qualifies. One hundred is an arbitrary number and as time goes on more books could be added, but I wanted to give the reader a reasonable goal. I don't expect everyone to agree with these one hundred. Somebody is inevitably going to say, "How could he include book x and not y?" I understand this. My main hope is that someone reading this book will come across a book he or she hasn't read and be interested enough to seek it out. Luckily, most of these books are readily available in reprints or from dealers specializing in Lincoln and the Civil War.

I picked the books on what I considered relevant grounds. The one hundred are notable for their originality, use of primary sources, interpretations, writing style, and definitiveness. I wanted to separate "influential" from this list. A book like *Why Was Lincoln Murdered?* is both influential and incredibly bad at the same time. This 1937 book argued that Lincoln was killed at the behest of his secretary of war,

Edwin Stanton. Experts on the assassination, such as members of the Surratt Society, are still trying to fight the hold this absurd theory has on the public mind.[3]

The one hundred are in chronological order of their first publication. They range in date from 1866 to 2002. If books were published during the same year, the order is alphabetical according to the author. Reflecting the upswing in Lincoln scholarship in the 1990s, almost a third are from 1990 to the present. Each chapter concerns one book. I do not attempt to give a full synopsis of the book or a biography of the author. Instead, I try to point out its most salient points and explain what makes this book "essential" in understanding our greatest president. I also did not feel it was necessary to edit what I was quoting from a book. I have left what the authors said untouched.

Since Lincoln books cover a wide range of topics, these are classified according to genre. The genres I picked are *Assassination, Biography, Family and Genealogy, Historiography, The Lincoln Image, Places Associated with Lincoln, Prepresidential Years, Presidency, Psychology and Religion, Reminiscences,* and if a book didn't fit in one of those, *General.* Once again, there is nothing scientific about putting something in a particular genre. Some could have fit in two or three. Many times, in the end it came down to a simple value call.

Lincoln scholar Paul Angle first attempted a project like this in 1946. It has been almost sixty years since his *A Shelf of Lincoln Books: A Critical Selective Bibliography of Lincolniana* was published. With the large amount of scholarship that has appeared since then, a new version is needed. My sincere wish is this present volume will supply it.[4]

NOTES

1. Mark E. Neely Jr., *The Abraham Lincoln Encyclopedia* (New York: Da Capo, 1982), 255; Jay Monaghan, *Lincoln Bibliography, 1839–1939,* 2 vols. (Springfield: Illinois State Historical Library, 1943).
2. Abraham Lincoln Online and the Abraham Lincoln Bookshop (Chicago, Illinois) have their own respective lists.
3. Otto Eisenschiml, *Why Was Lincoln Murdered?* (Boston: Little, Brown, 1937).
4. Paul M. Angle, *A Shelf of Lincoln Books: A Critical Selective Bibliography of Lincolniana* (New Brunswick: Rutgers University Press, 1946).

100 *Lincoln* ESSENTIAL BOOKS

The Inner Life of Abraham Lincoln: Six Months at the White House

AUTHOR: Francis B. Carpenter
PUBLISHED: 1866
GENRE: Reminiscences

A MEMOIR that has personal anecdotes of Lincoln published so soon after his death is extremely valuable. Francis B. Carpenter had access to President Lincoln during the crucial year of 1864 and reported what he saw soon afterward. *The Inner Life of Abraham Lincoln: Six Months in the White House* is not without its faults and biases, but because of its immediacy and witness to some memorable scenes, it deserves to be called essential.

Carpenter was a warm admirer of Lincoln. He went to Washington to paint what he regarded as a great moment in Western civilization, the Emancipation Proclamation. To Carpenter, it was "an act unparalleled for moral grandeur in the history of mankind." Given access to the White House through congressional friends, Carpenter wanted to capture the great event on canvas. Fortunately for history, he recorded much of what he saw for the six months he was present from February to July 1864.[1]

Carpenter stressed his access to the inner sanctum of the government. He recorded Lincoln as saying, "We will turn you loose here." Carpenter went on to say, "[Lincoln] proved to be an 'open sesame' to me during the subsequent months of my occupation of the White House. My access to the official chamber was made nearly as free as that of the private secretaries, unless social business was being transacted." Lincoln humored Carpenter and told visitors who objected to him, "You need not mind him; he is but a painter."[2]

Despite this, there is evidence that Lincoln found Carpenter to be somewhat of a burden. In a letter written in 1867 Mary Todd Lincoln seems taken aback by Carpenter's claims. "This man Carpenter never had a dozen interviews with the late president and the latter complained more than once to me that C. presumed upon the privilege he had given C. . . . . C. intruded frequently into Mr L's office, when time was too precious to be idled."[3] Whether Lincoln felt negatively about Carpenter or not, he was always unfailingly kind to him, a fact that Carpenter records in the book.

Carpenter recalls many incidents that highlight Lincoln's compassion. When watching the Ninth Corps reinforce the Army of the Potomac, Lincoln could only sadly remark about the many thousands who would not be returning home. The Wilderness campaign started in May and lasted a month. Carpenter paints with words an unforgettable picture of Lincoln during this period: "During the first weeks of the battles of the Wilderness he hardly slept at all. Passing through the main hall of the domestic apartment on one of those days, I met him, clad in a long morning wrapper, pacing back and forth a narrow passage leading to one of the windows, his hands behind him, great black rings under his eyes, his head bent forward upon his breast,— altogether such a picture of the effects of sorrow, care, and anxiety as would have melted the hearts of the worst adversaries."[4]

Carpenter could record shocking incidents of Lincoln as well. These have great probability of being true because Carpenter would not go out of his way to invent negative stories about a man he so respected. He relates a surprisingly angry president at times. When Pennsylvania governor Andrew Curtin and Lincoln were discussing gold speculators, both were equally mad. They felt these financial dealings were hurting the cause of the Union. Curtin called them "a set of sharks." Lincoln said, "For my part . . . I wish every one of them had his devilish head shot off!" Carpenter even tells of an incident in which Lincoln physically ejected a man from his presence. A cashiered officer who had insulted Lincoln was grabbed by his collar and marched out of the room personally by Lincoln.[5]

Unfortunately, the book is not without its faults. There is too much filler. If Lincoln's wife is right about the amount of personal interviews with Lincoln, this is to be expected. The last part of the book simply reprints much about Lincoln that was in the popular media at the time. Also, Carpenter has a strong need to make Lincoln into a believing Christian. He relates every anecdote that would show this, no matter how dubious. He relates the highly unlikely episode the Reverend Francis Vinton of New York told of Lincoln embracing him after the death of Lincoln's son Willie and screaming that Willie was really "alive!"[6]

Take this book with a grain of salt then, but take it nevertheless. It is an important source for Lincoln's years in the White House. It offers a valuable record of Lincoln's actions both official and unofficial during that crucial year. Because of its faults, many Lincoln scholars in the past have dismissed the book. That is not the case anymore. Lincoln scholar Mark Neely calls it "an indispensable source." He goes on to say, "All Lincoln sources must be used with care, but unlike many of them, Carpenter's book *must* be used."[7]

NOTES

1. Francis B. Carpenter, *The Inner Life of Abraham Lincoln: Six Months at the White House* (Lincoln: University of Nebraska Press, 1995), 10–11.
2. Abraham Lincoln as quoted in ibid., 30; Carpenter, 30; Lincoln as quoted in ibid., 30.
3. Mary Todd Lincoln to Henry C. Denning, December 16, 1867, in Justin G. Turner and Linda Levitt Turner, *Mary Todd Lincoln: Her Life and Letters* (New York: Knopf, 1972), 464.
4. Carpenter, 82, 30–31.
5. Andrew Curtin as quoted in Carpenter, 84; Abraham Lincoln as quoted in ibid., 84; Carpenter, 106.
6. Carpenter, 116–19; Abraham Lincoln as quoted in ibid., 118.
7. Mark E. Neely Jr., introduction to Carpenter, xi; xi.

The Life of
Abraham Lincoln

AUTHOR: Josiah G. Holland
PUBLISHED: 1866
GENRE: Biography

AFTER LINCOLN'S assassination, Josiah G. Holland produced the
first serious biography of Abraham Lincoln. *The Life of Abraham Lincoln* fits in the hagiographic mold of biographies. One look
at the table of contents shows this. Some of the subtitles under
chapter 5 include, "Mr. Lincoln was a self-made man—Loyal to his
Convictions . . . He was Respected and Loved." Before dismissing
the book, it helps to remember there is more to it than that. Not a
simple homily, *The Life of Abraham Lincoln* influenced many Lincoln
books, and echoes of it are still felt today. Lincoln is still looked at as
a hero by most Americans, though perhaps not as uncomplicatedly
as Holland does.[1]

Holland was a New Englander who took his Puritanism seriously. He was editor of the *Springfield Republican* when he decided
to write a biography of Lincoln. Instead of merely patching some
speeches together and throwing in a little narrative, like many of
the biographies produced right after Lincoln's death, he did serious
research. He visited Illinois and interviewed a number of Lincoln's
associates. He was the first to introduce a wide audience to some of
the well-known facets of Lincoln's life, such as Lincoln's love of his
stepmother and his years at New Salem. Holland's section on the
White House is also complete and includes all the major events of
Lincoln's administration.[2]

The book's prose may sound flowery to a modern reader not attuned to Victorian sensibilities. Holland wrote of Lincoln's mother, "Long after her sensitive heart and weary hands had crumbled into dust, and had climbed to life again in forest flowers, he said to a friend with tears in his eyes: 'All that I am or ever hope to be I owe to my angel mother—blessings on her memory!'" One of the more amusing parts of Holland's book is his need to defend Lincoln's famed storytelling. Victorian men of achievement were supposed to be serious. While Lincoln's storytelling is celebrated today, Holland felt the need to explain it away.[3]

One is also struck by the constant references to Lincoln's Christianity. If Lincoln's law partner, Herndon, can be believed, Holland certainly had an agenda. Herndon reported that Holland had asked if Lincoln was a Christian. Herndon replied, "The less said about that the better." Herndon then remembered Holland saying with a wink, "Oh never mind. I will fix that!" Holland, a Sunday school teacher, was not going to let Lincoln go down in history as an infidel.[4]

Holland based his opinions of Lincoln's Christianity on a highly disputed interview Lincoln had with the Illinois superintendent of education, Newton Bateman, while Lincoln was president-elect. Holland quotes Bateman's story of Lincoln telling him about his personal religious beliefs. "Stopping at last, he said, with a trembling voice and his cheeks wet with tears: 'I know there is a God, and that He hates injustice and slavery. I see the storm coming and I know that His hand is in it. . . . I know that liberty is right, for Christ teaches it, and Christ is God.'" This interview is suspect for a number of reasons. First, it would be odd for Lincoln to unburden himself so openly to a stranger, especially on religious matters. Second, while Lincoln is on record believing in God, he never made a confession that Christ was God. He may have believed that Christ was God, yet none of his close friends remember him saying so. While this is an argument from silence, Herndon's quote from Holland leads one to believe Holland may have either exaggerated what Bateman said, or pushed him to say more than he remembered. What Holland has to say about Lincoln's religion tells us more about him than it does Abraham Lincoln.[5]

Holland's view of Lincoln's religion might have had a more lasting influence had not William Herndon taken such an interest in disproving Holland on this point. The public, however, preferred the Holland view of the matter. When published in 1866, the book was a bestseller. Eighty thousand copies were sold, which was a phenomenal number for the time.[6]

Holland's book is in large part a eulogy, yet that is to be expected so soon after the president's death. Lincoln and the Republican Party are seen as always caring and right. It is therefore tempting to dismiss Holland's book as having no current value in the study of Lincoln. This is unfair. Holland was charting unknown territory. Lincoln biographers since Holland have had a vast amount of secondary literature to work with. Holland had almost none, and he had to make the effort to go and interview those who knew Lincoln. Sadly, Holland's biography is not well read today. Still, as Lincoln scholar David Herbert Donald said, "It was by far the best of the early biographies, and even today it has a quaint flavor of the era." Those wanting to get the feel of the country shortly after the death of Lincoln need look no further than Holland's *Life of Lincoln*.[7]

NOTES

1. Josiah G. Holland, *The Life of Abraham Lincoln* (Springfield: Samuel Bowles and Co., 1866), 10.
2. Benjamin P. Thomas, *Portrait for Posterity: Lincoln and His Biographers* (New Brunswick: Rutgers University Press, 1947), 3–4.
3. Holland, 23.
4. William Herndon to Isaac Arnold as quoted in David Herbert Donald, *Lincoln's Herndon* (New York: Knopf, 1948), 212–13.
5. Holland, 237.
6. Merrill D. Peterson, *Lincoln in American Memory* (New York: Oxford University Press, 1994), 68.
7. Donald, 212.

Behind the Scenes, or, Thirty Years a Slave, and Four Years in the White House

AUTHOR: Elizabeth H. Keckley
PUBLISHED: 1868
GENRE: Reminiscences

*B*EHIND THE SCENES, *or, Thirty Years a Slave, and Four Years in the White House* offers an inside view of life in the White House during the Civil War. It is particularly important because it offers an intimate view of the Lincoln family from a confidante during the war. A drawback that prevents the book from being the one undisputed and most useful source for the Lincoln marriage during the war years is that the book was most likely ghostwritten by James Redpath or Hamilton Busbey. Even so, there are many nuggets of truth to be gleaned from the book, and its narrative is compelling at points.[1]

The book can be considered chiefly an autobiography. It is the story of Elizabeth Keckley, a slave born around 1818. Her book recounts the many horrors she underwent as a slave, sometimes in very graphic fashion. She recounts the separation of her father and mother, who are briefly reunited, only to be cruelly separated again on a master's whim a mere two hours later. She also speaks of when, at eighteen years of age, a man used to force her to strip in order to whip her for what appears to be his own sexual gratification. Her only child, a son, was the result of being raped by a white man in the neighborhood. Strangely, despite all this, Keckley can say, "Slavery had its dark side as well as its bright side."[2]

Keckley's skill as a seamstress bought her freedom and the freedom of her son. It also put her in a prominent place in Washington. One of her main clients was Varina Davis, wife of the later Confederate president. The book recounts a prewar Christmas spent with the Davises. When the Lincolns came to Washington, she was hired to make dresses for Mary Todd Lincoln, and they became confidantes.[3]

The book is generally sympathetic toward Mrs. Lincoln. There is a charming section on the banter between Mr. Lincoln and Mrs. Lincoln as they get dressed and ready to attend a formal function. This includes the unforgettable line Lincoln states when he sees her long train. "Whew! Our cat has a long tail to-night." However, Mary Todd Lincoln felt the book betrayed a trust. It is hard to argue with her when a chapter is titled "Candid Opinions" and contains many things Mary obviously told Keckley in confidence, such as her negative opinions on the various public figures of the era. Keckley also recounted Mary's embarrassing efforts to sell her clothes to raise money after the death of her husband and reprints personal letters exchanged between them. After the book's publication, Mary cut off contact with Keckley and referred to her derisively as that "colored historian."[4]

The book is used by many Lincoln biographers for its memorable scenes between the Lincolns. The most lurid of these are the scenes Keckley recounts after the death of Willie Lincoln, probably the favorite son of the Lincolns. She recalls Lincoln at the deathbed of his son. "He came to the bed, lifted the cover from the face of his child gazed at it long and earnestly, murmuring, 'My poor boy, he was too good for this earth. God has called him home. I know that he is much better off in heaven, but then we loved him so. It is hard, hard to have him die!'" Even if Keckley got the words wrong, she was still witness to Lincoln's awesome grief at the death of Willie. Much more controversial is the recounting of Lincoln taking his grief-stricken wife to a window and pointing in the direction of an asylum. Lincoln supposedly said, "Mother, do you see that large white building on the hill yonder? Try to control your grief, or it will drive you mad, and we may have to send you there." Historians will long debate the truth of that episode.[5]

There is another aspect of the book that might recommend it to people. It is very hard to find a book about Mary Todd Lincoln that is not either apologetic in tone or critical of her. This book is one of few that reach a sort of balance. (This does not mean it is any more accurate than other books. It is just more neutral.) The book does show Mrs. Lincoln's intense love of her husband, but it highlights her many faults as well, particularly her often intense jealousy of her husband. It also has the added benefit of being written by a woman who was a friend of Mrs. Lincoln and can offer a woman's perspective.

The book is fascinating literature, whether one is interested in Lincoln or not. It is interesting for its insights into both slavery and the role of Victorian women in society. Its novel-like writing style makes it an easy read. However, mostly it is valuable for its glimpse into the Lincoln family and marriage, whether one believes everything one reads or not.

NOTES

1. Mark E. Neely Jr., *The Abraham Lincoln Encyclopedia* (New York: Da Capo, 1982), 172.
2. Neely, 171; Elizabeth H. Keckley, *Behind the Scenes, or, Thirty Years a Slave, and Four Years in the White House* (New York: Oxford University Press, 1988), 22–23, 33–38, 39, 30.
3. Keckley, 63–75.
4. Abraham Lincoln as quoted in ibid., 101, 127–38, 267–331, 332–71; Mary Todd Lincoln to Rhoda White, May 2, 1868, in Justin G. Turner and Linda Levitt Turner, *Mary Todd Lincoln: Her Life and Letters* (New York: Knopf, 1972), 476.
5. Keckley, 103; Abraham Lincoln as quoted in ibid., 104–5.

The Life of Abraham Lincoln

AUTHOR: Isaac N. Arnold
PUBLISHED: 1884
GENRE: Biography

Isaac N. Arnold was a close friend of Lincoln's. He had been a fellow member of the Illinois Bar and both had practiced law together, sometimes on opposing sides. Arnold went on to become a Republican congressman for Illinois during the war and was a strong supporter of the Lincoln administration. He was even the defense attorney at the insanity trial of Mrs. Lincoln. This intimacy put Arnold in a privileged position to see many of the important events of the Lincoln administration he recorded in his *The Life of Abraham Lincoln*.[1]

Arnold was an unabashed admirer of Lincoln. He was strongly antislavery and saw Lincoln as the man chosen by God to end slavery. After the assassination, he wrote a book titled *The History of Abraham Lincoln and the Overthrow of Slavery*. The book is not a biography and was more about the history of the era. Arnold might not have written this biography were it not for Ward Hill Lamon's biography published in 1872. The biography, actually written by Chauncey Black using notes collected by Lincoln's law partner, William Herndon, was shocking to many. What bothered Arnold most was the idea in the book that Lincoln was an infidel and not a Christian.[2]

Arnold set out to correct the record. His feelings on Lincoln's religion were intense. He did not think they were even up for debate. "All his writings prove that he was a religious man, reverent, humble, prayerful, charitable, conscientious, otherwise his whole life was a sham, and he himself a hypocrite." Arnold continued, "When the unbeliever shall convince the people that this man, whose whole life was straightforward, truthful, clear, and honest, was a sham and a hypocrite then, but not before, may he make the world doubt his Christianity." Arnold backed all this up with the many references to God in Lincoln's papers. He also uses the dubious Newton Bateman interview in which Lincoln supposedly confessed his Christianity.[3]

Despite his disgust at the Lamon book, Arnold seems to have kept close connections with Herndon. Herndon wrote Arnold a letter soon after Lincoln's death, scolding him not to cover up things about Lincoln. Arnold did not heed Herndon's advice, for while he did use some of the more controversial parts of Herndon's lectures, he tempered many of his conclusions. For instance, he did give full credence to the supposed romance between Lincoln and Ann Rutledge during Lincoln's New Salem years. Herndon had given this romance and the effect of Ann's death on Lincoln a prominent place in his lectures. Arnold treats it more circumspectly though. As Arnold states, "The picture has been somewhat too highly colored, and the story made rather too tragic."[4]

Another point stressed throughout the book is Lincoln's intense antislavery stance. Arnold is on much safer ground here. The book would deserve to be called essential if only for the recording of an interview Arnold had with fellow congressman Owen Lovejoy and Lincoln. Lincoln was discussing his plan for gradual emancipation of the Border States. Lincoln said, "Oh, how I wish the border states would accept my proposition. Then . . . you, Lovejoy, and you Arnold and all of us, would not have lived in vain! The labor of your life, Lovejoy, would be crowned with success. You would live to see the end of slavery." Arnold also recalls and quotes many of the congressional debates regarding the passage of the Thirteenth Amendment, which abolished slavery. Still, he gives full credit to Lincoln: "Yes, and it was but the brave heart, the clear, sagacious brain, the indomitable but patient will of Abraham Lincoln that carried through the great revolution."[5]

One possible criticism of the book is that it contains a bit too much history and not enough biography. There are long sections dealing with the various campaigns of the Civil War that do not really touch on Lincoln in a significant way. Since Arnold did know Lincoln well, one could have hoped for more of Lincoln's words and a more intimate view of him. Arnold's rigid morality and Victorian sense of propriety probably prevented this.[6]

Modern commentators have often felt that the book is too simplistic and turns Lincoln into an abolitionist. After reading this book, Lincoln does seem to be faultless. Commentators also feel the book could have focused more on race. One stated, "Much of the work of twentieth-century biographers would be aimed at qualifying this influential but over-simple interpretation." While there is truth in that comment, one needs to take Arnold's book on its own terms. Too much "presentism" can be a danger. Here was a man who was earnestly antislavery and admired tremendously the man he saw as responsible for ending the monstrous injustice of the institution. On these terms, the book is worthwhile.[7]

NOTES

1. Mark E. Neely Jr., *The Abraham Lincoln Encyclopedia* (New York: Da Capo, 1982), 8–10.
2. Ibid., 9; James A. Rawley, introduction to Isaac N. Arnold, *The Life of Abraham Lincoln* (Lincoln: University of Nebraska Press, 1994), xii; Neely, 178; see Ward Hill Lamon, *The Life of Abraham Lincoln* (Boston: James R. Osgood & Co., 1872).
3. Arnold, 448–49.
4. William Herndon to Isaac Arnold, November 20, 1866, in *The Hidden Lincoln: From the Letters and Papers of William H. Herndon,* ed. Emmanuel Hertz (Garden City, N.Y.: Blue Ribbon Books, 1938), 36–39; Arnold, 42.
5. Abraham Lincoln as quoted in Arnold, 251, 366.
6. See especially Arnold, 271–341.
7. Neely, 10.

Reminiscences of Abraham Lincoln by Distinguished Men of His Time

AUTHOR: Allen Thorndike Rice, editor
PUBLISHED: 1886
GENRE: Reminiscences

REMINISCENCES FROM anyone can be misleading. There is a natural tendency to place more importance on oneself. With Lincoln, the temptation is to make oneself more intimate with him than one actually was. This happens a few times in Allen Thorndike Rice's *Reminiscences of Abraham Lincoln by Distinguished Men of His Time,* especially in the case of Benjamin Butler. However, there is just too much of value in this book for it to be ignored. It is true there are selections from people who do not really have much to offer, yet there are also selections that are invaluable to Lincoln scholarship.

The most important reminiscence in this book is from Frederick Douglass. Douglass's writing of Lincoln's dealings with him is so telling that his entry alone would make the book worthy of being deemed essential. Douglass's section is called "Lincoln and the Colored Troops." In it Douglass recounts a Lincoln fully in sympathy with raising black troops and with promoting them to officers. The most important part of this selection is the interview he had at the president's Second Inaugural reception. Douglass was being forced out of the White House because of his color when Lincoln intervened. Lincoln earnestly asked Douglass what he thought of his Second Inaugural Address. In fact, Lincoln asked twice to hear Douglass's opinion. Douglass told him it was a "sacred effort."[1]

There is one point Douglass makes that those who seek to portray Lincoln as a racist would do well to remember. "In all my interviews

with Mr. Lincoln I was impressed with his entire freedom from popular prejudice against the colored race. He was the first great man that I
talked with in the United States freely, who in no single instance
reminded me of the difference between himself and myself, of the difference of color, and I thought that all the more remarkable because
he came from a State where there was black laws."[2]

Close behind Douglass's selection in value is Leonard Swett's. Swett
was a personal friend of Lincoln and had traveled the legal circuit in
Illinois with him. Swett recounts an interesting conversation he had
with Lincoln as they rode together in a buggy across the Illinois
prairies in 1853. Most descriptions of Lincoln's early life are bleak,
and Lincoln himself referred negatively to it. Swett, though, recalls
Lincoln remembering it in a more positive fashion. "Mr. Lincoln told
this story as the story of a happy childhood. There was nothing of
want, and no allusions to want, in any part of it. His own description
of his youth was that of a joyous, happy boyhood. It was told with
mirth and glee, and illustrated by pointed anecdote, often interrupted
by his jocund laugh which echoed over the prairies." It is hard to reconcile this with Lincoln's other descriptions of his childhood. It may
be that Swett caught Lincoln in a sentimental mood. Swett goes on to
praise boyhood life on the frontier, so he may have put more of an
emphasis on the positive things Lincoln said to fit that.[3]

As already stated, the low point of the book is Benjamin Butler's
selection. He gives an account of a conversation that is so bizarre and
at odds with other events that it defies belief. Butler recounts himself
selflessly turning down the vice-presidency. Far stranger is Butler's
assertion that right before Lincoln's death, he asked Butler to use his
great skill to deport the freed slaves. Lincoln supposedly was worried
about the black troops forming "guerrilla parties" after the war.
Butler raises objections to Lincoln's plan, and Lincoln's death stops
the enterprise. Historians have rightly rejected this story. It makes no
sense when Lincoln at the time was publicly supporting the right of
suffrage for black veterans. The best answer to why Butler said what
he did is that he wanted to solidify his place as a friend to the freedman. In order to do this, he probably thought it would be wise to
hurt Lincoln's reputation in comparison to his own.[4]

There are other fine selections. The most moving is journalist Charles Coffin's picture of Lincoln as he heard about the death of his old friend from Illinois, Edward Baker, at the battle of Ball's Bluff in 1861. Lincoln and George B. McClellan had gone to the telegraph office to hear of the battle. "Five minutes passed, and then Mr. Lincoln, unattended, with bowed head, and tears rolling down his furrowed cheeks, his face pale and wan, his heart heaving with emotion, passed through the room. He almost fell as he stepped into the street, and we sprang involuntarily from our seats to render assistance, but he did not fall. With both hands pressed upon his heart he walked down the street, not returning the salute of the sentinel pacing his beat before the door."[5]

Biographers of Lincoln have long used this book as a source, and it is no wonder. Some of the material in the book is priceless. While some of it is not so good, the good far outweighs the bad. This book rightly deserves to be read and treasured as it has been for more than a hundred years.

NOTES

1. Frederick Douglas, "Lincoln and the Colored Troops" in *Reminiscences of Abraham Lincoln by Distinguished Men of His Time,* ed. Allen Thorndike Rice (New York: Harper and Brothers, 1909), 317–18, 322.
2. Douglas in ibid., 323.
3. Leonard Swett, "Lincoln's Story of His Own Life" in ibid., 80.
4. Benjamin F. Butler, "Some of Lincoln's Problems" in ibid., 267, 258. For an excellent rebuttal of what Butler says, see Mark E. Neely Jr., *The Abraham Lincoln Encyclopedia* (New York: Da Capo, 1982), 43.
5. Charles Carleton Coffin, "Lincoln's First Nomination and His Visit to Richmond in 1865" in Rice, 176–77.

Herndon's Lincoln: The True Story of a Great Life

AUTHORS: William H. Herndon and
Jesse W. Weik
PUBLISHED: 1889
GENRE: Biography

I T WOULD be impossible to overestimate the lasting effects of this
book on Lincoln biography. *Herndon's Lincoln: The True Story of a
Great Life* has served as a template for many of the biographies that
have appeared after it. Even more than one hundred years later, the
biography of Lincoln by David Herbert Donald starts exactly as Herndon's starts—with the famous carriage ride in which Lincoln confesses his mother was illegitimate. Chances are, any information about
Lincoln's early life found in subsequent biographies has this book as
its source. Whether he or she likes it or not, no biographer can ignore
this book, and no serious Lincoln collection can be without it.[1]

The book was controversial from its publication. It addresses
many issues Lincoln admirers felt would be better left forgotten. Lincoln's supposed lazy father, his undying love for Ann Rutledge, and
his horrific married life are things that should never have seen the
light of day, according to many of Lincoln's friends who were still
alive at this book's publication. The book is also quite candid about
Lincoln's political ambition. There is the much-quoted statement
"The man that thinks that Lincoln quietly sat down and gathered his
robes about him, waiting for the people to call him, has a very erroneous knowledge of Lincoln. He was always calculating, and planning ahead. His ambition was a little engine that knew no rest."[2]

Due to the intimacy of the relationship between Lincoln and Herndon, his law partner for some twenty years, the portrait of Lincoln

presented here has become a staple not only for Lincoln literature but for American popular culture as well. The image of Lincoln as the son of the frontier has fixed itself in the American mind. It may seem odd, but this book suffered a severe blow during the 1940s and 1950s. Lincoln scholarship in large part ignored it for decades. This was due to the work of both James and Ruth Painter Randall, who went out of their way to discredit Herndon because of his negative view of Mary Todd Lincoln. It took Lincoln scholars such as Douglas Wilson, Rodney Davis, and Michael Burlingame in the 1990s to rescue Herndon's book and reputation from obscurity.[3]

Why is this book so valuable? The main reason, surprisingly, is not Herndon's own recollections of Lincoln but the information he gathered from various sources in the years following Lincoln's death. The information he acquired from people who knew Lincoln during his youth in Indiana is invaluable. Here we hear of Lincoln borrowing Parson Mason Weem's *Life of Washington* from his neighbor Josiah Crawford. The book gets wet by accident in the rain, and Lincoln has to "pull fodder" on Crawford's farm for three days to pay for the damage to the book. Here we also have Lincoln composing a ribald piece of writing to celebrate a practical joke he played at the wedding of some neighbors. Finally, we have Lincoln's ubiquitous honesty as he tells his sister, who is hurt playfully tackling him, "Tell the whole truth, 'Tilda, and trust your good mother for the rest.'"[4]

There are certain areas of the book that have been highly controversial and frankly wrong. Herndon spends some time musing on Lincoln's own possible illegitimacy. Herndon also has Lincoln failing to show up at his own wedding. Herndon went on to speculate that the reason the Lincoln marriage was so tempestuous was because Mary Todd was taking revenge on Lincoln for standing her up at their first attempt at marriage. "Love fled at the approach of revenge." These errors have been corrected by subsequent research and scholarship. They form a fair-sized part of the book but do not take away from the book's usefulness.[5]

In the years after Lincoln's death, Herndon wrote the letters that were the basis for much of the book. Jesse Weik, his literary partner, wrote the readable prose from Herndon's sometimes frantic letters.

Weik also wrote a short chapter on Lincoln's role as president. It seems useless and tacked on, since the book's primary focus is on Lincoln before his presidency. Nevertheless, one has to admire Weik's literary skill throughout the book. It moves quickly and can never be said to be boring.[6]

What is the overall impression one gets about Lincoln from the book? It is that Lincoln's life was a series of severe trials. They tested him, and he was not found wanting. The book has one of the best closings of any Lincoln book. "The central figure of our national history, the sublime type of our civilization, posterity, with the record of his career and actions before it, will decree that, whether Providence so ordained it or not, Abraham Lincoln was the man for the hour."[7]

NOTES

1. David Herbert Donald, *Lincoln* (New York: Simon and Schuster, 1995), 19–20; William H. Herndon and Jesse W. Weik, *Herndon's Life of Lincoln* (New York: Da Capo, 1983), 2–3.
2. Herndon and Weik, 304.
3. For the anti-Herndon literature, see both James G. Randall, *Lincoln the President: Springfield to Gettysburg,* 2 vols. (New York: Dodd, Mead and Co., 1945), 2:321–42; and Ruth Painter Randall, *Mary Todd Lincoln: Biography of a Marriage* (Boston: Little, Brown and Co., 1953). Examples of the literature that did the most to resurrect Herndon are Douglas L. Wilson and Rodney O. Davis, eds., *Herndon's Informants: Letters, Interviews, and Statements About Abraham Lincoln* (Urbana: University of Illinois Press, 1998); and Michael Burlingame, *The Inner World of Abraham Lincoln* (Urbana: University of Illinois Press, 1994).
4. Herndon and Weik, 36, 44–50; Abraham Lincoln as quoted in ibid., 31.
5. Herndon and Weik, 6–8, 169–70, 182.
6. David Herbert Donald, *Lincoln's Herndon* (New York: Knopf, 1948), 318; Herndon and Weik, 434–67.
7. Herndon and Weik, 490.

Inside the White House in War Times: Memoirs and Reports of Lincoln's Secretary

AUTHOR: William O. Stoddard
PUBLISHED: 1890
GENRE: Reminiscences

B Y ITSELF, William O. Stoddard's *Inside the White House in War Times: Memoirs and Reports of Lincoln's Secretary* might not have been considered essential. However, Lincoln scholar Michael Burlingame breathed new life into it by editing a new edition in the year 2000. He included other primary source material that, together with the original book, made it an important addition to a Lincoln collection. Good primary sources about Lincoln are the building blocks of any serious Lincoln collection, and this book supplies those in abundance.

Stoddard was a clerk for the Interior Department. His job was to sign Lincoln's name to land patents. He was eventually transferred to the White House and became "Lincoln's third secretary" behind John Nicolay and John Hay. This did not lead him to a position of intimacy with Lincoln. His main job was to open and sort through the White House mail. The sheer volume of mail became too arduous for Stoddard, and he was forced to retire from this job in 1864. Lincoln then sent him to Arkansas to serve as a marshal.[1]

Stoddard wrote many books after the war, most of them children's books. He did write a biography of Lincoln, but the more important book was his memoirs, which appeared in 1890. The book is artfully written. Stoddard was a journalist before the war, and using that style, he paints a picture of a busy and hectic White House during the Civil War. Stoddard humorously describes one of the many inventors who have come to see the president: "All sorts of people come upon all sorts of errands, and the broad-shouldered, plain-looking fellow sitting there seems to have his lap full of joiner-work, painted black. It reminds one of Noah's arks he used to get at Christmas, only that it is low and wide, and has no procession of wooden animals. There are toy cannon, too, looking out of the windows, instead of giraffes." Stoddard also records an individual who is mad that most of the president's mail ends up in the wastebasket at the hands of Stoddard. The man asked, "Is this the way you treat the President's mail? Mr. Lincoln does not know this! What would the people say if they knew that their communications to their Chief Magistrate are dealt with in this shameful manner?" When Stoddard showed the man the letter that had just been thrown out, the man changed his attitude. It was one of the many abusive letters the president received during his administration. The man could only reply, "You are right, young man! You are right! He ought not to see a line of that stuff! Burn it, sir! Burn it! What devils there are!"[2]

Stoddard's book is valuable for its more positive view of Mary Todd Lincoln than is the norm from people who dealt with her in the White House. Stoddard was a bit of a politician himself and knew well how to deal with the first lady. While his work is not wholly positive, it does present a defense against the worst charges, such as disloyalty to her country. Stoddard could with some justice say, "People in great need of something spicy to talk or write about are picking up all sorts of stray gossip relating to asserted occurrences under this roof, and they are making strange work out of some of it. It is a work which they will not cease from."[3]

The sketches Burlingame included in his edited version of the book were written in 1866 and are therefore closer in time to the actual events. Stoddard would use them to write his book almost thirty-five years later. They are not put together as a literary whole, yet they are valuable for their closeness to the events narrated. In one sketch, Stoddard gives an unusual description of Lincoln's mental processes. "He was a most teachable man, and asked questions with a childlike simplicity which would have been too much for the false pride of many a man far less well informed. His fund of knowledge was, as he himself declared, very largely made up of information obtained in conversation, and if not so well arranged and digested as if it had been the accumulation of careful and exact research, it included a vast amount of material hardly to be found in books." Stoddard also remembers that "he needed fewer 'explanations' than any other man I ever knew."[4]

Stoddard's book and the sketches provided in the newest edition give another precious view of the White House during the war years. We see Lincoln from somewhat of a distance, yet we see him all the same. The White House is a busy place, and Lincoln is supremely in control. Luckily, Stoddard was a journalist who could write his memoirs in a way the modern reader will find enjoyable.

NOTES

1. Michael Burlingame, editor's introduction to William O. Stoddard, *Inside the White House in War Times: Memoirs and Reports of Lincoln's Secretary* (Lincoln: University of Nebraska Press, 2000), vii, xi, xix.
2. Stoddard, 20; Anonymous as quoted in ibid., 15, 16.
3. Stoddard, 33.
4. Ibid., 184, 185.

Abraham Lincoln and Men of War-Times

AUTHOR: Alexander McClure
PUBLISHED: 1892
GENRE: Presidency

A LEXANDER MCCLURE was a journalist and political wirepuller. He was a leading Republican in the crucial state of Pennsylvania and was always fighting for his faction of the party in the state. His chief Republican rival in Pennsylvania was Simon A. Cameron, a member of Lincoln's cabinet. During the 1860 Republican convention, McClure moved his state's delegates away from Cameron to Lincoln rather than Lincoln's chief rival, William Seward. McClure went on to have many political dealings with Lincoln throughout the administration. He may have been following Lincoln's secret instructions to campaign for Andrew Johnson as Lincoln's running mate in the 1864 Republican convention rather than Hannibal Hamlin, the incumbent.[1]

McClure sets out a modest goal for his *Lincoln and Men of War-Times*. He wanted to correct some of the misconceptions about Lincoln. McClure makes no claim to a special intimacy with Lincoln. "My own limited intercourse with him taught me, in the early period of our acquaintance, that those who assumed that they enjoyed Lincoln's confidence had little knowledge of the man." This is refreshing candor, considering so many of his contemporaries were trying to claim Lincoln had unburdened himself to them intimately.[2]

McClure is an ardent admirer of Lincoln throughout the book. "Abraham Lincoln achieved more in American statesmanship than any other president, legislator, or diplomat in the history of the Republic; and what he achieved brought no borrowed plumes to his crown. Compelled to meet and solve the most momentous problems of our government, and beset by confused counsels and intensified jealousies, he has written the most lustrous record in American history; and his name and fame must be immortal while liberty shall have worshipers in any land." One can excuse the late Victorian style of prose, but one would be hard pressed to argue with the conclusion.[3]

McClure saw Lincoln's success to be primarily that of managing men and using his vast political skill. *Politician* may be a "dirty" word in the twenty-first century, but to McClure, a fellow politician, Lincoln was a master of its art. In a memorable line, McClure states, "If Abraham Lincoln was not a master politician, I am entirely ignorant of the qualities which make up such a character." Throughout the book McClure has chapters that deal with Lincoln's interactions with the leading politicians and military figures of the day. McClure's focus is a bit provincial in that he focuses on Pennsylvania politicians. This is to be expected, though, since that is what McClure knew and was privy to. There is also a long chapter on the Pennsylvania Reserve Corps. The corps was one of the great Union Civil War units, yet the chapter seems out of place in a book about Lincoln, since he had no real dealings with them. McClure can also be forgiven for writing about the experiences of his town, Chambersburg, during the war, since it was under Confederate occupation three times and was finally burned down by Confederate troops.[4]

McClure gives positive assessments to two people who usually do not fare well in Lincoln books: President James Buchanan and Gen. George B. McClellan. McClure gives them both high marks. Of McClellan he writes, "He was one of the great military geniuses of his day, one of the purest patriots, and one of the most loyal of men in the great battle for the preservation of the Union." To be sure, he blames McClellan's distrust of Lincoln as the reason McClellan was not as successful a commander as he might have been. Buchanan is also seen as a patriot. "He is entitled to justice from every honest American citizen, and I have sought to give him justice—nothing more, nothing less."[5]

There is one final part of the book that needs to be mentioned. The book has an appendix that includes letters exchanged between

McClure and Lincoln's secretary, John Nicolay. They concern the subject of whether Lincoln intervened in the nomination of Andrew Johnson for vice president in 1864. McClure speaks of a conference he had with Lincoln in which Lincoln urged the nomination of Johnson as being stronger for the ticket than Hamlin. Hamlin, being from Maine and seen as a Radical Republican, did not bring any War Democrats with him. Nicolay believed Lincoln was entirely neutral. Though certainty is impossible, it seems more likely that Nicolay, a political novice, was wrong, and McClure, the politician, recorded faithfully what Lincoln's feelings were at the time.[6]

McClure's book is a fascinating read from an old pol. It highlights an aspect of Lincoln that some would prefer remain forgotten. Being a politician is sometimes seen as a less attractive aspect of Lincoln's personality. Lincoln the master politician does not easily fit with the image of a homespun backwoodsman. It is an integral part of him though. McClure saw this and wanted to make sure history faithfully recorded it as part of Lincoln's character.

NOTES

1. Mark E. Neely Jr., *The Abraham Lincoln Encyclopedia* (New York: Da Capo, 1982), 202.
2. Alexander McClure, *Abraham Lincoln and Men of War-Times: Some Personal Recollections of War and Politics During the Lincoln Administration* (Philadelphia: Times Publishing, 1892), 8.
3. Ibid., 9.
4. Ibid., 85, 423–56, 390–422.
5. Ibid., 225, 311.
6. Ibid., 457–81.

Washington in Lincoln's Time

AUTHOR: Noah Brooks
PUBLISHED: 1895
GENRE: Places Associated with Lincoln

NOAH BROOKS was a journalist during the Civil War. As a writer for a Republican newspaper, the *Sacramento Daily Union*, he was given unique access to the White House when he arrived in Washington in 1862. The fact that he had made Lincoln's acquaintance back in the 1856 presidential campaign helped him in this regard. Had Lincoln not been assassinated, Brooks may have become his personal secretary, since John Nicolay was going to Europe and both Lincoln's wife and his friend Dr. Anson G. Henry urged Brooks's appointment. Brooks already had the experience of being a clerk in the House of Representatives, a position he attained late in 1863.[1]

While a journalist, Brooks sent 258 dispatches back to California about what was going on in the White House. He sent them under the pseudonym of Castine, the place of his birth. He worked with these dispatches and turned them into *Washington in Lincoln's Time* late in life. As the title of the book suggests, there is a large amount of information about wartime Washington. There is a chapter called "The Capital As a Camp." In this chapter Brooks gives an outline of how Washington had really become the center of a military enterprise with hospitals and forts. Brooks's skill as a descriptive writer can be seen in the following passage: "The streets were crowded by day and night, and the continual passage of heavily loaded quartermasters' trains, artillery, and vehicles of kinds before unknown in

Washington, churned the unpaved streets into muddy thoroughfares in winter, or cut them deep with impalpable dust in summer. It was a favorite joke of Washingtonians that 'real estate was high in dry weather, as it was for the most part all in the air.'"[2] Brooks also provides an excellent account of the end of slavery in the city and the country as a whole.

What students of Lincoln are really looking for is a record of Brooks's dealings with the president. Brooks does provide some of the most memorable reminiscences of Lincoln. Biographers of the president have found this book to be a rich source of Lincoln's words. On hearing a mule driver let loose a stream of oaths in frustration, Brooks records Lincoln asking the man a peculiar question: "Excuse me, my friend, are you an Episcopalian?" The driver replied in the negative. Lincoln then said, "Well I thought you must be an Episcopalian, because you swear just like Governor Seward, who is a churchwarden."

The most telling remark Brooks records is an example of the anguish the president felt at the lack of progress in the war. Brooks read Lincoln a telegram announcing that the Army of the Potomac had retreated after the battle in the wilderness around Chancellorsville. "Never as long as I knew him, did he seem to be so broken, so dispirited, and so ghostlike. Clasping his hands behind his back, he walked up and down the room, saying, 'My God! my God! What will the country say! What will the country say!'"[3]

There is also a revealing chapter on the domestic side of life in the White House. Brooks records just how permissive Lincoln was with his youngest son, Tad. Brooks even records a case of Lincoln attempting to bribe his son to behave! Tad went with his father to visit the Army of the Potomac. He soon became bored and pestered his father to take him home. Lincoln got tired of the boy's pestering. He offered his son a dollar if he would be quiet. Tad accepted the deal but continued to bother his father about going home. When it was time to leave, Tad asked for the dollar. Lincoln did give Tad the dollar and said, "'Now, Taddie, my son, do you think you have earned this?' The lad hung his head, and answered not a word. 'Well, my son,' said the indulgent father, 'although I don't think you have kept your part of the bargain, I will keep mine, and you cannot reproach me with breaking faith, anyway.'"[4]

This book is so well written and packed with so much important information about Lincoln as president that it is little wonder it has become indispensable to biographers. It is true that Brooks is a partisan of Lincoln. He tells of his own personal sense of loss when the president died. When told of the assassination, Brooks remembered, "I sank back into my bed, cold and shivering with horror, and for a time it seemed as though the end of all things had come." This sense of personal friendship does not mar the quality of the book though. Perhaps being a journalist allowed Brooks to see and record what was important. It also gave him the skill as a writer later in life to string together his dispatches into a classic piece of Lincoln writing.[5]

NOTES

1. Mark E. Neely Jr., *The Abraham Lincoln Encyclopedia* (New York: Da Capo, 1982), 38.
2. Ibid., 38; Noah Brooks, *Washington in Lincoln's Time* (New York: Reinhart and Co., 1958), 13–44, 20, 178–93.
3. Abraham Lincoln as quoted in Brooks, 55; Brooks, 61.
4. Brooks, 244–69, 251.
5. Ibid., 230.

Recollections of Abraham Lincoln: 1847–1865

AUTHOR: Ward Hill Lamon
PUBLISHED: 1895
GENRE: Reminiscences

WARD HILL LAMON has not fared well in Lincoln scholarship, perhaps deservedly so. He loaned his name to a biography of Lincoln he did not write. Lamon's *Life of Lincoln* is an almost wholly negative book. One wonders how Lamon's Lincoln could become president. Lamon's own character also does not endear him to Lincoln students. When Lincoln had appointed Lamon marshal of the District of Columbia, he was accused of profiting illicitly.[1]

All of this obscures the fact that during his lifetime, Lamon was intensely loyal to the president. Lincoln had befriended him in Illinois, and the physically powerful Lamon accompanied Lincoln as a bodyguard to Washington in 1861. When Lincoln sneaked into Washington fearing assassination, Lamon attempted to attack the first person who talked to Lincoln. "We were instantly alarmed, and would have struck the stranger had not Mr. Lincoln hastily said, 'Don't strike him!'" The man turned out to be a congressman and an old friend of Lincoln's. After Lincoln's reelection as president, Lamon spent the night at the White House on his own volition to guard the president. Lincoln's secretary, John Hay, records the event in his diary: "He took a glass of whisky and then, refusing my offer of a bed, went out &, and rolling himself up in a cloak, lay down at the President's door; passing the night in that attitude of touching and dumb fidelity, with a small arsenal of pistols & bowie knives around him. In the morning he went away leaving my blankets at my door, before I or the President were awake."[2]

Just as he did not write the biography that bears his name, Lamon did not write this book of his recollections. His daughter Dorothy Lamon Teillard pieced together stray scraps of paper that contained jottings Lamon had made about Lincoln. She then turned the scraps into *Recollections of Abraham Lincoln: 1847–1865* by skillfully arranging the material in chapters and adding links to make the book flow. She added more material when the book was reissued in 1911. This is the version that has been reprinted a number of times and that most are familiar with.[3]

Lamon's lowbrow humor was enjoyed by the president on occasion. "I had often recalled him from a pit of melancholy into which he was prone to descend, by a jest, a comic song, or a provoking sally of a startling kind; and Mr. Lincoln always thanked me afterward for my well-timed rudeness 'of kind intent.'" This would get Lincoln into trouble when the story got out that Lamon had sung a silly song to cheer up the president after singing a sad song when they were both visiting the battlefield of Antietam. Lamon defends Lincoln of any wrongdoing in this incident: "But enough has been given to show that Mr. Lincoln was as incapable of insulting the dead, in the manner credited to him in the Antietam episode, as he was of committing mean and unmanly outrages upon the living. If hypercritical and self-appointed judges are still disposed to award blame for anything that happened on that occasion, let their censure fall upon me, and not upon the memory of the illustrious dead, who was guiltless of wrong and without the shadow of blame for the part he bore in that misjudged affair."[4]

This book has the important reactions of Lincoln following his Gettysburg Address. Lamon was in a unique position to see this, since he was the marshal of the ceremony. Lamon records Lincoln saying soon after the speech, "Lamon, that speech won't scour! It is a flat failure, and the people are disappointed." *Scour* was a term for a plow that dirt did not stick to and thus plowed well. Lamon also remembers Lincoln saying that the speech "fell on the audience like a wet blanket." Some historians have questioned these anecdotes. Lincoln historian David Herbert Donald sums up the debate the best: "Lamon's detailed account of the Gettysburg ceremonies (pp. 169–179) is highly unreliable, but the quoted sentence does sound like Lincoln."[5]

Lamon's book is far from perfect. Some of the material in it comes from other sources. Lamon's daughter was forced to look elsewhere to find material to fill the book. She even uses some of painter Francis Carpenter's book of reminiscences to pad the book. All of this does not mean the book doesn't have serious value. Lamon was a friend of Lincoln. He cared deeply for the safety of Lincoln. His recollections of important events like the visits to Antietam and Gettysburg are not obtainable from any other source. Lamon was not a smart man, but he had more foresight than Lincoln in one respect. He remembers Lincoln stating to cabinet member John Usher, "Usher, this boy is a monomaniac on the subject of my safety. I can hear him or hear of his being around, at all times of the night, to prevent someone from murdering me. He thinks I shall be killed; and we think he is going crazy." Passages like this lead one to believe that maybe Lamon and this book deserve a kinder reconsideration from historians.[6]

NOTES

1. Mark E. Neely Jr., *The Abraham Lincoln Encyclopedia* (New York: Da Capo, 1982), 178.
2. Ward Hill Lamon, *Recollections of Abraham Lincoln: 1847–1865,* ed. Dorothy Lamon Teillard (Lincoln: University of Nebraska Press, 1994), 45–47; John Hay, 1864, in Tyler Dennet, ed., *Lincoln and the Civil War: In the Diaries and Letters of John Hay* (New York: Da Capo, 1988), 236.
3. James Rawley, introduction to Lamon, xii.
4. Lamon, 151, 156.
5. Abraham Lincoln as quoted in ibid., 173, 175; David Herbert Donald, *Lincoln* (New York: Simon & Schuster, 1995), 666.
6. Lamon, 162–65; Abraham Lincoln as quoted in ibid., 280–81.

Lincoln in the Telegraph Office: Recollections of the United States Military Telegraph Corps During the Civil War

AUTHOR: David Homer Bates
PUBLISHED: 1907
GENRE: Reminiscences

THIS IS one of the finest books in Lincoln studies. *Lincoln in the Telegraph Office: Recollections of the United States Military Telegraph Corps During the Civil War* combines a little-known subject of the Civil War with firsthand accounts of the president's words and actions during the war. David Homer Bates was only eighteen years old in 1861. He worked as a telegraph operator for the Pennsylvania Railroad. At the start of the war, Bates was sent with three others to work for the War Department in Washington. In that position he saw Lincoln almost daily and left this rich record of personal reminiscences of the president. Bates makes the point that "while in the telegraph office he was comparatively free from official cares, and therefore more apt to disclose his natural traits and disposition than elsewhere under other conditions."[1]

Lincoln would often go to the War Department building, which was a short walk from the White House, to see the news from the various fronts of the war. The telegraph office was housed in the building, so Lincoln was a frequent visitor. Bates remembers a number of humorous stories Lincoln would tell as he checked on the latest dispatches. "Lincoln's habit was to go immediately to the drawer each time he came into our room, and read over the telegrams, beginning at the top, until he came to the one he had last seen at his previous visit. When the point was reached he almost always said, 'Well, boys, I am down to raisins.' After we heard this curious remark, a number of times, one of us ventured to ask him what it meant. He thereupon told us the story of the little girl who celebrated freely of many good things, topping off with raisins for dessert. During the night she was taken violently ill, and when the doctor arrived she was busy casting up her accounts. The genial doctor, scrutinizing the contents of the vessel, noticed some small black objects that had appeared, and remarked to the anxious parent that all danger was past, as the child was 'down to raisins.'" Lincoln equated his being at the bottom of the pile of telegraphs with the young girl's experience. Bates remembers other jokes, and he definitely fell under the magnetic personality of the president.[2]

Bates does remember one time that Lincoln lost his temper and swore. After the crushing defeat at Chickamauga, the Union Army of the Cumberland was forced to retreat to Chattanooga. Lincoln ordered reinforcements to Chattanooga. The closest forces were under Ambrose E. Burnside. Lincoln ordered Burnside to march with all haste to Chattanooga. When he saw that Burnside had instead marched to the strategically insignificant Jonesboro, Lincoln lost his temper. After reading Burnside's latest dispatch, he said, "Damn Jonesboro!" It is a testament to the president's good nature that this is the only time Bates remembers him swearing. This is incredible when one remembers all the bad news Lincoln had to read from his generals.[3]

This book serves as the source for the information that Lincoln wrote the Emancipation Proclamation while in the telegraph office. Bates quotes his immediate superior, Maj. Thomas T. Eckert, for the story. After the Seven Days' battles in which the Union army was pushed back from Richmond, Lincoln was in the telegraph office and asked Eckert for some paper. "He would look out the window a while and then put his pen to paper, but he did not write much at once. He would study between times and when he had made up his mind he would put down a line or two, and then sit quiet for a few minutes. After a time he would resume his writing, only to stop again at intervals to make some remark to me or to one of the cipher-operators as a fresh despatch from the front was handed to him." Eckert also remembers that Lincoln would ask him to lock up what he had written so nobody could see what he was doing.[4]

Bates also has much to say about the assassination. He was in Washington and was relaying telegraphs with Major Eckert to the various military commanders. Bates has some interesting surmises about the Confederate government's involvement in the assassination. As a telegraph operator, Bates realized the significance of the Confederate cipher code found in Booth's hotel room. Subsequent historians have forgotten what Bates thought was so significant. Bates also has a chapter on the secret workings of the Confederate agents in Canada to undermine the Northern war effort.[5]

This book is full of so much important information that it is impossible to do the book justice in this short sketch. Bates left us a wonderful book that gives witness to important actions of Lincoln that might have been lost to history. It also gives us a picture of Lincoln that shows his charm and his ability to make admirers out of his contemporaries.

NOTES

1. David Homer Bates, *Lincoln in the Telegraph Office: Recollections of the United States Military Telegraph Corps During the Civil War* (Lincoln: University of Nebraska Press, 1995), 15–16, 3–4.
2. Ibid., 40.
3. Abraham Lincoln as quoted in ibid., 202.
4. Bates, 138–40.
5. Ibid., 83–85, 287–98.

A Reporter's Lincoln

AUTHOR: Walter B. Stevens
PUBLISHED: 1916
GENRE: Reminiscences

L IKE THE Stoddard book *Inside the White House in War Times,* this book would not have made the list of essential books were it not for the efforts of Lincoln scholar Michael Burlingame. *A Reporter's Lincoln* was originally published in 1916 by the Missouri Historical Society. The original book was a limited affair with only six hundred copies being printed. The book was a compilation of articles by Walter B. Stevens that ran in the *St. Louis Globe-Democrat* in 1909 for the centennial of Lincoln's birth. The articles were reminiscences of Lincoln that Stevens had collected. Stevens had started collecting this material in 1886 and continued for twenty-three years. When the book was published in 1916 it contained only about half of Stevens's articles that appeared in 1909. Burlingame, in a new edition of the book published in 1998, went back to the original series and reprinted all the left-out articles as a supplement to Stevens's original book. Burlingame also reprinted some other recollections of Lincoln and an essay written by himself on the Lincoln-Douglas debates.[1]

It is important to note that not all of the material was gathered directly by Stevens through interviews. Some of the material came from other sources such as the Historical Society of Bloomington, Illinois, and the Lincoln Centennial Association of Springfield, Illinois. Like many collections of reminiscences, there is a great variation in the quality of the material. Some of it is very good, and some so untrustworthy as to be useless. This book is still valuable because it does contain enough quality reminiscences that cannot be found anywhere else.[2]

The longest and most important reminiscence is from Illinois Congressman Robert R. Hitt, who had covered the Lincoln-Douglas debates as a shorthand reporter for a Republican organ, the *Press and Tribune of Chicago.* Hitt complains about the way a Democratic organ, the *Chicago Times,* covered the debates. He felt they were mangling what Lincoln had said. "The controversy over the Democratic reports of Lincoln's speech was waged with great bitterness until long after the seven debates were finished. Republicans were very sore about it. They held Douglas in a large degree responsible for the unjust treatment. There was something in it which created great sympathy for Lincoln. The American sense of fair play was outraged."

In an appendix Burlingame shows that the Democratic paper had indeed shortened what Lincoln said in the debates and left him often unintelligible. Both Burlingame and Hitt, though, absolve Douglas of personal responsibility. The reason this is important is that an influential book written by Harold Holzer in 1993 argued that the *Times* version of what Lincoln said was more accurate than the standard version. Both Hitt and Burlingame destroy this notion.[3]

There are other reminiscences that are both informative and charming. Marshall S. Snow recalls when Lincoln visited his son Robert in 1860 at Phillips-Exeter Academy. Snow recalls the students supported William Seward for president but turned out to see Lincoln make a speech. The students were taken aback by Lincoln's unkempt appearance. "One of the boys leaned over and whispered: 'Look here! Don't you feel kind of sorry for Bob?'" Snow recalls that all of the negative feeling faded away after the students heard ten minutes of Lincoln's speech. "Every part fitted into the whole argument perfectly." Snow then recalls, "We went up to the platform and shook hands with Mr. Lincoln, telling him how proud we were having the honor of meeting Bob's father."[4]

William B. Thompson recalls Lincoln as a friend to all the boys of Springfield rather than as the famous politician he became. He remembers, "He would put the neighbors' boys into the family carryall, as many could be crowded in, and drive away to the banks of the Sangamon." Thompson continues, "If the boy was small Mr. Lincoln would often take him up in his arms and talk to him. If the boy was larger Mr. Lincoln would shake hands and talk with him. If he didn't recall the face, he would ask the name, and if he recognized it he would say, 'Oh yes; I remember you.' If the boy was a comparative stranger Mr. Lincoln would treat him so pleasantly that the boy always wanted to speak to Mr. Lincoln after that whenever he met him."[5]

Stevens, with the help of Burlingame, has left a worthwhile addition to any Lincoln bookshelf. The sheer quantity of the reminiscences attest to that. It must be noted that quality is not sacrificed for quantity though. Stevens's work was neglected for a long time because it was not widely published in 1916. This was a mistake. The book has a charm to it that many other collections of reminiscences do not have.

NOTES

1. See William O. Stoddard, *Inside the White House in War-Times: Memoirs and Reports of Lincoln's Secretary* (Lincoln: University of Nebraska Press, 2000); Michael Burlingame, editor's introduction to Walter B. Stevens, *A Reporter's Lincoln* (Lincoln: University of Nebraska Press, 1998), xiv, xiii, 229–36.
2. Burlingame in Stevens, xiii.
3. Robert R. Hitt in ibid., 71; Burlingame, appendix 2 in ibid., 229–36; see Harold Holzer, *The Lincoln-Douglas Debates: The First Complete, Unexpurgated Text* (New York: HarperCollins, 1993).
4. Marshall S. Snow in Stevens, 55, 56.
5. William B. Thompson in ibid., 98.

Abraham Lincoln

AUTHOR: Lord Charnwood
PUBLISHED: 1917
GENRE: Biography

T HIS IS one of the finest single-volume biographies ever written on Abraham Lincoln. It has withstood the test of time and is as powerful today as it was in 1917. In 1952 Benjamin Thomas could say the reason he wrote his biography of Lincoln was because "no satisfactory life of Lincoln within the covers of a single volume has been published since Godfrey Rathbone Benson, Lord Charnwood's in 1917." Lord Charnwood was an Englishman writing for an English audience. It may be this detachment that makes *Abraham Lincoln* so wonderful. Lord Charnwood sees Lincoln as a universal statesman and champion of democracy, not just a parochial American hero. The United Kingdom was in a death struggle with Germany at the time of the writing of this book. Charnwood hoped that the shared values of the United States and his own country would lead to a common effort against Germany. To Charnwood, Lincoln could be a unifying figure between the two countries in that he expressed the best democracy had to offer.[1]

While the book is an acknowledged classic, it will never be popular with the majority of modern readers. They will wince at some of Charnwood's assertions about race. Charnwood was writing in the period of English colonialism, and there is bit of the "White Man's Burden" attitude in his book. When talking about the "amalgamation" between the races, Charnwood defends the prevailing disgust of intermarriage in the Civil War era by stating, "We might perhaps add that as the inferior race becomes educated and rises in status it is likely itself to share the same disgust." This does not mean Charnwood is a hater of the black population in America. Charnwood is vehemently antislavery. He praises Lincoln for seeing slavery as inherently immoral. "And here there was the distinction between Lincoln and many Republicans, which again may seem subtle, but was really far wider than that which separated him from the Abolitionists. Slavery must be stopped from spreading into Kansas not because, as it turned out, the immigrants into Kansas mostly did not want it, but because it was wrong."[2]

There are long stretches of the book that do not deal with Lincoln in particular, but rather with American history. This can be explained because Charnwood was writing to an audience that was not familiar with the background of the events leading to the Civil War. These sections of the book are well written, though, and provide a foreign perspective on antebellum America that is not readily available elsewhere. It is true that Charnwood did no original research as did other Lincoln biographers and relies mainly on what others have written about Lincoln. He did not know Lincoln as other biographers such as Arnold and Herndon knew him, yet he so ably blends their material that he creates a Lincoln who is both memorable and noble.

Charnwood's view of Lincoln's religion is an important part of the book. Charnwood was a Christian. He does not accept Herndon's view of Lincoln's infidelity. The major evidence that Charnwood has for Lincoln's basic Christianity is Lincoln's own words in his Second Inaugural Address. "Probably no other speech of a modern statesman uses so unreservedly the language of intense religious feeling." After reprinting the speech, Charnwood adds, "The reader whose piety knows no questions will not be pained to think that this man had professed no faith." In this section of his book, Charnwood makes one of the best defenses of the view that Lincoln was indeed a religious man.[3]

Charnwood's admiration of the character of Lincoln is an integral part of his view of the man. He closes his book with a short sketch of Lincoln's thoughts and actions: "He faced the difficulties and terrors of his high office with that same mind which he had paid his way as a poor man or navigated a boat in rapids or in floods. If he had a theory of democracy it was contained in this condensed note which he wrote, perhaps as an autograph, a year or two before his presidency: 'As I would not be a slave, so I would not be a master. This expresses my idea of democracy. Whatever differs from this, to the extent of the difference is no democracy.—A. Lincoln.'"[4]

The words of Benjamin Thomas best describe Charnwood's book. Thomas can be viewed as an authority on the quality of Lincoln biography, and his description of Charnwood's work is near perfect. "Charnwood unearthed no new facts—he relied on the writings of others—and he changed no major conclusions. His originality consisted in the detached and balanced judgment he brought to bear, in the delineation of Lincoln as a towering native growth rather than an unintelligible prodigy, and in his appreciation not merely of Lincoln's determination to save the Union but of his larger purpose of demonstrating democracy to the world as a workable political philosophy." It would be hard to improve on Thomas's assessment.[5]

NOTES

1. Benjamin P. Thomas, *Abraham Lincoln: A Biography* (New York: Random House, 1968), 524.
2. Lord Charnwood, *Abraham Lincoln* (Garden City, N.Y.: Garden City Publishing Co., 1917), 124, 128–29.
3. Ibid., 439, 441.
4. Ibid., 456.
5. Benjamin P. Thomas, *Portrait for Posterity: Lincoln and His Biographers* (New Brunswick: Rutgers University Press, 1947), 209.

The Real Lincoln: A Portrait

AUTHOR: Jesse W. Weik
PUBLISHED: 1922
GENRE: Biography

JESSE WEIK was Herndon's collaborator on his biography of Lincoln. Herndon struck up a casual correspondence with the young man, and eventually they became close friends. Weik worked hard with Herndon. He rewrote most of Herndon's original work. He also helped gather information from people who had known Lincoln. Herndon had done most of his interviews in the years immediately following Lincoln's death. Weik interviewed some of the same people in the 1880s for the biography they would write together. After Herndon's death in 1889, Weik kept the notes they had collected. *The Real Lincoln: A Portrait* is the result of Weik's revisiting those notes and adding some of his own memories.[1]

Weik's book is something of a neglected gold mine. There is quite a bit of important information in the book that not only helps us understand Lincoln but also his most important biographer, Herndon. Herndon prided himself on being a truth teller. "I claim no literary power taste, etc., but I do claim to possess the wish to tell the truth." According to Weik's book, there were some things Herndon told Weik that were not included in their biography out of embarrassment for Herndon. The last meeting between Lincoln and Herndon before Lincoln goes to Washington to become president is a well-known story from Herndon's biography. However, there was an important part left out. Weik recalls Herndon telling him the whole story in private. "It was near sunset. We had finished the details of our business and for a while were engaged in the exchange of reminiscences when suddenly without rising from his seat, he blurted out: 'Billy, there's one thing I have, for some time, wanted you to tell me, but I reckon I ought to apologize for my nerve and curiosity in asking it even now.' 'What is it?' I inquired. 'I want you to tell me,' he said, 'how many times you have been drunk.'" Herndon was an alcoholic at that point in his life. He then said he expected a lecture from Lincoln, but Lincoln merely told him that others had tried to replace Herndon in the law partnership for his insobriety. This anecdote shows that Herndon could understandably conceal a little, yet it also shows Lincoln's understanding of his partner's shortcoming.[2]

Weik relates a humorous story about Herndon's behavior toward women. Herndon told Weik that Lincoln was passionate about women and could hardly keep his hands off them, though he did resist the temptation. Weik went and found a female client who had run a bordello at one point. Weik asked if Lincoln had ever said anything improper toward her; she said that Lincoln hadn't. "But that is more than I can say for Bill Herndon."[3]

Weik's book also sheds light on why Herndon included the false story about Lincoln failing to show up for his wedding to Mary Todd on January 1, 1841. Weik went back in 1883 and interviewed Elizabeth Edwards, Mary Todd's sister and the person whose house Lincoln and Mary were eventually wed in. He gives his diary entry for the day in the book: "Called on N. W. Edwards and wife. Asked about marriage Mary Todd to Lincoln—Mrs. E. said arrangements for wedding made—even cakes baked but Lincoln failed to appear. At this point Mr. Edwards interrupted—cautioned his wife she was talking to newspaper man—she declined to say more—had said Mary greatly mortified by Mr. Lincoln's strange conduct. Latter were reunited—finally married."[4]

It is easy to see why Herndon would believe the story when the chief witness herself is so confused about the matter.

There is a telling incident in the book that shows just how indulgent Lincoln was as a father. Judge Samuel H. Treat of Springfield told Weik about a game of chess that he and Lincoln were playing. When one of Lincoln's sons came to tell his father to come to dinner,

Lincoln agreed yet got lost in the game. In frustration the boy kicked the chess table, and the pieces went flying everywhere. Judge Treat was amazed at Lincoln's reaction. "Instead of the animated scene between an irate father and an impudent youth which I expected, Mr. Lincoln without a word of reproof calmly arose, took the boy by the hand, and started for dinner. Reaching the door he turned, smiled good-naturedly, and exclaimed, 'Well Judge, I reckon we'll have to finish this game some other time,' and passed out." Scenes like this one abound regarding Lincoln's parenting; this one may be the most extreme and comical.[5]

It is a testament to this book's success that so much of the information in it has been incorporated into other Lincoln books. Weik in many ways is an unsung contributor to the Lincoln field. He has been overshadowed by his connection with Herndon. This book allows Weik to be Weik and to speak about both Lincoln and Herndon authoritatively.

NOTES

1. David Herbert Donald, *Lincoln's Herndon* (New York: Knopf, 1948), 296.
2. William Herndon to Charles H. Hart, April 13, 1866, in *The Hidden Lincoln: From the Letters and Papers of William H. Herndon,* ed. Emmanuel Hertz (New York: Viking Press, 1938), 32–33; Jesse W. Weik, *The Real Lincoln: A Portrait* (Boston: Houghton Mifflin, 1922), 301.
3. Weik, 81, 85.
4. Ibid., 63.
5. Ibid., 102; Judge Treat as quoted in ibid., 103.

In the Footsteps of the Lincolns

AUTHOR: Ida M. Tarbell
PUBLISHED: 1924
GENRE: Family and Genealogy

IDA M. TARBELL is most famous for her exposés of Standard Oil at the beginning of the twentieth century. She was one of the great "muckrakers" of the era. Tarbell had other interests, though, and for decades one of them was Abraham Lincoln. Tarbell wrote many books on Lincoln, including a biography. However, by most accounts, her greatest Lincoln book was *In the Footsteps of the Lincolns*.[1]

In this book Tarbell covers a long time period. The book begins with the first Lincoln in America, Samuel Lincoln, who arrived in Massachusetts in 1637, and continues through many generations until it reaches Abraham Lincoln. As the book title suggests, it also follows the many migrations of Lincoln's ancestors. Tarbell did do some original research, including an interview with the reclusive Robert Todd Lincoln, but the main reason this book is essential is the literary skill that went into it. One expert put it this way: "Tarbell uncovered whole new layers of stories. This was valuable, but placed at the service of her literary talent, it also had unusual popular appeal."[2]

The sentimental way Tarbell writes about the grave of Lincoln's mother, Nancy Hanks, is a case in point: "I know of no woman's grave in this or any other country which more deeply—and rightfully so—touches the heart than that of this simple pioneer woman, the mother of our greatest American. How worthily and beautifully is the place marked! The hilltop on which she lies with the group of little graves which gradually grew around hers has been turned into a park—not a pretentious park, but a rarely lovely one. Hundreds of beautiful trees cover the knoll. Between them one looks upon the fertile, well-developed valleys, distant farms—the kind of thing which Thomas and Nancy Lincoln had in mind when they started overland into the new country."

Tarbell could certainly paint a picture with words. She also movingly writes about the effects on Lincoln of the death of Ann Rutledge, his first serious romance. "The death of Ann Rutledge opened wide the vein of melancholy in Abraham Lincoln's nature. His mind must have gone back again and again to the summer of 1818, when Pigeon Creek Valley of Indiana had been swept by a scourge of disease not unlike that from which the Sangamon country had just suffered. Then it was his mother who had been taken from him—now it was his love."[3]

The book shows signs of having been written during Prohibition. Tarbell is at pains to explain away Lincoln's selling of alcohol when he was the co-owner of a general store. "The fact that he undoubtedly sold liquor in his general store in New Salem in 1833, that he and his partner Berry took out a license to sell, that he once worked in a distillery, may be used to confuse the discussion, but it cannot by any fair process of argument destroy his position as an out-and-out believer in the wisdom of destroying the liquor business." Tarbell even believes that the famous carriage ride in which Lincoln told Herndon his mother was illegitimate was the result of an alcohol-induced hallucination! "Personally, I have never believed that Mr. Herndon would have accepted and insisted on the story if it had not been that at the time he set it down, and for long after, his mind was confused and weakened by alcoholism." It is unlikely that such a judgment would be passed today.[4]

The best part of Tarbell's book is the story of Lincoln's progenitors. Tarbell wishes to make Lincoln's ancestors as respectable as possible, hence her wanting to believe that Nancy Hanks was legitimate. She writes of a long line of hardworking and solid Lincolns in America. In this she is right, and she tells the story well. In addition, Tarbell seeks to paint a more positive picture of Lincoln's own father, Thomas. The common picture of Thomas was that he moved frequently because he was shiftless. Tarbell begs to differ. "This move of Thomas Lincoln from Elizabethtown has often been cited as a proof of shiftlessness. It does not necessarily mean anything of the kind. A working man in those days went—as he does now—to the point where he thought he could get the steadiest and best paying job, and then, as now, he took his family with him; and in these changes, made to better his situation, it was no sign of shiftlessness that he rented a home, as Thomas did, at the start." To Tarbell, Thomas Lincoln was a sturdy pioneer, not the lazy man Herndon had written about.[5]

Tarbell's book is a good example of the romantic picture of Lincoln's upbringing on the frontier that was so prevalent in her day. This does not take away from the book; in fact, it adds to its charm. Ultimately, Tarbell's book stands out for the excellence with which it presents the stories of the Lincolns in America. Nobody has ever surpassed her in writing a more enjoyable telling of those stories.

NOTES

1. Merrill D. Peterson, *Lincoln in American Memory* (New York: Oxford University Press, 1994), 149.
2. Ida M. Tarbell, *In the Footsteps of the Lincolns* (New York: Harper and Brothers, 1924), 1; Peterson, 151, 149.
3. Tarbell, 126, 222–23.
4. Ibid., 193, 86.
5. Ibid., 91–92.

Abraham Lincoln: The Prairie Years

AUTHOR: Carl Sandburg
PUBLISHED: 1926
GENRE: Prepresidential Years

THERE ARE two parts to Carl Sandburg's massive biography of Lincoln. The first part, *Abraham Lincoln: The Prairie Years*, came out in two volumes in 1926, and the second, *Abraham Lincoln: The War Years*, came out more than a decade later. The two works are so dissimilar, they could be from different authors. It is the first part of Sandburg's work that captures why it is so important to the Lincoln legend. The work has rightfully been called "the most imaginative and humanly flavorful of the biographies." Carl Sandburg, who was a poet, writes a poetic take on Lincoln from his birth to his leaving for Washington to become president. *The War Years* is less poetic and more factual. It is seldom read today. This can't be said about *The Prairie Years*. It was the inspiration for many movie and television portrayals of Lincoln. Even today it holds some sway with the imagination of the American people.[1]

A few examples will give the reader a taste of how Sandburg wrote about Lincoln. Sandburg records Lincoln's thoughts as he moved from Kentucky to Indiana as a small boy: "The boy, Abe, had his thoughts, some running ahead wondering how Indiana would look, some going back to his seven little years in Kentucky. Here he had curled around his mother's apron, watched her face and listened to her reading the Bible at the cabin log-fire, her fingers rambling through his hair, the hands patting him on the check and under the chin." Sandburg wrote a chapter on the Lincoln and Ann Rutledge romance and waxed poetic on the possibilities. "He was twenty-six, she was twenty-two; the earth was their footstool; the sky was a sheaf of blue dreams; the rise of the blood-gold rim of a full moon in the evening was almost too much to live, see, and remember." After Ann's death, Sandburg writes of Lincoln, "A week after the burial of Ann Rutledge, Bill Green found him rambling in the woods along the Sangamon River, mumbling sentences Bill couldn't make out. They watched him and tried to keep him safe among the friends at New Salem. And he rambled darkly and idly past their circle to the bury-ing ground seven miles away, where he lay with an arm across the one grave." These are examples more of poetry rather than sober his-torical writing.[2]

Sandburg's Lincoln is a homespun frontiersman. He is earthy and kind. "He laughed at himself for helping a pig in a gate or lifting a fledgling bird up into a nest, and philosophized intricately to the effect that he wasn't moral; he was selfish; his peace of heart would have been disturbed all day if he had not helped the pig or the bird; he was paid in good feeling." Sandburg writes of an incident in which an old farmer was interrupting a Lincoln speech: "The old hunter sat twisting his hat; wind and weather had worn the brim off of it; he saw Lincoln's stovepipe hat under the chair, full of letters, papers, notes; there he shoved his hat; it was out of his restless fin-gers. Yet he had forgotten something; he couldn't keep quiet; he leaned forward, hands on his knees and elbows out, and called 'Abe! Abe! I forgot to ax you about how Mary and the babies were.' And Lincoln turned from his speech and said in a low voice: 'All well when I left them at Springfield yesterday morning, Uncle Jimmy; all very well, thank you.'" Sandburg describes Lincoln at fifty-one years of age this way: "So tall with so peculiar a slouch and so easy a saunter, so bony and sad, so quizzical and comic, sort of hiding a funny lantern that lighted and went out and that he lighted again— he was the Strange Friend and he was the Friendly Stranger." Sand-burg's Lincoln is a man who is of the common people and thus admires them so much.[3]

Sandburg's style has irked more than a few Lincoln scholars. "For Edmund Wilson, Sandburg's biography was the cruelest thing that

has happened to Lincoln since he was shot by Booth." Wilson reacted
to a line in the book in which Ann Rutledge remarks to Lincoln, "The
corn is getting high, isn't it?" by saying, "The corn is getting high
indeed!" Much of this criticism misses the point of Sandburg's books.
He was a popularizer and probably the greatest popularizer of Lincoln ever. Sandburg's books also show that he was well familiar with
the basic outline and details of the Lincoln story. It may be an unwar-
ranted intrusion to put thoughts in Lincoln's head, yet one can forgive Sandburg because he does this type of thing so well.[4]

NOTES

1. David Herbert Donald, *Lincoln* (New York: Simon & Schuster, 1995), 601; see
    Carl Sandburg, *Abraham Lincoln: The War Years*, 4 vols. (New York: Harcourt,
    Brace & Co., 1939).
2. Carl Sandburg, *Abraham Lincoln: The Prairie Years*, 2 vols. (New York: Harcourt,
    Brace & Co., 1926), 1:26, 186, 189–90.
3. Ibid., 2:252, 70, 284.
4. Edmund Wilson quoted in Stephen B. Oates, *Abraham Lincoln: The Man Behind
    the Myths* (New York: HarperPerennial, 1984), 193, 12.

Lincoln's Parentage and Childhood: A History of the Kentucky Lincolns Supported by Documentary Evidence

AUTHOR: Louis A. Warren
PUBLISHED: 1926
GENRE: Family and Genealogy

*L*INCOLN'S *P*ARENTAGE *AND* *C*HILDHOOD: *A History of the Kentucky Lincolns Supported by Documentary Evidence* is the best and fullest account of the Lincolns' experience in Kentucky. As such it covers not just the short seven years Abraham Lincoln spent in Kentucky as a young boy but also the experiences of his father, mother, and grandparents. The subtitle of the book is absolutely correct. Author Louis Warren did the hard work of combing old courthouse records to obtain a clearer picture of the Lincolns. What he found goes against the grain of most Lincoln biographies, and his findings are discounted by many. Still, his book is valuable because of its status of being the most complete study of this obscure part of Lincoln's life and background. It is also the strongest defense mounted of Lincoln's father, Thomas.

The book opens with Abraham Lincoln's grandfather being killed by Indians as a pioneer in the 1780s. Warren then follows with the almost never told story of Lincoln's paternal grandmother, Bersheba (sometimes spelled Bathsheba) Lincoln. Warren's tendency to romanticize and make thoroughly respectful anyone related to Lincoln is first seen here. Not much can be known about this woman. "The scarcity of women in Kentucky at that date must have brought many suitors to the door of Bersheba Lincoln, but her life was evidently lived in the interest of her children." Warren is not necessarily wrong in saying this, but it soon becomes a pattern, and it is evidently the main reason for this book.[1]

The most controversial part of the book follows. Warren does not believe Lincoln's mother, Nancy Hanks, was illegitimate. He believes instead that Nancy Hanks was the daughter of a first marriage that Lucy Shipley had with a Joseph Hanks. Warren may be chasing windmills here, but he does a heroic job making the possible connections in the documentary record. He makes much of a highly disputed document that may read, "Widoy," which he interprets as "widow." He labors under many difficulties though. To accept his complicated chain of events, one has to believe the people who knew Lincoln's mother best were ignorant of her ancestry. This includes not only two of her cousins but her son as well! Warren writes that Lincoln believed erroneous information about his mother told to him by his cousins. Both John and Dennis Hanks didn't want Lincoln's mother to go down in history as illegitimate or "baseborn." They invented an easily disprovable story that Nancy Hanks was really Nancy Sparrow, the legitimate daughter of Henry Sparrow and Lucy Hanks. One has to ask why, if the Warren genealogy is true, did they bother to invent that story?[2]

Most of the rest of the book is a solid defense of Thomas Lincoln's life and work habits. Warren's chief foil in this is Lamon's biography of Lincoln. Warren calls Lamon "the chief instigator in defaming the character of Thomas Lincoln." It is evident that Lamon and his ghostwriter, Chauncey Black, did not do their homework on certain things. They insist that while in Kentucky, Thomas Lincoln housed his bride in a cabin that was so bad it had been used as a slaughterhouse and stable when they were first married. Warren shows that Lamon is completely wrong about that. The cabin in question had been the cabin of the widowed and poor second wife of Thomas Lincoln before she married him. Warren is at his best on these points in the book.[3]

Warren continues his defense of Thomas Lincoln in a chapter titled "The Citizen." Thomas Lincoln was at the height of his fortune during Lincoln's years in Kentucky. Warren gives some of his duties as a citizen. "The Indian Fighter," "The Guardsman," "The Jury-man," "The Patroller," "The Road Surveyor," and "The Freeholder" are ways Thomas Lincoln can be described while he lived in Kentucky. Warren backs up his assertions with documents from the time period. Warren's research in this area is something all historians of Lincoln should be grateful for.[4]

Warren also has a chapter titled "Educational Advantages." This is a rare account of Lincoln's years of schooling in Kentucky. Warren gives brief biographies of Zachariah Riney and Caleb Hazel, Lincoln's two teachers in Kentucky. Even Warren's skill at research cannot flesh out these men, yet he makes a valiant effort. Clearly, though, one may question the idea that Lincoln had educational advantages, since he left Kentucky at the age of seven.[5]

Warren's book is unique and a good defense brief for Thomas Lincoln and Lincoln's relatives in Kentucky. Still, one feels the book has an agenda and an ax to grind. Warren is correct in dispelling some of the most tendentious things written about Thomas Lincoln by people like Lamon. His zeal in this regard may have tipped him from being an impartial historian into the realm of advocacy. One may not always agree with his conclusions, but his book is essential nonetheless.

NOTES

1. Louis A. Warren, *Lincoln's Parentage and Childhood: A History of the Kentucky Lincolns Supported by Documentary Evidence* (New York: Century, 1926), 4–9, 14.
2. Warren, 17–37, 36–37, 24, 28. The author realizes that this controversy has not been settled completely and eagerly awaits coming books on Lincoln's lineage.
3. Warren, 125, 126–27.
4. Ibid., 180–91, 180, 181, 182, 184, 185, 188.
5. Ibid., 195–217, 210–17.

The Women Lincoln Loved

AUTHOR: William E. Barton
PUBLISHED: 1927
GENRE: Family and Genealogy

WILLIAM E. BARTON was a Congregational minister who at about the age of forty decided to begin writing Lincoln books. His writing has been called "antiquarian." Barton was most interested in the minutiae of Lincoln. Most historians would consider Barton's focus on relatively unimportant matters amateurish. For example, Barton's book *Lincoln at Gettysburg* goes into excruciating detail about inconsequential matters such as where most of the speech was written, instead of more important matters like what the words of the speech meant for the country.[1]

Barton was a good researcher, though, and a prolific author. Two of his books have made this list, the first being *The Women Lincoln Loved*. This book is essential because of its completeness in looking at the women in Lincoln's life. In order to write this book, Barton had to stretch the meaning of the word *love*. His list of women, with a chapter devoted to each, includes: "Lucy Hanks," "Betsy Sparrow," "Bathsheba Lincoln," "Nancy Hanks," "Sarah Bush Lincoln," "Sarah Lincoln Grigsby," "The Johnston Girls," "The Girl in the Covered Wagon," "Katie Roby," "Caroline Meeker," "Polly Warnick," "Ann Rutledge," "Mary Owens," and "Mary Todd Lincoln."[2]

The first woman Lincoln "loved" is his maternal grandmother, Lucy Hanks. Barton differs widely with Louis Warren on the illegitimacy of her daughter, Nancy, Lincoln's mother. Barton believes she was illegitimate. He creates fanciful scenes involving Lucy Hanks and Lincoln's unknown maternal grandfather, who is supposedly a Virginia nobleman. "We can not help wondering if he was interested in the fact that this attractive girl, nearly eighteen years of age, could read, and whether he brought books or otherwise encouraged her education. If so the case was not an isolated one; all the way from Eve to Heloise the woman has seen the fruit of the tree of knowledge as something to be desired to make one wise, and the teacher has become the tempter." This is enjoyable reading yet sheds no real light on the matter.[3]

For many of the women in the book, Barton admittedly does not have a lot to work with: "But I do not know. I have told you all I know about it, and a very little besides. But not very much." He is also forced to make assumptions for readability. Barton assumes that Lincoln's paternal grandmother had a special interest in him. "She did not let this lad pass out of Kentucky and into the wilderness of Indiana and pay no heed to his appearance and character. He and his name meant too much to her. The name had been borne by one she remembered as a tall young ranger whom she married six years before they stopped paying taxes to King George, and who, at the close of the Revolution, bore the title Captain."[4]

The Ann Rutledge chapter's tone is different from the rest of the book. Barton is very critical of the story. He believes in the romance between Lincoln and Ann, yet he is skeptical of much of it: "The author of this volume has followed to its very limit every avenue of known information on this subject. He has crossed the continent to interview the last remaining sister of Ann Rutledge. He has made what he supposes to be the most careful examination ever made of all the evidence in the case, and he presents here what he supposes to be the most careful examination ever made of all the evidence in the case, and he presents here what in his judgment is the truth, the whole truth, and nothing but the truth about Abraham Lincoln and Ann Rutledge."

This is odd, considering Barton weaves dramatic narratives out of almost nothing for other women. In this Barton foreshadows James

Randall, who almost twenty years later felt the need to be hyper-critical of the sources of the Ann Rutledge story.[5]

It may be that the reason for Barton's and Randall's skepticism has to do with another thing they have in common. Both are apologists for Mary Todd Lincoln. For some reason, attacking the Ann Rutledge romance is a prerequisite for Mary Todd Lincoln apologetics. Barton is not as uncritical in his defense of Mary as Randall is, and his long Mary Todd Lincoln chapter is the best in the book. Barton relates a domestic disturbance but adds a caveat: "But such occasions were rare. Lincoln did not often find himself under the necessity of explanation. He bore his burden in silence; and his domestic life was not always a burden. Mrs. Lincoln's periods of passion alternated with others in which she was passionately affectionate. Far from hating her husband, she loved him with a love that was exacting and furious."[6]

The Women Lincoln Loved is the most readable of all Barton's books. It is an enjoyable read. Barton was not a great historian, but he did leave a book that is, to this day, the fullest account of all the women Lincoln may have loved.

NOTES

1. Mark E. Neely Jr., *The Abraham Lincoln Encyclopedia* (New York: Da Capo, 1982), 20; William E. Barton, *Lincoln at Gettysburg: What He Intended to Say; What He Said; What He Was Reported to Have Said; What He Wished He Had Said* (Indianapolis: Bobbs-Merrill, 1930).

2. William E. Barton, *The Women Lincoln Loved* (Indianapolis: Bobbs-Merrill, 1927), contents.

3. Ibid., 24.

4. Ibid., 156, 58.

5. Ibid., 185; James G. Randall, *Lincoln the President: Springfield to Gettysburg*, 2 vols. (New York: Dodd, Mead & Co., 1945), 2:321–42.

6. Barton, 289.

Lincoln at New Salem

AUTHOR: Thomas P. Reep
PUBLISHED: 1927
GENRE: Places Associated with Lincoln

THERE IS no Lincoln site that captures the public's imagination as New Salem does. There is just so much that happened there that has entered the Lincoln legend. Lincoln's wrestling match with Jack Armstrong, Lincoln's romance with Ann Rutledge, Lincoln's first political campaigns, and Lincoln's election to captain in the Black Hawk War are all things that spring to mind when one hears of New Salem. The six years young Lincoln spent in New Salem were so productive that biographer William Barton called New Salem "Lincoln's Alma Mater."[1]

Thomas P. Reep's *Lincoln at New Salem* is in part an advertisement for the restoration of New Salem. New Salem had become a ghost town within Lincoln's own lifetime. Reep was a member of the Old Salem Lincoln League, a group dedicated to the memory of the town. The book ends with a heartfelt appeal to the reader to pressure the state of Illinois to act: "With the aid of your influence, Dear Reader, the State of Illinois will complete its work of restoration now, instead of delaying it for another generation. Won't you ask your representatives in the State Legislature to see to it that this work is done now?"[2]

Even if the book was produced on one level to persuade, it is still full of facts that are unavailable elsewhere. Despite the book's title, it is not just about Lincoln's experience at New Salem, though this makes up the bulk of the book. It starts with the founding of the town and goes all the way to the efforts of restoration and an account of a picnic there in 1918 to commemorate the centennial of the state.[3]

One of the highlights of the book is the photographs. There is a photograph of the remains of the old dam that Lincoln's flatboat became stuck on in 1831. Part of the dam was still visible at low water when this book was produced. There is also a wonderful fold-out map that shows the locations of the various buildings in the village of New Salem and who occupied them. There is a poignant picture of where the main part of New Salem had been. The picture shows how the Illinois prairie has reclaimed the land to the point where there are hardly any signs there once was a village on that site. There is even a picture of the original stone foundation of the Lincoln-Berry store, which had been excavated for the restoration. The most moving picture is of the grave of Ann Rutledge. The grave had been moved in 1890 and an impressive stone added at the new site. The stone contains the famous poem from Edgar Lee Masters commemorating Ann's life.[4]

The best part about the book is the descriptions of the lives of the people who lived at New Salem while Lincoln was there. The book does not treat them as merely actors for a short period in Lincoln's life but follows their later lives and careers. Of course, most biographies do not have the space to devote to these stories, so it is nice there is a source for this information. For example, "Uncle Jimmy" Short was a good friend of Lincoln in New Salem. When Lincoln's horse and surveying instruments were seized by the sheriff because of Lincoln's business debts, Short bid on them and gave them back to Lincoln. The book fleshes out the rest of his life: "A few years later he moved to Iowa and settled near the town of Winterset. He made a number of trips to California seeking to better his fortune, but was living on a farm in Iowa at the close of the Civil War." The author goes on to describe his father's visit to Short's farm. "'Uncle Jimmy,' as he was called, boasted about his fine farm and declared he had six miles of fence on it. He took much pride in showing him over it and pointing out its excellences." It is sad that some people did disappear without a trace. Lincoln's friend Jack Kelso is one of them. "But the country was getting too thickly settled for him and wild game scarcer and Jack, instead of moving to Petersburg with most of the other inhabitants, trekked westward to a newer and wilder country. Where he went or what became of him is not known." The Old Salem Lincoln League took a touching amount of care to preserve every aspect of the town and its people for posterity.[5]

Reep's book is not readily available, and it's a shame. It is a great example of those books on Lincoln one finds oneself constantly returning to for their charm and warmth. Maybe because the book was produced as an Illinois venture to promote the preservation of New Salem, it did not reach as wide an audience as it might have. The book has been superseded by other books on this time period of Lincoln's life, though none have all the stories and biographies included in this one.

NOTES

1. William E. Barton, *The Life of Abraham Lincoln,* 2 vols. (Indianapolis: Bobbs-Merrill, 1925), 1:192–201.
2. Thomas P. Reep, *Lincoln at New Salem* (Petersburg: Old Salem Lincoln League, 1927), 140.
3. Ibid., 132–37.
4. Ibid., 14, foldout, 86, 44, 76.
5. Ibid., 124, 118.

Abraham Lincoln: 1809–1858

AUTHOR: Albert J. Beveridge
PUBLISHED: 1928
GENRE: Prepresidential Years

THIS IS an unfinished work. U.S. Senator Albert J. Beveridge set out to write a full biography of Abraham Lincoln. He had already written a mutivolume biography on Chief Justice John Marshall. Beveridge did not live to complete his Lincoln biography. He got as far as the Lincoln-Douglas debates before he died in 1927. What he did leave were two volumes that have become a classic for the study of the years before Lincoln became president.[1]

What makes Beveridge's study different from others of Lincoln's earlier years is the amount of research he did. Comparing the amount of footnotes in the books to actual text is incredible. As one scholar has put it: "Even academic readers boggled at the 'rivulet of text' in 'a meadow of footnotes.'" Beveridge was thorough if nothing else.[2]

The first volume of Beveridge's work follows Lincoln from his birth to the repeal of the Missouri Compromise in 1854. In this volume, Beveridge uses the material that Lincoln's law partner, Herndon, had collected. He also did original research into Lincoln's early political career. Surprisingly, Beveridge does not like what he sees. His chapters on Lincoln's years in the Illinois legislature are negative in tone. He does not see any statesmanship. According to Beveridge, Lincoln and his colleges had traded votes in favor of expensive and irrational internal improvements in order to have the capital of the state moved to Springfield: "The husbandry of the 'Long Nine' in the fields of vote-trading has yielded its harvest. Writing years later, just

after the collapse of the internal improvement scheme, in explanation of the methods used to secure it and the location of the capital,
Governor Thomas Ford bitterly concludes: 'Thus it was made to cost
the State about six million of dollars to remove the seat of the
government from Vandalia to Springfield, half which sum would
have purchased all the real estate in that town at three prices.'" As we
shall presently see, the resentment of this impartial observer was
cherished by many.

This conclusion of Beveridge has been questioned by historians.
Beveridge wrongly believed that the Democratic governor of Illinois
was an impartial witness against the Whigs of Sangamon County.[3]

Beveridge's harshest criticism concerns Lincoln's one term in Congress. A strong nationalist, he was dismayed by Lincoln's opposition
to the Mexican War and scours Lincoln's speech against the war for
being too legalistic. Beveridge attacks Lincoln's rebuttal of President
James K. Polk's justification of the war: "Here Lincoln came perilously
close to pettifogging." Beveridge seems to feel that Lincoln should
have adopted the old attitude of "My country, right or wrong!"[4]

In the second volume, Beveridge moves away from Lincoln and
toward Douglas. A picture of Douglas is the frontispiece of the
second volume. This foreshadows the content of the volume. Beveridge begins with a long defense of Southern society prior to the
war. Beveridge has a very benign view of slavery: "Moreover care was
taken that slaves should not be overworked—this too, was the result
of self-interest as well as humanity, and public opinion also enforced
moderation. If the indolent and unruly were chastised, the industrious and provident were actually paid for extra work. 'You justly
observe if punishment is in one hand, reward should be in the other,'
wrote the overseer of a big plantation to this employer. The fact was,
the defenders of slavery stated, the slaves of a good master were his
warmest friends, rejoicing in his prosperity and success, grieving at
his adversity and failure. They were given as many holidays as white
laborers in the North enjoyed, and the slaves had a better time at
such seasons, particularly during Christmas week." Beveridge continues with a history of the sectional struggle that is quite favorable
toward the South.[5]

It was this understanding attitude toward slavery that made Beveridge think so highly of Douglas. Douglas was a man who tried to compromise the slavery issue. It was the Republicans, one of whom was Lincoln, that pushed the South into secession. Had Douglas's plan been followed, there would have been no Civil War and America would not have been threatened with disunion. One wonders if Beveridge wished he could have gone back and changed his project to a biography of Douglas rather than Lincoln. It is impossible to know if Beveridge's tone would have changed had he lived to write about Lincoln's presidency. The best guess is that it would have, since Lincoln was defending American power through the Union in the war.

Beveridge, like Louis Warren, made his great contribution not so much in his conclusions but rather in his research. Beveridge did the hard work of looking at the old records in the legislature and elsewhere. Modern writers do not share his attitudes about slavery and Douglas, yet Beveridge's book is worthwhile for the vast amount of material he was able to gather and apply to his look at Lincoln's career before the presidency.

NOTES

1. Mark E. Neely Jr., *The Abraham Lincoln Encyclopedia* (New York: Da Capo, 1982), 23–24.
2. Neely, 26.
3. Albert J. Beveridge, *Abraham Lincoln: 1809–1858*, 2 vols. (Boston: Houghton Mifflin, 1928), 1:205; see Paul Simon, *Lincoln's Preparation for Greatness: The Illinois Legislative Years* (Norman: University of Oklahoma Press, 1965).
4. Beveridge, 1:425.
5. Beveridge, 2:39–40.

The Lineage of Lincoln

AUTHOR: William E. Barton
PUBLISHED: 1929
GENRE: Family and Genealogy

WILLIAM E. BARTON'S second book on the list is similar to his first in that its focus is antiquarian. *The Lineage of Lincoln* doesn't have the fanciful narratives the other has. It is a solid look at the ancestors of Lincoln, and here once again Barton shows his strength as a researcher. He divides his book into three parts. The first deals with Lincoln's paternal ancestors, the second deals with his maternal ancestors, and the third is a mass of documents that Barton unearthed in his research into Lincoln's progenitors.

The book today is most referred to as an answer to Louis Warren's claims about Nancy Hanks. Warren's book, *Lincoln's Parentage and Childhood,* argued that Lincoln's mother was legitimate. Barton lays out a strong case for illegitimacy in this book. Barton feels that the story should be told, no matter how many people object to the airing of dirty laundry in Lincoln's past. "Something of this story I published in my *Life of Abraham Lincoln,* and something also in *The Women Lincoln Loved.* Not every reader likes this story, and because they do not like it, some people think that I ought not to have told it. My own conviction, however, is that it is the duty of an author to tell the truth."[1]

It is hard to argue with the logic of Barton's case. He shows that the cousins of Lincoln were lying to cover up Nancy Hank's illegitimacy. When Dennis Hanks said Nancy Hanks was really Nancy Sparrow, he was trying to pretend that Nancy's birth fell under the time that Lucy Hanks was married to Henry Sparrow. In fact, Nancy had been born some years before the marriage. Herndon had asked Dennis why she was called Nancy Hanks, if this was so. The semi-literate Dennis answered with a transparent lie: "All I can say in this She was Deep in the Stalk of the Hanks family. Calling her Hanks probily is My Fault. I always told hir she Looked more Like the Hankses than Sparrow. I think this is the way; if you call hir Hanks, you make hir Base born Child which is not trew." Barton rightfully sees through Dennis and understands his true motive. "So wrote Dennis early in February, 1866. The last sentence shows the motive. Dennis was desperately trying to protect the name of his cousin, the president's mother, from the stain of illegitimacy."[2]

Barton also effectively rebuts Warren's contention that the word *widoy,* meaning "widow," was prefixed before Lucy Hanks's name in the marriage bond between her and Henry Sparrow. This would make Nancy the legitimate child from a previous marriage. Barton will have none of this: "A futile and fatuous attempt has been made to prove that Lucy Hanks was a widow when she married Henry Sparrow, and credulity has gone to far lengths in this abortive effort. The argument rests upon imaginary letters alleged to be prefixed to the word 'day' in a document relating to her. By means of these non-existent letters, the word 'day' is transformed into 'widow.' Of the five letters in one word and three in the other, one letter is common to the two words. There are no such letters in the document as the argument assumes, and, whatever may have been done to the repro-duction, there was in the original, as carefully examined and twice reproduced by the camera, no scratch, blur, stain or erasure. No such letters or any others are there or ever were."[3]

A strange and unnecessary chapter in the book tries to connect Abraham Lincoln with Robert E. Lee. Barton even includes pictures of the two men to show physical similarities. Barton is really reaching in this chapter, and his motive is clear. "These two men present con-trasts enough, but both were intellectual, both had unusual ability, both were men of magnanimity, who emerged from a cruel war with-out the hatred, and who sought the welfare of a reunited country. Both were men of great heart and unsullied honor. Both were Virginians, and both belong to the whole of America. Both North and South should be proud to know that these two great and noble Americans were kinsman."[4] Barton is engaging in sectional reconciliation here rather than sound genealogy.

It is true that this type of book might not interest everyone. It can be dull reading, and reading all the documents Barton provides might make the reader's eyes glaze over. The modern reader may also find the status of Lucy Hanks when she gave birth to Lincoln's mother irrelevant. However, this book is the best and most complete source on Lincoln's ancestors. It also presents the most convincing scenario about the birth of Lincoln's mother, Nancy. Barton can be admired for his research and his detective work, and this book is his greatest contribution to the Lincoln field.

NOTES

1. See Louis A. Warren, *Lincoln's Parentage and Childhood: A History of the Kentucky Lincolns Supported by the Documentary Evidence* (New York: Century, 1926); William E. Barton, *The Lineage of Lincoln* (Indianapolis: Bobbs-Merrill, 1929), 230.
2. Denis Hanks as quoted in Barton, 221; Barton, 221.
3. Barton, 230–31.
4. Ibid., leaf after 204, 211.

Lincoln's New Salem

AUTHOR: Benjamin P. Thomas
PUBLISHED: 1934
GENRE: Places Associated with Lincoln

BENJAMIN P. THOMAS is one of the giants of the Lincoln field. While he was not an academic historian, he was active in Lincoln groups like the Abraham Lincoln Association. *Lincoln's New Salem* has become the authoritative book on Lincoln's years at New Salem. Thomas's skill as a writer has never been surpassed in Lincoln literature. Thomas knows how to tell a good story, and there is no better Lincoln story than the six years he spent in New Salem.[1]

Thomas describes the little village that influenced Lincoln so much: "It was a typical pioneer town. Almost everything needed was produced in the village or surrounding countryside. Cattle, sheep, and goats grazed on the hillsides. Hogs rooted in the woods and wallowed in the dust and mud on the road. Gardens were planted about the houses, and wheat, oats, corn, cotton, and tobacco grew in the surrounding field." Thomas's skill as a descriptive writer can be seen in the following passage: "Sunflowers bloomed profusely on the prairie. In the spring and summer, bass, sunfish, catfish, and suckers could be caught near the dam. Sometimes there was good seining below the mill, and occasionally fish could be gigged. Wild turkeys abounded in the woods, and deer, while becoming scarce, could still be had. Quail, prairie hens, ducks, and wild geese were plentiful. Prairie wolves, a small species about the size of a fox, though rapidly being exterminated, were still a menace to sheep."[2]

The life of the average person on the Illinois prairies is also well described: "The women worked harder than the men. Clarke wrote that 'a man can get corn and pork enough to last his family a fortnight for a single day's work, while a woman must keep scrubbing from morning till night the same in this country as in any other.' Women prepared the food, bore and cared for the children, spun thread, wove cloth and made soap and candles, and performed most of the humble, humdrum, necessary tasks. An English traveler noted that central Illinois was 'a hard country for women and cattle.'"[3] Despite the romantic nature of what is usually said about New Salem, life was tough, especially for women.

New Salem would never have been heard of today were it not for Lincoln's stay in the village. This stay is covered in detail by Thomas. He describes Lincoln's first experience in New Salem, when the twenty-two-year-old Lincoln freed his boat from the town dam: "One of the crew, a long, ungainly-looking individual, took charge. He was dressed in 'a pair of blue jeans trowsers indefinitely rolled up, a cotton shirt, striped white and blue, . . . and a buckeye-chip hat for which a demand of twelve cents would have been exorbitant.' Under his direction the cargo in the stern was unloaded until the weight of the cargo in the bow caused the boat to right itself. The young man then went ashore, borrowed an augur at Onstot's cooper shop, bored a hole in the bow, and let the water run out. He then plugged the hole; and the boat, with lightened cargo, was eased over the dam."[4] Thomas relates countless incidents like this throughout the book.

For all its primitiveness, New Salem was not an intellectual wasteland. "There was even a budding intellectuality in the place. James Rutledge is said to have had a library of twenty-five or thirty volumes. Dr. Allen was a graduate of Dartmouth. Jack Kelso, a lazy dreamer who knew where to catch the best fish, how best to snare small game, and who was an expert rifleman, was familiar with the works of Shakespeare and Burns and could quote long passages." Lincoln was not stifled in New Salem but instead was able to grow both intellectually and professionally. Lincoln first honed his skill in politics in New Salem. He did quite well there. In his first election, he was able to attain 277 votes out of the 300 votes cast.[5]

The importance of New Salem in Lincoln's life is recognized by Thomas: "The New Salem environment, typical of the west in general, offered opportunities that Lincoln would not have had in an older community. Humble origin and lack of schooling were no handicaps, for they were common deficiencies. A newcomer had no difficulty in establishing himself, for no one had been there long, no propertied class had emerged, and social castes were unknown. Equality of opportunity was in large degree a fact, and democracy and nationalism were the political ideas."[6]

Benjamin Thomas left as his first great book a study not just of New Salem but how it shaped our nation's greatest president. The combination of the great story of New Salem and a great writer like Thomas make this book a real find.

NOTES

1. Ralph G. Newman, foreword to Benjamin P. Thomas, *Lincoln's New Salem* (Carbondale: Southern Illinois University Press, 1987), vi.
2. Thomas, 25, 26.
3. Ibid., 33.
4. Ibid., 59–60.
5. Ibid., 44, 87.
6. Ibid., 135.

"Here I Have Lived": A History of Lincoln's Springfield 1821–1865

AUTHOR: Paul M. Angle
PUBLISHED: 1935
GENRE: Places Associated with Lincoln

T HE TITLE of the book has its origin in the tearful speech Lincoln made from the back of a train as he left his hometown for Washington in 1861. In that speech, Lincoln reminisced about the town of Springfield, "Here I have lived for a quarter of a century."[1] Lincoln's home was in Springfield twenty-four out of his fifty-six years, a longer time than at any other place. Despite this, the town of Springfield has never captured the imagination the way the six years he spent in New Salem has. Thankfully, Lincoln historian Paul M. Angle wrote a solid history of the town from its inception to Lincoln's assassination. *"Here I Have Lived": A History of Lincoln's Springfield 1821–1865* also covers the rich social history of the town.

Springfield, like other towns on the frontier, could easily have failed. Other towns in Sangamon County, notably New Salem, did fail. The founders of the town were hard workers, though, and the town flourished through their efforts in promoting it. One of the town fathers, Charles R. Matheny, was a good promoter. Five years after the founding of Springfield, the town's lots were all bought up, "a fact which indicated that a growing number of people were convinced that the town was there to stay. Their confidence was soon justified, for in the following year its population more than doubled. When Charles R. Matheny composed a second advertisement early in 1826, he was able to announce the presence of 500 inhabitants 'in a prosperous and thriving condition,' and to assert, in calm confidence, that 'if town property is to be valuable in any county town in the Western Country, it doubtless must be here.'"[2] Angle is the only available book-length source of the town's founding for the general reader.

Angle is particularly good at describing the effects the internal-improvement plan had on Springfield. Lincoln had been influential in getting this law passed. The state as a whole was not ready for it. Springfield fared better than most places with the Northern Cross Railroad being built, but even that was not very helpful to the town. "As time went on, the failure of the Northern Cross became glaringly apparent. Its physical equipment was primitive. In building the road ties had been laid on mud sills without ballast. Spiked to the ties were oak 'stringers,' on which narrow strap iron were mitred so that each rail would take the weight of the wheel before it had left the preceding rail. . . . Underrun by the wheels, they shot up through the flimsy cars, and sometimes through an unfortunate passenger or member of the train crew."[3] This was certainly not on par with the Erie Canal. Lincoln's attempt to be the "DeWitt Clinton" of Illinois was not a dream he fulfilled.

The most astonishing thing Angle covers in this book is the political evolution of Springfield. For most of its history, Springfield was solidly Whig, so it backed Lincoln throughout most of his career. With the dissolution of the Whig Party and the rise of the Republican Party, the town abandoned Lincoln. Springfield was generally conservative on the slavery issue. "So far as the people of Springfield were concerned, colonization was the respectable way of dealing with the slavery question. The local society has been functioning for several years, and numbered many of the town's leading citizens among its members. But let the opponents of the 'peculiar institution' go further, let them even mention with approval the dread word 'abolition'—and a sharp rebuke was quick to follow." The town could not follow Lincoln into a party that was tainted with too much abolitionism. This is apparent when one looks at the returns for Lincoln in his two presidential elections in Springfield. In 1860, Lincoln polled 1,395 votes. Douglas polled 1,326 votes. Breckenridge and Bell together got 47. In 1864, Lincoln received 1,324 votes, and McClellan received 1,314. It is true that Lincoln narrowly squeaked by each time, but one must remember that Springfield was his hometown. He should have polled a huge majority.[4]

Springfield to this day retains the spirit of Lincoln. One can visit the only home he ever owned on Eighth and Jackson Streets. The station where Lincoln last saw Springfield as he boarded the train still stands. He is buried there in Oak Ridge Cemetery with his wife and three of his sons. Angle has given us the story of this town that meant so much to Lincoln. One can feel this importance to Lincoln when reading the speech he spoke as the train pulled away: "To this place, and the kindness of these people, I owe everything. . . . To His care commending you, as I hope in your prayers you will commend me, I bid you an affectionate farewell."[5]

NOTES

1. Abraham Lincoln, February 11, 1861, in Paul M. Angle, *"Here I Have Lived": A History of Lincoln's Springfield 1821–1865* (Crawfordsville, Ill.: R. R. Donnelly and Sons, 1935), 260.
2. Ibid., 17.
3. Ibid., 147.
4. Ibid., 79, 253, 287.
5. Abraham Lincoln, February 11, 1861, as quoted in ibid., 260.

The Unlocked Book: A Memoir of John Wilkes Booth by His Sister Asia Clarke Booth

AUTHOR: Asia Clarke Booth
PUBLISHED: 1938
GENRE: Assassination

A N OLDER sister of John Wilkes Booth wrote a memoir of him in 1874. Hard feelings from the assassination were still held by many. *The Unlocked Book: A Memoir of John Wilkes Booth by His Sister Asia Clarke Booth* could simply not be published in her lifetime. In fact, the book lay dormant for more than sixty years before it saw the light of day. The sympathetic way in which the assassin of Lincoln is held in the book is disconcerting even today. Asia Clarke Booth holds both Lincoln's and her brother's violent deaths as moral equivalents. "The South avenged the wrongs inflicted by the North. A life inexpressively dear was sacrificed wildly for what its possessor deemed best. The life best loved by the North was dashed madly out when most triumphant. Let the blood of both cement the indissoluble union of our country." She goes on further to state, "The light of reason will show that success alone makes the hero or the outlaw." She is saying the only difference between Lincoln and Booth was that Lincoln's side won the war. Speaking of her brother, she writes, "This man was noble in his life, he periled his immortal soul, and he was brave in death. Already his hidden remains are given Christian burial, and strangers have piled his grave with flowers."[1] While one can expect this type of writing from a family member, it is still an odd comparison and in poor taste.

The book is valuable for its intimate view of John Wilkes Booth. The story is told by a sympathetic witness, so it is also unique among

Lincoln assassination books. This book has been resurrected from obscurity by Lincoln assassination expert Terry Alford. He has added biographical material about the author as well as Booth family letters and documents. He also cleaned up the text by correcting the author's often erratic punctuation. With this added material, the book is a must for the student of the Lincoln assassination.[2]

Asia loved her brother intensely. "He was once stopping at Edwin's New York house, and suffering from a diseased arm [an erisyphilis attack in August 1864], he fainted from acute pain, and Junius carried him and laid him on the bed. As he lay there in his shirt-sleeves so pale and death-like, we all felt how wondrously beautiful he was. It was a picture that took hold deeply of our hearts, for soon he was to lie dead among his foes, and not one of us should gaze upon his face."[3] The book has many other scenes like this where a sister's love is on prominent display.

The picture the book paints of Booth is sympathetic, yet traces of an egotistical and hateful personality are discernible. Booth is thoroughly aristocratic from the account left by his sister: "The first evidence of an undemocratic feeling in Wilkes was shown when we were expected to sit down with our hired workman. It was the custom for members of the family to dine and sup with the white men who did the harvesting. Wilkes had a struggle with his pride and knew not which to abide by, his love of equality and brotherhood, or that southern reservation which jealousy kept the white laborer from free association with his employer or his superior." Booth seems to have made lip service to democracy, for whites at least, yet in practice was a man who saw himself in a privileged position.[4]

Booth's feeling toward slaves and blacks is on display throughout the book. Booth saw slaves as perpetual children. When Booth returned from a trip to Baltimore he greeted the slaves with presents. "He had a greeting for all and threw a packet of candies from his saddle-case far beyond where he stood, saying, 'After it, Nigs! Don't let the dogs get it!'" Booth thought candy was an appropriate gift for adult slaves and gave it to them in a patronizing way. John Wilkes Booth could tolerate the black population as long as they knew their place and acted accordingly. This is not surprising from a man who wrote, "The country was formed for the *white,* not for the black man. And looking upon *African Slavery* from the same stand-point held by most of the framers of our Constitution, I for one have ever considered *it* one of the greatest blessings (both for themselves and us) that God ever bestowed upon a favored nation."[5]

There are some today who question Lincoln's commitment to emancipation and his care for the future of the black race. From this book it is quite clear that one person who did not question Lincoln's commitment to those issues was John Wilkes Booth. Booth was a firm believer in the peculiar institution, so much so that it ultimately led him to murder the man he saw responsible for freeing an inferior race.

NOTES

1. Terry Alford in preface to Asia Clarke Booth, *John Wilkes Booth: A Sister's Memoir* (Jackson: University Press of Mississippi, 1996), xi; Booth, 100, 100, 100.
2. Terry Alford, introduction to Booth, 25.
3. Booth, 84.
4. Ibid., 48.
5. Ibid., 76; John Wilkes Booth, November 1864, as quoted in ibid., 107.

The Hidden Lincoln: From the Letters and Papers of William H. Herndon

AUTHOR: Emmanuel Hertz, editor
PUBLISHED: 1938
GENRE: Reminiscences

THIS IS one of the most shocking Lincoln books ever released to the general public. It includes many letters from Lincoln's law partner, William Herndon. Herndon unburdens himself to others about Lincoln in a very open way in *The Hidden Lincoln: From the Letters and Papers of William H. Herndon*. Some of the material is a tad risqué, to say the least. The editor, Emmanuel Hertz, must have sought out the most controversial material. This book's release may have started the decline in Herndon's reputation that continued until the 1990s. It is not that Herndon set out to destroy Lincoln; he just wanted to tell the truth as best he could. Some of the things he states in his letters have turned out not to be true, but it is fascinating reading nonetheless. Herndon knew Lincoln better than most, and his observations are of immense value.

The book also contains some letters written to Herndon as well as interviews he conducted concerning Lincoln. In 1998 Lincoln scholars Douglas L. Wilson and Rodney O. Davis produced all of these letters and interviews in a more accurate fashion. However, Herndon's own letters are not available elsewhere. The book also contains a brief autobiographical statement from Herndon that is valuable.[1]

In the book Herndon makes some assertions about Lincoln's sexuality that are very controversial. Herndon repeats a story that was told to him by Lincoln's friend Joshua Speed. In the story, Lincoln goes to a prostitute, strips, and gets into bed. After finding out the prostitute's services cost five dollars and he only had three, Lincoln got out of bed and told the woman he could not go on credit because he was so poor and could not pay her soon. She supposedly replied, "Mr. Lincoln, you are the most conscientious man I ever saw." Lincoln scholar Charles Strozier got it right when he said, "Somehow one senses a Lincoln joke that got lost in translation." Herndon also states Lincoln told him that as a young boy he had contracted syphilis and wrote a prominent doctor about it. Lincoln's best friend, Speed, thought Lincoln wrote the doctor about his love for Ann Rutledge. Since there is no physical evidence that Lincoln suffered from the disease, Speed, who was on more intimate terms with Lincoln than Herndon, is probably correct.[2]

Fastidious readers were probably taken aback by some of Lincoln's earthy humor in the book. Lincoln used to tell a story about an audacious man at a party. The party was a large affair, and when it came time to dine, the man was asked to carve the turkey. "The men and women surrounded the table to carve the turkeys, chickens, and pigs. The men and women surrounded the table, and the audacious man, being chosen carver, whetted his great carving knife with the steel and got down to business and commenced carving the turkey, but he expanded too much force and let a f—t, a loud f—t so that all the people heard it distinctly." Lincoln stated the man played it cool and pretended nothing happened. He then went back to carving the turkey and said, "Now by God, I'll see if I can't cut up the turkey without f—ting." The people all laughed, and the man was even more popular for his audacity. Many might ask how the man who wrote the Gettysburg Address could be telling such stories, yet to deny Lincoln did tell stories like this is to deny an integral part of his personality. This book lets us view that earthy side of Lincoln a book like Josiah G. Holland's biography would not.[3]

Herndon's musings on Lincoln are sometimes unintelligible. "In philosophy Mr. Lincoln was a realist as opposed to an idealist, was a sensationalist, as opposed to an institutionalist, a materialist as opposed to a spiritualist. . . . I said to you in private that Mr. Lincoln was at all times and places and under all circumstances deeply and a thoroughly religious man, sincerely, firmly, broadly, and grandly, so.

I do not say he was a Christian. I do not say that he was not. I give no opinion the one way or the other. I simply state the facts and let each person judge for himself." Herndon's musings cannot be taken as the final word on Lincoln's thought, since they themselves are often confused.[4]

This book is at times redundant. Many times Herndon repeats the same thoughts in letters to different people. This is to be expected and says something about his honesty. He did not change the story but stuck to his version of Lincoln, no matter to whom he was talking. Herndon's biography is one of the most influential books on Lincoln. Herndon's thoughts on Lincoln, in an unpolished form, are in this book. They all may not be pretty, but one can't deny that they are important.

NOTES

1. Douglas Wilson and Rodney Davis, eds., *Herndon's Informants: Letters, Interviews, and Statements About Abraham Lincoln* (Urbana: University of Illinois Press, 1998); William Herndon in *The Hidden Lincoln: From the Letters and Papers of William H. Herndon,* ed. Emmanuel Hertz (Garden City, N.Y.: Blue Ribbon Books, 1938), 395–96.
2. William Herndon to Jesse Weik, January 5, 1889, in Hertz, 233; Charles B. Strozier, *Lincoln's Quest for Union: Public and Private Meanings* (New York: Basic Books, 1982), 48; William Herndon to Jesse Weik, January 1891, in Hertz, 259.
3. Hertz, 399; Abraham Lincoln as quoted in ibid., 399; see Josiah G. Holland, *The Life of Abraham Lincoln* (Springfield: Samuel Bowles and Co., 1866).
4. William Herndon to Jesse Weik, November, 24, 1882, in Hertz, 91.

Lincoln and the Civil War: In the Diaries and Letters of John Hay

AUTHOR: Tyler Dennett, editor
PUBLISHED: 1939
GENRE: Presidency

JOHN HAY was one of Lincoln's secretaries during the Civil War. During that time he became an ardent admirer of the president. Hay wrote to Herndon shortly after the war, "I consider Lincoln Republicanism incarnate—with all its faults and all its virtues. As in spite of some rudeness, Republicanism is the sole hope of a sick world, so Lincoln with all his foibles, is the greatest character since Christ."[1]

During the war Hay kept a diary. Tyler Dennett gives us the most relevant passages concerning Lincoln in *Lincoln and the Civil War: In the Diaries and Letters of John Hay.* He also includes letters written by Hay during and shortly after the war. Hay's diary is one of the great sources for Lincoln in the White House because there is an immediacy only a diary can give. John Hay's proximity to the president on occasions such as his reelection night makes this book essential in understanding those important events. Furthermore, John Hay is very skilled in the use of the pen, so his diary is a good read. It is full of gossip about the leading characters of the war, and it has many vignettes of Lincoln in his more unguarded moments. "A little after midnight as I was writing those last lines, the President came into the office laughing, with a volume of Hood's works in his hand, to show Nico and me the little caricature 'An unfortunate Bee-ing,' seemingly utterly unconscious that he with his short shirt hanging above his long legs & setting out behind like the tail feathers of an enormous ostrich was infinitely more funnier than anything in the book he was laughing at." Hay also has some unflattering things to say about Mary Todd Lincoln after seeing her close-up. "Hellcat" is his preferred name for her. "The devil is abroad having great wrath. His daughter, the Hellcat, sent Stackpole in to blackguard me about the feed of her horses. She thinks there is cheating round the board and with that candor so charming in the young does not hesitate to say so. I declined opening communications on the subject."[2]

This book is also valuable for its recounting of Lincoln's views on important political issues of the day. In June 1864 Hay wrote, "I am glad the President has sloughed off that idea of colonization." This puts a lie to the notion that Lincoln wanted to deport all the former slaves after the war, a notion that is still aired by both Neo-Confederates and Black Nationalists. The book also shows that Lincoln was not in constant battle with the Radicals of his own party, a notion that was popular among revisionist historians of the 1930s and 1940s. Hay records Lincoln's view of the Radical Republicans in Missouri: "The President added, 'I believe, after all, those radicals will carry the State & I do not object to it. They are nearer to me than the other side, in thought and sentiment, though bitterly hostile personally. They are utterly lawless—the unhandiest devils in the world to deal with—but after all their faces are set Zionwards.'"[3] As stated above, Hay's writing has an immediacy that makes it more likely to be true than later recollections about these controversial matters.

It is interesting to see the effect the president had on his young secretary. Hay borders on hero worship in his diary. He refers respectfully to the president as the "Tycoon." Hay writes, "The Tycoon is a fine whack. I have rarely seen him more serene & busy. He is managing the war, the draft, foreign relations, and planning a reconstruction of the Union, all at once. I never knew with what tyrannous authority he rules the Cabinet, till now. The most important things he decides & there is no cavil. I am growing more and more firmly convinced that the good of the country absolutely demands that he should be kept where he is till this thing is over. There is no man in the country, so wise, so gentle and so firm. I believe the hand of God placed him where he is." Hay also railed against the ideas that Lincoln was being controlled by others or should stay out of military affairs. "You may talk as you please of the Abolition Cabal directing affairs from Washington: Some well-meaning newspapers advise the president to keep his fingers out of the military pie: and all that sort of thing. The truth is, if he did, the pie would be a sorry mess. The old man sits here and wields like a backwoods Jupiter the bolts of war and the machinery of government with a hand equally steady & equally firm."[4]

Since its publication, every biographer has had to use Hay as a source to be credible. We are all fortunate that John Hay was in the right place at the right time and that he left us so valuable a record as his diary.

NOTES

1. John Hay to William Herndon, September 5, 1866, in Douglas L. Wilson and Rodney O. Davis, eds., *Herndon's Informants: Letters, Interviews, and Statements About Abraham Lincoln* (Urbana: University of Illinois Press, 1998), 332.
2. Tyler Dennett, ed., *Lincoln and the Civil War: In the Diaries and Letters of John Hay* (New York: Da Capo, 1988), 179; John Hay to John Nicolay, April 5, 1862, in ibid., 40. Michael Burlingame has published an edition of Hay's diary that is more complete but does not have the letters.
3. John Hay in ibid., 203, 108.
4. John Hay in ibid., 76, 91.

The Great American Myth: The True Story of Lincoln's Murder

AUTHOR: George S. Bryan
PUBLISHED: 1940
GENRE: Assassination

THERE HAVE been many horrible books on the Lincoln assassination. Some of them are downright awful and full of wild speculation. *The Great American Myth: The True Story of Lincoln's Murder* is one of the exceptions to that rule. Lincoln assassination expert William Hanchett has stated, "No writer could be more eager than Bryan to set the record straight." George S. Bryan sees the assassination as a simple conspiracy by John Wilkes Booth to avenge the South. "After the demoralizing winter of 1864–1865 and the collapse of the abduction plot, Booth determined upon murder—which he called 'sacrifice.' It was to him the way of duty; it might also be the path of glory; but something 'decisive and great must be done.'" More recent works have challenged this interpretation and have argued that Booth had a strong connection to the Confederate government. Whether Bryan or the new thesis is right, this book is important because it is the best work that argues for a simple conspiracy of Booth and his cohorts.[1]

Bryan treats Booth not as a madman and failure but as a successful and intelligent actor. "It should be obvious that this young player—not only sought by managers as 'good box office' but greeted in such fashion by the press of the leading theatrical centers of the East and acclaimed by seasoned patrons of the drama in an era of gifted actors—was not, as has been misrepresented, either a foolish tyro or an empty swashbuckler."[2] In other words, Booth was a substantial person.

Bryan also treats Booth as a brave man. Booth's end at the Garrett farm is captured well by Bryan. He describes the scene as the Union cavalry get ready to burn Booth out of the tobacco barn. When given a time limit to leave, Booth remained defiant. "'Well Captain' was the reply, 'that is the damned hard, to burn an innocent man's barn. I'm lame. Give me a chance. Draw up your men before the door and I'll come out and fight the whole command.'" Later, Booth shouts, "Well, my brave boys, you can prepare a stretcher for me." Booth is sometimes portrayed as a man who was too cowardly to fight for the South in the regular Confederate army. A cowardly Booth is hard to square with Booth's last few moments. "They threw water in his face; his lips stirred. 'Tell mother,' he whispered faintly—'tell mother I die for my country.'" Booth was many negative things, but a coward was not one of them.[3]

The most useful part of the book is the last chapter, "False Colors and Shapes." There have been many "documentaries" that have trotted out the tired falsehood that Booth did not really die in the barn but escaped and lived the rest of his life under a false identity. This is one of those tired canards that gets more attention than it deserves. Bryan takes a look at the most prominent of these stories and shows that there is nothing substantial behind it.[4]

The most famous of these false Booths is John St. Helen. St. Helen supposedly made a deathbed confession in 1903 that he was truly John Wilkes Booth. There is really nothing to this except for those who want to believe a good story. F. L. Bates was the chief promoter of this story. He wrote a number of articles and books about it. Bates went so far as to have St. Helen's mummified corpse tour the country. "After some years, the body was turned over to Finis Bates; presumably with the understanding that he would give it a decent burial. Instead of that, Bates stored his dear old friend in the Bates garage at Memphis. And when Bates could, he rented him and leased him and let him out for hire." Bryan shows that Bates's research is lacking. "Bates did not make notes of St. Helen's 'confession' at the time but thirty-five years afterward he published it *verbatim*. The story that Bates puts into St. Helen's mouth must have been Bates' own synthesis. He found material for it in 1897 in a reporter's interview with David Dana, in the *Boston Sunday Globe* of December 12, 1897. The feature article 'He almost saved Lincoln' yielded many particulars that Bates later wove into his book."[5] As one can see, Bryan is a good resource to have when the inevitable story of Booth's escape comes up.

Bryan's book is sometimes hard to read. His sentences occasionally run together, and one finds oneself reading paragraphs over again to get the meaning. Bryan's book has also been superseded to some extent by books written by academic historians. However, it is useful in clearing up many of the myths of the assassination. Furthermore, the simple conspiracy of Booth and his accomplices has no better defender than Bryan. Those inclined to accept that view should have this book as their chief resource.[6]

NOTES

1. William Hanchett, introduction to George S. Bryan, *The Great American Myth: The True Story of Lincoln's Murder* (Chicago: Americana House, 1990), xxv; Bryan, 392; see William Tidwell, James O. Hall, and David Winfred Gaddy, *Come Retribution: The Confederate Secret Service and the Assassination of Lincoln* (Jackson: University Press of Mississippi, 1988).
2. Bryan, 91.
3. Ibid., 264, 264, 265.
4. Ibid., 324–81.
5. Ibid., 340, 340.
6. See Thomas A. Turner, *Beware the Public Weeping: Public Opinion and the Assassination of Abraham Lincoln* (Baton Rouge: Louisiana State University Press, 1982).

Lincoln and the Radicals

AUTHOR: T. Harry Williams
PUBLISHED: 1941
GENRE: Presidency

*L*INCOLN AND THE RADICALS is a book whose time, in large part, has come and gone. The author confesses as much some twenty years after its publication. "The book has become, in fact, something of a whipping boy for revisionist writers who, influenced by the ideals of their own time, cannot resist revising the picture of an earlier time to make it accord with their ideals." T. Harry Williams's book is the harshest on the Radical Republicans ever written. Even Williams admits he may have been wrong to some degree. "Looking at these judgments now, I can now see that a few of them are extreme and, looking at these cases, I can see that some of them are overstated." This book did have a long period of influence on Lincoln writings during the 1940s and 1950s though. Williams's book can be said to be out of date, yet it cannot be said to be useless. There are information and interpretations still of value in the book.[1]

Williams's thesis is that Lincoln's greatest enemies were the Radical Republicans, which he sometimes calls "Jacobins" after the radicals in the French Revolution. Members of his own party were thwarting him and hurting the war effort. The book makes the point that General McClellan was defeated not by the Confederates but by the Radicals back in Washington who undermined him. The seven members of the Joint Committee on the Conduct of War are seen as almost demonic in this book. When McClellan was retreating after the Seven Days' battles, they are seen as jubilant for they now can put their own general in command. "The committee sprang into action. This was the moment for which it had been waiting. The king was dead, long live the heir! And Wade and Chandler had an heir. They had prepared him for the succession and anointed him with the radical oil. Now they led him out for Lincoln to see. It was General John Pope, just lately come out of the West." Pope was badly defeated at Second Bull Run, so the implication is that this was the committee's fault.[2]

The book takes a cue from Beveridge and praises Southern civilization at the expense of the fanatical North. "Northern propagandists found their task immeasurably facilitated by the existence of a convenient stereotype—the cruel slaveholder epitomized by Simon Legree. Thirty years of abolitionist preachings had installed in the popular mind definite patterns and reactions regarding the Southern people and their social system. . . . Such intense emotional fixations needed only the impetus of a flood of atrocity stories to unleash a venomous hatred of the South that carried through the war and persisted long after the conflict itself had ended."[3] Williams fails to realize that he himself is using a stereotype of the people in the North.

There is one section in the book that is still valuable. During the 1864 presidential election, there was indeed an attempt to replace Lincoln with John C. Frémont, someone more advanced in his racial views. "Early in May they sent out a call for a convention to meet in Cleveland. The important party bosses stood coldly aloof from the movement, although some of them, such as Greeley and Andrew, secretly urged the Frémont men on." When they found that Frémont's candidacy could not possibly win, they had to reluctantly support Lincoln. "Most Jacobins shared Wade's feelings of sullen resentment as they settled down to the job of beating McClellan. One congressman said the Republicans had to defeat 'a creature that owes its strength—as does the rebellion itself—to the fact that he was so long tolerated—along with the Border State counselors—by the President himself.'" It is true that Lincoln was closer to the "Jacobins" in his own party than he was to McClellan and the Democrats, yet there were some differences that cannot be completely forgotten. Williams's book is the best book available concerning the attempts of the Radical Republicans to run a different candidate in 1864.[4]

Williams's book is overwritten, and he is hardly fair to the Radical Republicans. His ending soars to an absurd rhetorical height. After the death of Lincoln, the Radicals faced a president who did not agree with them in Johnson. "Once again the Jacobins faced a hostile president. Once again they knew they must fight the battle of reconstruction. But they felt no misgivings, only a fierce joy. They had conquered Lincoln, they would conquer Johnson. With a grim confidence, they entered the savage years of the tragic era."[5] Williams, as above, is apologetic for some of the language he used. He admits that had he the chance to write the book again, he "would also make somewhat more positive the portrait of the Radicals, stressing that they were the firmest of nationalists, the men who would never give up the Union, and recognizing that they represented a powerful moral urge in American society."[6]

NOTES

1. T. Harry Williams. *Lincoln and the Radicals* (Madison: University of Wisconsin Press, 1972), x, vii.
2. Ibid., 140.
3. Ibid., 254–55.
4. Ibid., 314, 332.
5. Ibid., 254–55.
6. Ibid., 384, xi.

Lincoln and His Party in the Secession Crisis

AUTHOR: David M. Potter
PUBLISHED: 1942
GENRE: Presidency

L INCOLN'S ACTIONS as president-elect have long been controversial. Southerners have seen Lincoln as a tyrant who tried his best to force war on them. Revisionist historians of the era in which this book was written felt that Lincoln should have compromised and avoided the war. These viewpoints are not prominent in today's scholarship, which feels the war was ultimately inevitable. David M. Potter's thesis in *Lincoln and His Party in the Secession Crisis* is that Lincoln did his best to avoid the war without abandoning his principles.

There were many attempts at compromise to avoid the war after Lincoln's election. The most famous of these was the Crittenden Compromise. This compromise would have allowed slavery to spread into the territories below the old Missouri Compromise line. Lincoln had been elected on a platform of halting the expansion of slavery. To endorse the compromise, Lincoln would have had to give up the very principles he stood for in his election. Lincoln effectively shut the door on this and other compromises. When some members of his party wished to accept the Crittenden plan, Lincoln intervened. "In consequence he abandoned his policy of remaining inactive until his inauguration, and quietly but effectively he brought the vast weight of his influence to bear. Assuming a momentous responsibility, he intervened to arrest the growing sentiment for compromise among the Republicans in Congress."[1]

Much of the older controversy has also focused on Lincoln's handling of the Fort Sumter crisis. Did Lincoln pursue an aggressive posture in order to force the South into firing the first shot, or did Lincoln and the Republican Party try their best to maintain the peace? Potter feels that Lincoln ordered the resupply of Fort Sumter in order to keep the fort as a symbol of Unionism but not to deliberately start a conflict. Lincoln's hand had been forced by a message from the fort's commander, Maj. Robert Anderson, that the garrison was running low on food: "It had been the original purpose to hold Sumter without changing the status there. Anderson's necessity had frustrated this purpose, and he sought some device by which he might abandon the fort without abandoning his policy. But as these efforts failed, he reverted, in effect, to his original policy. He would not disturb the status of Sumter, but, in order merely to preserve that status, he would send to the garrison such foodstuffs as were necessary to prevent it being starved out."[2] Lincoln was faced with the difficult choice of abandoning the Union or risking war. He risked war.

Potter feels that Lincoln did make one major mistake. He overestimated the number and strength of Southern Unionists. "It is distinctly pertinent to record that the President-elect had already showed and continued to show a complete misunderstanding of the Southern temper, and a complete misconception of the extent of the crisis. On this misconception, his later policy was constructed."[3] Potter's observation lends credence to the modern view that Lincoln's election made the war inevitable. Lincoln's actions, short of recognizing Southern independence, were not going to prevent war. There were no real Southern Unionists in any strength for Lincoln to work with, and Lincoln and the Republicans were not going to give up the Union.

It is interesting to note that Potter is well aware of the cost of the war that Lincoln ultimately accepted. He makes a valid point about modern students of the war who do not think highly of the attempts to compromise to avoid war: "Those who despise the advantages of a stopgap peace will point out, of course, that the Civil War did settle the basic issues. It saved the Union, and it freed 4,000,000 slaves. Certainly this is true, and it is important. But it can hardly be said that these immense values were purchased at a bargain. For every six slaves who were freed, approximately one soldier was killed; for every ten white Southerners who were held in the Union, one Yank and one Reb died. A person is entitled to wonder whether the Southerners could not have been held and the slaves could not have been freed at a smaller per-capita cost. Certainly few would have purchased these gains at the time if they had known the price, and the mere fact that it has already been paid is not a reason for historians to let it go without questioning now."[4] Potter gives the reader a good reminder of the cost of the war. A cost that is all too easy to forget.

In the end, Potter feels Lincoln did the right thing, and his book is the best book about this crucial time period in Lincoln's life and administration. One also gets the feeling from reading this book that events sometimes take control of themselves. Lincoln may have been right when he once said, "I claim not to have controlled events, but confess plainly that events have controlled me."[5]

NOTES

1. David M. Potter, *Lincoln and His Party in the Secession Crisis* (Baton Rouge: Louisiana State University, 1995), 133.
2. Ibid., 371.
3. Ibid., 245.
4. Ibid., xl–xli.
5. Abraham Lincoln to Albert G. Hodges, April 4, 1864, in *The Collected Works of Abraham Lincoln*, ed. Roy P. Basler, 8 vols. (New Brunswick: Rutgers University Press, 1953), 7:282.

Lincoln the President

AUTHORS: James G. Randall and
Richard N. Current
PUBLISHED: 1945–1955
GENRE: Presidency

THESE FOUR volumes, published over a period of ten years, are the largest and most in-depth scholarly treatment of the Lincoln presidency. James Randall has been called "the greatest Lincoln scholar of all time." Unfortunately, he did not live to finish the second half of the last volume of *Lincoln the President,* which was completed by Richard Current, another great Lincoln scholar. It is impossible to go through all the facets of these books in this chapter, so only some of the highlights of the books and where their perspective is unique will be discussed.[1]

Randall was a thorough revisionist, so he does not think highly of the Republican Party, a party he sees as bringing on an unnecessary war. He is especially disdainful of the Radicals in the party, so Randall all but turns Lincoln into a Democrat. One of the potential Democratic nominees for president in 1864 was Horatio Seymour, the governor of New York. Seymour had many problems with the Lincoln administration's handling of the war, but Randall glosses over them. "As to the actual 1863 situation the fact of the President being of one party and the New York governor being of another should not be misunderstood. Instead of treating this difference with a party slant as some writers have done, it would be more in keeping with Lincoln's thought to view the subject from a nonpartisan standpoint. Lincoln felt that he and Seymour had much in agreement in that they had the same stake in keeping the government going."[2] Randall may be projecting his own political views onto the president.

Along with revisionism comes a somewhat dismissive attitude toward slavery. Revisionists generally thought slavery was dying and not worth fighting over. Randall laments the zeal that all parties brought to the 1860 presidential election: "Except for the saner elements which seemed inadequately vocal, the campaign was waged in an emotional atmosphere of abnormal intensity. It was unreality made real—a conflict made inevitable by repeatedly and vociferously declaring it so." Unfortunately, along with his revisionism Randall brings a negative attitude toward blacks. He shows his patronizing attitude toward the black Union troops: "In guffawing antics they added a welcome touch of comedy to the army scene. In their tugging and chorusing gangs heavy labor became a pastime."[3]

Randall gives the most detailed study of Lincoln's first emancipation plan. This plan is often obscured by the Emancipation Proclamation. In the months before that, Lincoln had proposed a compensated emancipation program for the Border States. Not surprisingly, Randall admires its seemingly conservative approach. "This blueprint was envisaged not merely with reference to the war, though its integration with a broad war policy was a vital factor; beyond the war the President's solution was projected into a peace minded future with a view to the ultimate, statesmanlike elimination of an institution in which, as Lincoln felt, North and South had a common responsibility and a community of interest."[4] Randall covers the attempt of Lincoln to implement his plan well, yet he misreads it as conservative since it really was an enormous change in Federal policy toward slavery.

Randall is interesting in that he is an admirer of both Lincoln and McClellan. In most books Lincoln is portrayed as the better man both militarily and politically. Randall does not see it that way, and his recounting of the Peninsula campaign of 1862 gives high marks to McClellan. Randall makes a convincing case that interference from Washington prevented McClellan's capturing Richmond. He may go too far in this and underestimates McClellan's well-known shortcomings as a general, yet Randall's perspective is a valid one and he skillfully supports it. Randall also believes that Lincoln and

McClellan were almost on the same page politically. "The real issues, as between Lincoln and McClellan, were much less sharp than they had been made to appear to the voters."[5]

There is one part of the series that had a negative effect on Lincoln scholarship for almost fifty years. It is an unnecessary appendix that Randall included in his second volume. Randall, who was an apologist for Mary Todd Lincoln, tried to show that Lincoln's youthful romance with Ann Rutledge was a myth. He does this with selective quoting and questioning the motives of the people involved. In doing so, he hurt the credibility of everyone Herndon had interviewed about Lincoln's early life.[6] This appendix lies outside the scope of Randall's work and should not have been included. The unfortunate result is that scholars stayed away from the very valuable material Herndon had collected on Lincoln's early life out of deference to the prestige of Randall as a historian.

Randall's and Current's work is still valuable for the depth of scholarship and professionalism they bring to Lincoln's presidency. Many of the interpretations of the era have changed. Revisionism has died, yet *Lincoln the President* still stands as a mammoth work that no academic historian has replaced as a study of Lincoln's years as president.

NOTES

1. James G. Randall, *Lincoln the President: Springfield to Gettysburg*, 2 vols. (New York: Dodd, Mead & Co., 1945); James G. Randall, *Lincoln the President: Midstream* (New York: Dodd, Mead & Co., 1952); James G. Randall and Richard N. Current, *Lincoln the President: Last Full Measure* (New York: Dodd, Mead & Co., 1955); Mark E. Neely Jr., *The Abraham Lincoln Encyclopedia* (New York: Da Capo, 1982), 255.
2. Randall, *Midstream*, 313.
3. Randall, *Springfield to Gettysburg*, 1:190, 2:203.
4. Ibid., 2:142.
5. Ibid., 2:120; Randall and Current, *Last Full Measure*, 262.
6. Randall, *Springfield to Gettysburg*, 2:321–42.

Lincoln in Caricature

AUTHOR: Rufus Rockwell Wilson
PUBLISHED: 1945
GENRE: The Lincoln Image

W HEN ONE discusses the Lincoln image, photographs and paintings are the usual mediums that come up. However, in Lincoln's lifetime the most popular type of image was caricatures of him in newspapers and prints. They ranged in tone from showing Lincoln as either demonic or stupid to showing him as a great statesman. Rufus Rockwell Wilson has collected some of the best of these caricatures in *Lincoln in Caricature* and provided commentary on them. This book came out in a limited edition in 1945 and was reprinted in wider distribution in 1953. The later edition is more easily obtainable and is a good addition to a Lincoln bookshelf, since it is a subject that many are not familiar with.

The most brutal caricatures are from Maryland's Adalbert John Volck, who published a series of twenty-nine caricatures of Lincoln in 1864 under the pseudonym of V. Blada. He was a talented artist, and his hatred of Lincoln knew no bounds. The four caricatures of Lincoln in the book show an evil and cowardly man. Volck shows a frightened Lincoln sneaking into Washington in a freight car, scared even of a cat. Lincoln is seen in another drawing writing the Emancipation Proclamation as he puts his foot on the Constitution. There is a picture of John Brown as a saint in a frame, and Lincoln's inkstand is in the shape of a devil. Another drawing shows Lincoln playing a fool in a tragedy onstage. The final drawing shows the North as a whole worshiping a black man and sacrificing a white man to him.

Volck packs a lot of detail into his drawings to get his point across; whether one agrees with his extreme pro-Confederate views is another matter.[1]

Wilson provides many Currier and Ives prints from presidential campaigns. Currier and Ives produced prints for every political party, so Lincoln is seen in both a positive light and a negative light. Lincoln is usually seen as a rail-splitter in the 1860 campaign. When Currier and Ives were making prints for the Republicans, his rail-splitting image was seen as a testament to his honesty and humble beginnings. In the critical caricatures, Lincoln's rail-splitting is lampooned as proving he is a simpleton. One caricature has Lincoln riding a rail held up by a slave and Horace Greeley. The slave is a racist caricature who says, "Dis N-gger strong and willin, bub its awful hard work to carry Old Massa Abe on nothing but dis ere rail!!" Rails are present in many of these caricatures, and the opposition made light of the fact that the Republicans seemed to be running on Lincoln's laboring past, which, to them at least, was not an important qualification for the highest office in the land.[2]

The most powerful and moving caricature is from England. After Lincoln died, *London Punch* included a memorial in which a weeping Lady Britannica lays a wreath on Lincoln's bier. Slaves are seen weeping, too, as they sit next to broken chains suggesting mourning over the man who freed them. The tone of this caricature is a far cry from the usual caricatures in that publication. Their usual view of Lincoln was as an awkward and incompetent man guilty of letting the bloodshed of war continue. The previous December they had featured a caricature of Lincoln as a phoenix burning things like free press, constitution, and credit. In the preface to the collection, Wilson writes of *London Punch*, "These caricatures as a whole were animated by bitter hostility to the Northern cause and a strange misunderstanding of Mr. Lincoln's character and purpose. Too late editor and artist awoke to their unfairness and injustice."[3]

During the 1864 presidential campaign, the caricaturists liked to play off the height difference between Lincoln and McClellan. In one cartoon, a giant Lincoln holds a small McClellan and says, "This reminds me of a little joke." When Lincoln won the election there was a clever visual play on words in *Harper's Weekly,* which showed an elongated Lincoln with the caption "Long Abraham a Little Longer." That image is so memorable that Wilson put it on the cover of the book.[4]

Lincoln's humor is often a target of caricaturists. In a Currier and Ives cartoon the country is falling apart, and all a laughing Lincoln has to say is, "This reminds me of a most capital joke." In another Lincoln asks for a funny song at the Antietam battlefield, which is littered with corpses. Lincoln's humor was an easy target for the opposition.[5]

Lincoln's striking appearance made him a caricaturist's dream, and that might account for the number of memorable caricatures of the man. This book preserves some of the best of that material from the Civil War period. Even today the caricatures get their message across quickly and humorously, which was the point in the first place.

NOTES

1. Rufus Rockwell Wilson, *Lincoln in Caricature* (New York: Horizon Press, 1953), 109, 193, 141, 237.
2. Ibid., 27, 31.
3. Ibid., 325, 309, xv.
4. Ibid., 281, 305.
5. Ibid., 275, 293.

Lincoln's War Cabinet

AUTHOR: Burton J. Hendrick
PUBLISHED: 1946
GENRE: Presidency

THIS IS the only book to focus exclusively on Lincoln's cabinet. There have been individual biographies of the various members before, but none on the cabinet as a whole. This is surprising, since the cabinet is made up of such fascinating people as William Seward and Salmon P. Chase. Burton J. Hendrick has done a fine job in capturing the cabinet as an entity. He pictures them as a group of enormous egos that at times were almost at each other's throats. "That the cabinet disintegrated in 1864 was not surprising; the really astonishing thing was that it had held together so long. No such uncongenial or contentious group had ever assembled beneath the White House roof. Lincoln's conception of a coalition was politically sound, but on the personal side it inevitably led to trouble." *Lincoln's War Cabinet* stresses Lincoln's skill in managing this group of men. Hendrick breaks his book into seven separate sections, which he calls books, covering different phases of Lincoln's relationships with the various members, and in each he shows Lincoln gaining the upper hand.[1]

The most influential and important member of the cabinet was William Seward, the secretary of state. Seward originally saw himself as the "prime minister" of the administration and in the early days sought to carry out his own agenda in regard to the Southern states. On the first day of April 1861, Seward gave what amounts to an ultimatum to Lincoln: "In this paper Seward thus definitely proposed that Lincoln not only eliminate himself from the conduct of affairs, but the cabinet as well. The demand that supreme power be 'devolved' upon some member, and that 'once adopted, debates on it must end, and all agree and abide' could have no other meaning. He evidently desired no more discussions such as had recently taken place on Fort Sumter; one man—that is, Seward himself—was to settle all such problems and enforce his decisions with no interference from any other source." This was too much for Lincoln, and Seward was quickly put in his place with a letter of response. "Lincoln therefore replied to Seward's statements of his case with a quiet dignity that in itself amounted to a severe rebuke."[2] Hendrick's analysis of this strange episode in Seward's career is right on target.

Hendrick deems the resignation of Montgomery Blair, the postmaster general, as a necessary evil for Lincoln's election. The conservative Blair was an anathema to most of his fellow Republicans. The Republican platform subtly called for his resignation in 1864. Blair's loyalty to Lincoln had led him to write out his resignation and leave it undated. "Personally fond as Lincoln was of his Postmaster General and as he highly esteemed his abilities and his worth, his presence in the cabinet had been an embarrassment for a considerable time." Lincoln appears to have sacrificed Blair on the altar of political expediency. Hendrick is somewhat critical of this. He is writing in the time of revisionism, and he sees the Radicals as wrongfully pushing Blair out. Again, Lincoln's ability to win people over is evident in Blair's conduct for the rest of the 1864 campaign. One would expect Blair to be angry or indifferent to Lincoln's reelection. Hendrick records the opposite: "One week after leaving the cabinet Montgomery appeared at a great Lincoln rally in Cooper Union, New York. His speech was an eloquent eulogy of Lincoln and a plea for his overwhelming election." Furthermore, "Up till the day of his death, in 1883, any man who attacked Lincoln's memory invariably found Montgomery Blair a most aggressive defender."[3]

Lincoln's skillful handling of his competent yet disloyal secretary of the treasury is covered as well. Salmon Chase wished desperately to replace Lincoln as president in 1864. Due to Chase's dealings in this matter, Lincoln eventually had to force him to leave his cabinet that summer by accepting his resignation. Chase, unlike Blair, was bitter. "Montgomery's conduct and that of Chase after 'decapitation' brings out in bold contrast the two characters of the men." However, Chase saw the handwriting on the wall and had to support Lincoln. "By September 17, Chase no longer hesitated as to his course. He returned to Washington and called upon the President. . . . In the short time that remained before the voting, Chase made several speeches in Lincoln's favor, the most ambitious in his home town, Cincinnati." Lincoln would appoint Chase Chief Justice of the Supreme Court after the election. He skillfully left the position open in order to ensure Chase's loyalty.[4]

Lincoln's cabinet as a whole deserves greater scrutiny. The way he handled these difficult yet competent people is one of the reasons he is America's greatest president. Hendrick in this book gives us this side of Lincoln in more depth than anyone else has. The biographical information he supplies adds a human touch to these historical figures. Lincoln's cabinet certainly found a worthy biographer in Hendrick.

NOTES

1. For an alternative view of Lincoln's formation of his cabinet, see William E. Baringer, *A House Dividing: Lincoln As President Elect* (Springfield: Abraham Lincoln Association, 1945); Burton J. Hendrick, *Lincoln's War Cabinet* (Boston: Little, Brown, and Co., 1946), 369.
2. Hendrick, 125, 176, 177.
3. Ibid., 441, 458, 460, 460.
4. Ibid., 459, 457.

The Lincoln Reader

AUTHOR: Paul M. Angle, editor
PUBLISHED: 1947
GENRE: Biography

THIS BOOK is not so much a biography as an anthology. Paul M. Angle takes bits and pieces of Lincoln's story from sixty-five different authors. Angle has a total of 179 selections that tell Lincoln's story from his birth to death. Angle himself contributes commentary on the various selections. *The Lincoln Reader* is special since it gathers together so many different authors in one book. Angle had a good sense of selection, even if he could not explain it. "I wish I could formulate the standard selection by which I have been guided. It would be gratifying, though presumptuous, to be able to assert that here is the 'best' of Carl Sandburg, or Lord Charnwood, or Nicolay and Hay, but I make no such claim." Angle is too modest; he did pick his authors' selections in their areas of individual strength.[1]

It is no surprise that for Lincoln's childhood he picked authors like Ida M. Tarbell and William E. Barton. They were specialists on this part of Lincoln's life. Tarbell aptly describes the physical surroundings of Lincoln's mother, Nancy Hanks, in Kentucky: "Here, as there, the fireplace of the cabin was the very heart of this place. Nancy's fireplace, as we see it today, was deep and wide, with a long stone mantel and big hearthstone. The chimney was outside—a cant-and-clay chimney, as it was called, made by mixing cut straw or grass with stiff clay and laying it in alternative layers with split lathes of hard wood. Within, hooks were fitted and the long crane from which to suspend the pots." William E. Barton describes the milieu of Lincoln's father's life: "The pioneer did not fret because he could not cut down the whole forest in a single year. He accepted his situation, and when his day's work was done, he rested and visited and took life as comfortably as he was able."[2]

Angle's choices of authors on Lincoln's political career in Illinois are telling. Angle could have picked only eulogizers of Lincoln's political life. He makes a surprising choice in including a selection from Democratic governor Thomas Ford. Ford believed the Whigs of Sangamon County, of which Lincoln was one, had ruined the state's economy by supporting an unsustainable internal-improvement system. Ford believed that the Sangamon County delegation had used unscrupulous means to get the capital moved to Springfield in exchange for votes for internal improvements. "By distributing money to some of the counties, to be wasted by the county commissioners, and by giving the seat of government to Springfield, was the whole State bought up and bribed, to approve the most senseless and disastrous policy which ever crippled the energies of a growing country."[3] Ford may have been wrong, but Angle was right to include a not-so-favorable look at Lincoln's politics for balance.

For the famous Lincoln-Douglas debates, Angle made ten selections. His choices are again superb. Especially amusing are the headlines of a pro-Lincoln paper and a pro-Douglas paper concerning the Freeport debate. The pro-Douglas *Chicago Times* recounts, "Douglas and Lincoln.—15,000 present!—Lincoln on Pledges.—Lincoln 'Aint Pledged' to Anything! Lincoln Asks Questions! Lincoln Gets Answered!—A Leak Takes Place.—The 'Lion' Frightened the 'Dog'!—Lincoln Gets Weak! Lincoln a Fountain!!—Speeches of the Candidates." The pro-Lincoln *Chicago Tribune* has a different spin: "Fifteen Thousand Persons Present.—The Dred Scott Champion 'Trotted Out' and 'Brought to His Milk.'—It Proves to Be Stump-Tailed.—Great Caving-in on the Ottawa Forgery.—He Was 'Conscientious' about It.—Why Chase's Amendment Was Voted Down.—Lincoln Tumbles Him All over Stephenson County.—Verbatim Report of Lincoln's Speech.—Douglas' Reply and Lincoln's Rejoinder."[4] The reader will have to decide which headline was more accurate.

Lincoln's presidency is covered in great detail by people present during some of the most important moments. John Hay, Thomas T. Eckert, Gideon Welles, Salmon P. Chase, and Edward Bates are just some of the eyewitness accounts Angle includes. There are superior secondary works as well from James G. Randall, Lord Charnwood, Lloyd Lewis, and Margaret Leech. Leech writes of Washington as the news of Lee's surrender arrived. "While the illuminations turned a shrouding mist to gold, an immense throng gathered before the White House, filling the grounds and obstructing the sidewalks of Pennsylvania Avenue. As Lincoln stepped to the window, cheers surged and broke, and surged again."[5]

The epilogue of the book is left to the eloquent Lord Charnwood. "Many great deeds had been done in the war. The greatest was the keeping of the North together in an enterprise so arduous, and an enterprise for objects so confusedly related as the Union and Freedom. Abraham Lincoln did this; nobody else could have done it; to do it he bore on his sole shoulders such a weight of care and pain as few other men have borne."[6] Angle did indeed get the "best" of these authors.

NOTES

1. Paul M. Angle, ed., *The Lincoln Reader* (New Brunswick: Rutgers University Press, 1947), xi.
2. Ida M. Tarbell in ibid., 7–8; William E. Barton in ibid., 14.
3. Thomas Ford in ibid., 88.
4. *Chicago Times*, August 27, 1858, in ibid., 236; *Chicago Tribune*, August 27, 1858, in ibid., 237.
5. Angle, vii–viii; Margaret Leech in ibid., 518.
6. Lord Charnwood in ibid., 538.

Lincoln the Liberal Statesman

AUTHOR: James G. Randall
PUBLISHED: 1947
GENRE: General

JAMES G. RANDALL offers in *Lincoln the Liberal Statesman* a series of essays that cover many aspects of Lincoln's life and career. His book came out after the end of the Second World War and sees Lincoln as a true liberal who personifies the path the country should be taking in the postwar years. "To explore the thought of a liberal statesman fully enough to understand the interplay of motive and application in his own time is to lay the groundwork for conclusions and solutions in the present age. One cannot say that present factors are the same as those of Lincoln's day, though there are similarities." One problem with this is Randall's definition of *liberalism*. As was said in regard to *Lincoln the President,* Randall's Lincoln looks a lot like Randall.[1]

Randall was a Woodrow Wilson Democrat. He even worked in the Wilson administration. Wilson was a Southern Democrat whose views on race were hardly enlightened. He was an ardent segregationist. One Wilson biographer remarked, "In any case he permitted several of his cabinet to segregate, for the first time since the Civil War, whites and negroes within executive departments." Randall sees a special kinship between Lincoln and Wilson. He sees a similarity between Lincoln's supposedly generous peace toward the South and Wilson's Fourteen Points of Peace. Both were thwarted in their efforts by partisan radicals. Randall engages in hyperbole in discussing the foes of Wilson: "In years that should have been fruitful for peace the United States drifted down the anti-Wilson road through international anarchy to Hitler and world disaster." As to Lincoln, "The overthrow of Lincoln's plan by partisan radicals, in the vindictive period of exploitation and abuse that has been miscalled 'reconstruction,' cannot be reviewed here, though its sordidness should be remembered for those twinges of conscience that are good for the soul."[2] Randall, true to his Wilsonian leanings, doesn't think much of the efforts of the Radicals to gain civil rights for former slaves during this period. Randall's view of liberalism in regard to race would not be accepted today and would certainly not have been accepted by Abraham Lincoln.

Randall gives the revisionist case in a compact form in the essay "A Blundering Generation." He is quite emphatic about it. "The notion that you must have war when you have cultural variation, or economic competition, or sectional difference is an unhistorical misinterpretation which is stupid to promote. Yet some of the misinterpretations of the Civil War have tended to promote it." Randall sees the blundering as being done mainly by Northern Radicals, whom he defines as people who cared about slavery's spread. "Southerners cared little about taking slaves into the territories; Republicans cared so little in the opposite sense that they avoided prohibiting slavery in territorial laws passed in February and March of 1861."[3] Randall's views are not accepted by many today, yet they represent the dominant view of his generation.

There is a touch of egotism in Randall's writing that can be hard to swallow at times. In an appendix in *Lincoln the President,* Randall attacks the Ann Rutledge story. Randall does it again in this book. "The sentimental tradition as to Lincoln and Ann Rutledge still persists, but informed readers are by this time well advised of the thinness of its historical basis." To back up this assertion, Randall cites his own appendix! Apparently, the only people qualified as informed readers on this matter are the ones who read his work.[4]

Having said all this, there are positive things about this book that make it a valuable addition to a Lincoln bookshelf. The best essay in the book, "Lincoln and John Bright," brings to light a touching cross-Atlantic relationship between two progressive politicians. John

Bright was a Quaker who disregarded his religion's pacifism to support Lincoln and the Union cause in Parliament. "The Lincoln-
Bright friendship was not related to any particular setting nor
confined to a special episode. Its reference was to great and enduring
values. Its concern was the essential attitudes of whole people
towards each other." Randall makes the point that Bright and Lincoln
never met, but as Randall states, "Few friendships so indirect have
been so real."[5]

The last essay in the book is also well done. "Lincoln the Liberal
Statesman" sums up Lincoln's liberalism as seen by Randall. Randall
often misses the point about Lincoln, in particular concerning slavery, but he sometimes gets it just right. "Though primarily interested
in popular rights on these shores, Lincoln showed a vigorous sympathy for democracy in other lands. He declared that when he saw a
people borne down by tyranny he would do all in his power to raise
the yoke."[6] Randall was a great scholar, and this essay, like the
others, gives an important and valid, but perhaps not always correct,
view of Lincoln.

NOTES

1. James G. Randall, *Lincoln the Liberal Statesman* (New York: Dodd, Mead & Co.,
   1947), xiii; James G. Randall and Richard N. Current, *Lincoln the President*, 4
   vols. (New York: Dodd, Mead & Co., 1945–55).
2. Merrill D. Peterson, *Lincoln in American Memory* (New York: Oxford University
   Press, 1994), 300; John Morton Blum, *Woodrow Wilson and the Politics of Morality*
   (Boston: Little, Brown and Co., 1956), 115; Randall, 157, 153.
3. Randall, 36–64, 50, 48–49.
4. James G. Randall, *Lincoln the President: Springfield to Gettysburg,* 2 vols. (New
   York: Dodd, Mead & Co., 1945), 2:321–42; Randall, *Lincoln the Liberal Statesman,* 5, 208.
5. Randall, *Lincoln the Liberal Statesman,* 135–50, 137, 136.
6. Ibid., 175–206, 199.

Portrait for Posterity: Lincoln and His Biographers

AUTHOR: Benjamin P. Thomas
PUBLISHED: 1947
GENRE: Historiography

*P*ORTRAIT FOR POSTERITY: *Lincoln and His Biographers* is the second title from Benjamin P. Thomas to make this list. It is a valuable study of Lincoln biographers from 1865 until right after the Second World War. Thomas himself would write a biography a few years after this book was published that is still considered by some to be the best single-volume biography. Thomas probably prepared for writing this book by seeing where previous biographers had succeeded and failed. Thomas's great literary ability is again evident in this book. What could have been a dry topic is made interesting by Thomas's skilled storytelling.[1]

Thomas divides Lincoln biographers into two broad categories. They are either "realists" or "idealists." Thomas describes the situation shortly after Lincoln's death: "Here four years after Lincoln's death, it was as though two groups of artists had clustered about an easel, eager to paint a portrait for posterity. But they differed violently and volubly in concept. On the one hand were a few realists who would throw the highlights into bold relief against the shadows. Opposed were the far more numerous idealists who thought the features should be softened with a refracted light—the kind peculiar to a halo." Thomas sees Josiah Holland as the archetype of the "idealists" and William Herndon of the "realists." This distinction is artificial in some cases. Thomas might have allowed more categories. Many biographers do not fit neatly into the two.[2]

Thomas includes some biographers who have faded into obscurity. Henry Clay Whitney was a lawyer who practiced with Lincoln. His book *Life on the Circuit with Lincoln* was published in 1892. It is a book that tends to be rambling at times, yet it does take an honest look at Lincoln's legal career. "In a clear case of dishonesty he would hedge in some way so as to not, himself, partake of the dishonesty. In a doubtful case of dishonesty, he would give his client the benefit of the doubt, and in an ordinary case he would try the case, so far as he could, like any other lawyer, expect that he absolutely abjured technicality and went for justice and victory." Whitney also points out that Lincoln as a lawyer would not necessarily give up his client even if he knew the client was in the wrong. Being a lawyer was a business endeavor, and Lincoln had to pay attention to it.[3]

Thomas's book has some telling anecdotes about the most famous Lincoln biographers. He has an anecdote of William E. Barton that is humorous and seems very close to character. "Barton was not bashful of his eminence. One time, on a trip to New Salem, he alighted from the train at Petersburg and engaged a hackman for the day. The mud on New Salem was axle deep, the air was raw and penetrating, but the driver, proud to be of service to the great, was undeterred." Thomas finished the story with Barton simply promising the man a copy of his next book, instead of giving the man money for his hard work all day. Thomas also relates how William Herndon responded to criticism of his Lincoln lectures from a fellow lawyer: "William Herndon was never a man to duck a punch or take one without retaliating. His counterblow was short, sharp, and devastating. 'Mr. Goodrich, Sir,' he wrote. 'I thank you for the first part of your letter giving me an account of the patent case which Mr. Lincoln "tended" to. I say thank you for it. As to the second part of your letter, I guess I shall have to treat you as Lincoln always did treat you, as an exceedingly weak-headed brother. The more he kicked you the closer you clung to him. Do you remember? Analyze yourself.'"[4]

Toward the end of his book, Thomas mounts a vigorous defense of those who tend to excessively "eulogize" Lincoln. "Extreme eulogists of Lincoln sometimes go so far as to compare their hero with Jesus Christ; and while some realists may scoff, there is a valid comparison, in one respect at least, and it goes far to explain why books continue to be written. For both Christ and Lincoln symbolize great vibrant, living forces—the one Christianity, the other Democracy—and so long as these forces remain vital there will be no cessation of interest in either man."[5] Thomas may well be right about the reason for the continued fascination with the sixteenth president.

In the end, Thomas acknowledges the contributions of both the "realists" and the "idealists." He closes, "The realist's ruthless searching gives the necessary facts. Yet the realist is ill-advised to scorn the idealist's sensitivity to those soul-qualities of Lincoln which documentary facts alone may not disclose. The idealists, on their part, need not fear facts; time has shown this fear to be ridiculous. For as our portrait of Lincoln becomes true, it also becomes more superb."[6] Thomas is correct and shows once again with this book why he is one of the greatest Lincoln writers.

NOTES

1. Benjamin P. Thomas, *Abraham Lincoln: A Biography* (New York: Knopf, 1952); David Herbert Donald, *Lincoln* (New York, Simon & Schuster, 1995), 601.
2. Benjamin P. Thomas, *Portrait for Posterity: Lincoln and His Biographers* (New Brunswick: Rutgers University Press, 1947), 28, 4, 7.
3. Ibid., 165, 169–70.
4. Ibid., 220, 23–24.
5. Ibid., 309.
6. Ibid., 310.

Lincoln's Herndon

AUTHOR: David Herbert Donald
PUBLISHED: 1948
GENRE: Historiography

HERNDON'S INFLUENCE on Lincoln biography is immense, as has been shown throughout this current volume. To understand Lincoln, it is necessary to understand Herndon to a large degree. This is the only biography of William Herndon. Its author is one of the greatest Lincoln scholars of all time, and this biography was his first entry in the field.

David Herbert Donald wrote *Lincoln's Herndon* shortly after World War II. James Randall's revisionism influenced it heavily. That comes as no surprise, since Donald was a student of Randall. Donald writes negatively of the principal actors and the coming war in a way that mirrors Randall's "A Blundering Generation" essay. "Douglas would shortly dissolve the great national Democratic Party over the future of two slaves in Kansas; Lincoln would let a nation rise in arms to prevent the extension of slavery to regions where nature had already prohibited it; Herndon would willingly sit down to the bloody feast of civil war in order to forestall a hypothetical attempt on the part of an imaginary Southern despotism to extend slavery into Illinois." Herndon was a strong Republican before the war. As revisionism's favorite targets are Republicans, especially of the Radical type, Herndon does not fare well in this biography.[1]

It is important to note that in a later edition of this biography, Donald backtracked from this view. "As I look back, I think that my argument on this point—and it appears in several scattered passages in the first half of the book—had less to do with my understandings of the 1850s than with my concerns in the late 1940s. While writing Herndon's biography, I, like so many others, desperately feared that the Cold War between the United States and the Soviet Union might erupt into a shooting war."[2] Being a Lincoln scholar for so long has allowed Donald to see the larger sweep of history.

The first part of this biography covers Herndon's life up until Lincoln's death. In Donald's view, Herndon is an erratic man. For instance, during Lincoln's senatorial campaign in 1858, Herndon loyally stumped for Lincoln. Since most Irish supported Douglas, they were not thought highly of by Herndon. At one point in the campaign, Herndon turned violent. "Billy [Herndon] leaped from his seat, yelling 'God Damn the Irish, I want it distinctly understood that we [Republicans] . . . are willing to have war with them,' seized the noisy drunk and unceremoniously chucked him downstairs." Herndon's alcoholism was also a serious problem. "When Herndon and a couple of cronies celebrated so wildly one night that they broke the tavern windows, they turned to Lincoln to pay their fines, and that good man got out in the grey morning to collect the one hundred dollars needed to keep his partner from jail."[3] Herndon was far from a saint.

If Herndon was so erratic, why did Lincoln make him his law partner? The answer seems to lie in Herndon's loyalty. Donald recalls Lincoln's despondent mood after his defeat at the hands of Douglas. "When friends dropped by to see him, he complained mournfully: 'I expect everyone to desert me except Billy.'" Donald also gives Herndon credit for doing most of the drudgery of research Lincoln used in court.[4]

The second part of the book deals with Herndon's attempt to write a biography of Lincoln. This biography is the reason why Herndon is famous. Donald shows the importance of Herndon's literary partner, Jesse Weik. Herndon's writing often goes in many directions at once. Weik did his best to prune Herndon's prose, and his doing so helped to make *Herndon's Lincoln* a classic.[5]

Donald admires Herndon's honesty in writing his biography. "There is not to the present writer's knowledge, a single letter or other manuscript that reveals a desire or willingness to lie." Donald does question some of Herndon's judgments, though, such as his insistence that Lincoln failed to show up to his original wedding. According to Donald, the best part of Herndon's biography is the personal observations Herndon gives of his famous partner: "The heart of the Herndon-Weik biography is its brief, vivid glimpse, of Lincoln on the platform, in the law office, in the courts, walking Springfield's muddy streets. There are bits of description which have the precision of a Brady photograph: Lincoln bursting into uproarious guffaws over 'Nothing to Wear'; the future President 'stalking towards the market-house, basket on arm, his old gray shawl wrapped around his neck, his little boy Willie or Tad running along at his heels asking a thousand boyish questions'; the circuit lawyer sleeping in a short bed with enormous feet and bare shins projecting over the footboard."[6] One would have to agree with Donald on this point, since many of the characteristics of Lincoln that are so familiar come from Herndon.

Donald's book is the only book-length source for biographical details on this complicated man. A new biography of Herndon could be useful. The tone in this one is fairly negative. While Herndon is not perfect, he was honest and contributed greatly to our knowledge of Lincoln.

NOTES

1. See James G. Randall, *Lincoln the Liberal Statesman* (New York: Dodd, Mead & Co., 1947), 36–64; David Herbert Donald, *Lincoln's Herndon* (New York: Da Capo, 1989), 102.
2. Donald, vii.
3. Ibid., 125, 126.
4. Ibid., 126, 38.
5. Ibid., 366–67.
6. Ibid., 347, 358–60, 351.

Lincoln and the
War Governors

AUTHOR: William B. Hesseltine
PUBLISHED: 1948
GENRE: Presidency

O F ALL the books deemed essential, this one is the most negative in attitude about Abraham Lincoln. William B. Hesseltine was a Jeffersonian Democrat. His political interpretation of the war is evident in the preface of *Lincoln and the War Governors*. "Rather than a war among the American states, the conflict of 1861–1865 was a war between the states on one hand and the growing power of the national government on the other. In popular speech, the Southern Confederacy symbolized the particularist principles of states' rights, and the United States embodies the national creed." Slavery was not an important issue in the war, according to his analysis. Hesseltine's sympathies are generally with the South. In a book he edited about Civil War prisons, Hesseltine believed the North was far more culpable for prison deaths than the South. "Certainly Secretary of War E. M. Stanton ordered Northern prison authorities to reduce food, fuel, shelter, and clothing of prisoners to levels that he and propagandists of the North contended were parallel to conditions in the South."[1] One has to remember, Hesseltine does have a Southern ax to grind in this book.

It is not that Hesseltine sees Lincoln as wholly evil. He is somewhat ambiguous on that point. He feels that Lincoln was not above military intimidation at the polls, yet he believes Lincoln was still better than the Radical Republicans. On Lincoln's death Hesseltine writes, "On the night of April 14, in Ford's Theatre, insane John

Wilkes Booth brought to a sudden end the last best chance of moderate, conciliatory, reconstruction."[2] One wonders, after all the charges leveled against the Lincoln administration in this book, how the author could close with such a sentiment.

The book's worth sometimes overcomes its agenda. It covers a little-written-about area of Lincoln's political dealings during the war. Lincoln had to work with various chief executives of the Northern states in fighting the war. This was much more important then than it would be in a modern-day war. The troops were raised not by the Federal government but rather by the states. They were then mustered into Federal service. Lincoln had to massage a lot of egos in order to keep the war effort on track.

Hesseltine's thesis is that early in the war Lincoln was forced to depend on the governors. Later in the war, the governors were dependent on Lincoln. Hesseltine may be generalizing too much in this. Each state had a specific political complexion, and not all had to depend on Lincoln. For example, Massachusetts was going to elect Republican governors no matter what Lincoln did.

Revisionism also influenced the book. The governors who were Radical Republicans are seen as bloodthirsty men who thought only of themselves and not their country. "They had clamored for war upon the South, they had rejoiced over Sumter, and they had plunged with enthusiasm into their new roles as commanders-in-chiefs." Hesseltine views the governors' Altoona conference as having forced Lincoln to deal with slavery. He makes a bold assertion concerning the conference: "In Lincoln's desk the Emancipation Proclamation would probably have remained had it not been for the increased activities of the radicals and a new move from the governors." The fact is, the proclamation had been written months before, and Lincoln was waiting for a Union victory. He got one at Antietam; the Altoona conference really had nothing to do with it.[3]

Hesseltine's political sympathies naturally make him admire the Northern Democrats, particularly Horatio Seymour, the governor of New York. "In Horatio Seymour it was evident, the forces of national concentration had met a foeman worthy of their steel." Hesseltine also praises Seymour's inaugural, stating it had "a realism strange to the political oratory of war." Seymour's loss in his reelection bid is chalked up to fraud. "The Democrats diligently dug up several sick soldiers who, having voted earlier in the hospitals, got home in time to vote—and found Republican ballots in their envelopes."[4]

Lincoln's political skill and the underhanded methods of Stanton went on to save many Republican governors in 1864, according to Hesseltine. "The need for Lincoln's aid was illustrated in Pennsylvania. There it was not thought necessary to send the soldiers home. Early in the summer the legislature had provided for voting in the field. Under the law the Democratic minority had no rights." Democrats won local elections in Pennsylvania only because Republican governor Andrew Curtin had a conscience, in Hesseltine's view.[5]

The book's ultimate strength comes from its topic. Here, between two covers, one can get political information about Northern governors that is not easily obtainable. It also follows the political situations in the states themselves, which is an important story rarely discussed in Civil War literature. Former Speaker of the House Tip O'Neill once famously said, "All politics is local." That is true, and it underscores why this book is so valuable.

NOTES

1. William B. Hesseltine, *Lincoln and the War Governors* (New York: Knopf, 1948), v; William B. Hesseltine, ed., *Civil War Prisons* (Kent, Ohio: Kent State University Press, 1992), 7.
2. Hesseltine, *Lincoln and the War Governors*, 393.
3. Ibid., 167, 249.
4. Ibid., 284–85, 283.
5. Ibid., 379.

Lincoln Runs
for Congress

AUTHOR: Donald W. Riddle
PUBLISHED: 1948
GENRE: Prepresidential Years

L INCOLN'S EFFORTS to become a U.S. congressman were long and arduous. He was a Whig in the only Whig district in the state, so naturally there was a lot of competition from other ambitious Whigs for the seat. The story of Lincoln's efforts in the district to gain the seat is the topic of *Lincoln Runs for Congress*. Donald W. Riddle's book is an exciting account of the sometimes bitter political battles Lincoln had to wage to become a congressman. It is included here for its strong contribution to understanding Lincoln's Illinois political career.

Riddle provides background information of the political situation in Illinois. The state was overwhelmingly Democratic. Riddle shows how the settlement of the state influenced its political makeup. Illinois originally was settled mainly from the South. "When the Democratic and Whig parties, properly so-called appeared in Illinois, the distribution of adherents of the two parties was affected by the regional influence of settlement. . . . Most of the southern counties were (and remained) Democratic. The Whig counties tended to border the Wabash, Ohio, Mississippi, and Sangamon rivers." Riddle also blames the poor attempts at organization by the Whig Party in the state for their unfortunate showings. By the time Lincoln ran for Congress, there was only one Whig district out of seven in the state. Riddle makes the point that even it was not wholly Whig. There were some Democratic counties, but it was still a safe Whig seat.[1]

Lincoln made his first attempt for the Whig nomination in 1843, but he lost his county's delegation to his friend Edward Baker. It would seem that Lincoln's marriage hurt him because he was seen as marrying into the aristocracy. "Lincoln remarked that it would 'astonish, if not amuse the older citizens to learn that I (a stranger, friendless, uneducated, penniless boy, working on a flatboat for ten dollars per month) have been put down as the candidate of pride, wealth, and aristocratic distinction.'" Baker would lose the nomination to another rising star in Illinois politics, John Hardin. However, at the Whig convention Lincoln did something very clever. He had a resolution passed that nominated Baker for the next election. In doing so, Lincoln set up a revolving seat for the Whigs in the county. This ensured that after Baker had finished, Lincoln could get the nomination. Riddle covers this wirepulling, which could be confusing, in a clear and understandable way.[2]

Lincoln was to run in 1846. Hardin did not like this because he thought he was being maneuvered out of the nomination he had earned by his service. Riddle records Lincoln's skillful handling of the situation. Lincoln had made it seem that Hardin was reneging on a deal. "He (Hardin) could not fail to see that the slogan 'Turn about is fair play,' however indefensible it was to him and might be to others, had been subtly infused into the public mind and that it, too, was gaining in public acceptance. It was becoming clear to General Hardin that A. Lincoln, Esq., was a formidable opponent." Hardin was forced to withdraw. His story ends tragically when he was killed at the battle of Buena Vista during the Mexican War. Had he lived, he might have continued to be a powerful political figure in the state.[3]

Lincoln's opponent in the general election was Peter Cartwright, a Methodist preacher. "Lincoln's opponent was, indeed, a picturesque figure. Like Lincoln, Cartwright was an emigrant from Kentucky who had settled in the fertile Sangamo region. . . . The Democratic candidate for Congress was a preacher of tremendous energy and first rate ability. His industry seemed limitless in miles traveled while riding his circuits, in number of sermons preached, revivals and camp meetings held, conversions, and baptisms, his feats became legendary." Despite Cartwright's energy, the campaign was fairly quiet. The reason is that Cartwright never had a real chance. The Seventh was safe for the Whigs. It is telling that Riddle feels a short chapter can adequately cover this part of the campaign in comparison to his much longer chapters on Lincoln's maneuvering to get the Whig nomination.[4]

The only real attack Cartwright could make was on Lincoln's religious views. Cartwright tried a whispering campaign that painted Lincoln as an "infidel." Lincoln was forced to respond in a famous handbill in which he admits to not being a member of a church but denied that he ever questioned the truth of the Scriptures. Lincoln's handbill is confusing as to what his actual religious views were, but it didn't matter. "Lincoln's victory was by far the most conclusive of the Congressional elections in the Seventh District up to that time."[5]

Riddle's book is indispensable, not only for understanding Lincoln's tortuous path to Congress, but also in understanding the political makeup of the state and how the parties operated during that time period. There is not likely to be a better book on this subject.

NOTES

1. Donald W. Riddle, *Lincoln Runs for Congress* (New Brunswick: Rutgers University Press, 1948), 35–36, 43, 57.
2. Ibid., 64, 71.
3. Ibid., 90.
4. Ibid., 163–64, 160–75.
5. Ibid., 174, 177.

Lincoln's Vandalia: A Pioneer Portrait

AUTHOR: William E. Baringer
PUBLISHED: 1949
GENRE: Places Associated with Lincoln

THE TITLE to this book is ironic. Lincoln did more than anyone else to try to move the Illinois state capital from Vandalia to Springfield, thus ensuring Vandalia's relative obscurity. Author William E. Baringer writes with a wistful note of the town's obscurity. "Motorists on U.S. 40 between Terre Haute and St. Louis encounter modern Vandalia as a peaceful town in central Illinois, differing from a thousand others only in a vague tradition of historic events long past." That does not mean Vandalia is unimportant. Vandalia was the site of Lincoln's earliest political education, so it is an integral part of the Lincoln story: "In the muddy village of Vandalia he learned and practiced the subtleties of his trade under the example of the tutelage of experienced politicians. Here for the first time he mingled in polite society with men and women of wealth, culture, education; here he debated and discussed every phase of national and state politics and economic theory, probing problems of slavery and abolition, banking rights, executive powers and patronage, temperance, internal improvements, public lands, tariff, education, capital punishment, judicial procedure, financial panic."[1]

Vandalia was indeed a learning experience for Lincoln, and *Lincoln's Vandalia: A Frontier Portrait* covers extensively the political doings of the young Lincoln during his stay in the town. Vandalia, on the other hand, doesn't have much for which to be thankful to Lincoln.

Vandalia was founded a year after Illinois became a state in 1819. A new capital was needed that was farther north and not subject to the flooding that the territorial capital, Kaskaskia, experienced. Vandalia suffered the growing pains many frontier towns go through. Lincoln first arrived in 1834. Ten years before he got there, the statehouse had burned down. "All summer in 1824 gapers watched a new brick capital rise near the charred site of the old. Workmen and supplies of materials proceeded on faith that the state would pay them later. When the legislature met in November they found a two-story brick building, plain and badly constructed, ready to house the state government and to be paid for. By the time Lincoln arrived to represent Sangamon County, the second state house was nearly ready to fall down."[2] The people of Vandalia were scared of losing their status as state capital to other locations, and in their haste they hadn't constructed a very sturdy building.

The best sections of this book deal with little-known aspects of the town, such as its social life and its frontier economy. "Enforcement of municipal regulations against fighting would have been difficult if not impossible, had not the custom taken hold of settling arguments at a place called the 'Bull Pen.' At a pond on the northern edge of town contestants gathered when personal combat was imminent. Honor satisfied, the sporting event invariably ended at a nearby tavern." The town's economic growth was a rough-and-tumble thing as well. "Business establishments waxed and waned with astonishing rapidity. Partnerships of the twenties, which had often changed two or three times a year, had been replaced by new ones of evanescent character. The firms were still general stores; specialization had made but slight progress." Vandalia never developed a strong enough economy on its own. It depended too much on state expenditure.[3]

Vandalia did make a valiant effort to keep its status as state capital. It even built another new building, but as Baringer shows, it was still inadequate for the needs of the growing state. Vandalia suffered the same fate as its predecessor, Kaskaskia. The state's population was moving northward. Vandalia originally was moved northward to accommodate that fact, yet the movement of the state's population continued. Vandalia was now too far south. Lincoln and his friends in Sangamon County got their wish to locate the capital in the more central Springfield. Vandalia made attempts to stop this, but it was a lost cause.[4]

Mark Neely said rightfully, "The importance of Vandalia as a temporary residence for Abraham Lincoln, who was there for about 44 weeks altogether, has generally been underestimated. That is largely due to the restoration and subsequent promotion of New Salem as a tourist attraction." Vandalia did leave its marks on Lincoln. Baringer closes his book with these thoughts: "The Civil War President had good reason to remember his old colleagues in Vandalia. They had assisted in the winning of his first political triumph. Politics and politicians were not essentially different on the Potomac and on the Kaskaskia. In Washington, as in Vandalia, he won his victory, using in his handling of national affairs a skill in practical politics which he began to develop three decades earlier, back in the frontier capital."[5]

Thankfully, due to the efforts of Baringer and others, this frontier town is not forgotten.

NOTES

1. William E. Baringer, *Lincoln's Vandalia: A Pioneer Portrait* (New Brunswick: Rutgers University Press, 1949), 3, 4, 71–126.
2. Ibid., 12, 22–23.
3. Ibid., 23, 33.
4. Ibid., 86, 123.
5. Mark E. Neely Jr., *The Abraham Lincoln Encyclopedia* (New York: Da Capo, 1982), 319; Baringer, 126.

Abraham Lincoln: A Biography

AUTHOR: Benjamin P. Thomas
PUBLISHED: 1952
GENRE: Biography

A FTER BENJAMIN P. THOMAS had written about Lincoln's biographers, he decided to write his own biography. It was fortunate that he did, because the biography he left is an acknowledged classic. Thomas wrote his biography after the work of professional historians such as James Randall had dominated the field, but as Lincoln scholar Allen Guelzo states, "Ironically, what remains the finest one-volume survey biography of Lincoln, Benjamin Thomas's *Abraham Lincoln: A Biography* (1952), was written by a nonacademic, the executive secretary of the Abraham Lincoln Association."[1] The reason Thomas's biography is of such quality is that his vast knowledge of Lincoln was backed up by a literary skill few biographers possess.

A good example of that skill is Thomas's account of the death of Lincoln's mother. He relates the story of the milk sickness and how it was killing the neighbors of the Lincolns in Indiana. Unfortunately, it then struck Nancy Lincoln: "Soon afterward Nancy Hanks Lincoln became ill and died on October 5. Again Thomas put together a rude coffin, and again the awfulness of death afflicted the little group in the wilderness cabin. The body lay in the same room where they ate and slept. The family made all the preparations for burial, and conducted the simple funeral service, for no minister resided in the neighborhood. The woods were radiant with autumn's colors as they buried Nancy Lincoln beside the Sparrows."[2] No more haunting recounting of the death of Lincoln's mother has ever been written.

Thomas also gives a balanced description of the relationship between Lincoln and his wife: "Devoted, even possessive toward her husband, she was eager to make him happy. But small matters upset her and brought on fits of temper. Servants found her difficult to please; she quarreled with tradesmen and neighbors. She suffered violent headaches, known now to have been warnings of mental illness, and these sometimes made her utterly unreasonable. Lincoln bore it the best he could, taking her tongue-lashings, yielding to her whims whenever possible, offering excuses to the neighbors, trying to make allowances for the affectionate wife and mother he knew she was at heart."[3] It is rare that a writer on Lincoln could give such an evenhanded account of Mary Todd Lincoln.

Thomas's book fortunately is not weighted down with the revisionist thinking that was still popular in his day. Thomas sees what Beveridge and Randall failed to see in the Lincoln-Douglas debates. Speaking of the two, Thomas says, "Their fundamental difference was ethical." Thomas does not go as far as later writers did, but he did challenge the revisionist notion that there was hardly any difference between Lincoln and Douglas. He also is not contemptuous of the slaves themselves and does see Lincoln as taking an interest in them. "Whites and blacks must learn to live together as free men. Helping to bring Lincoln to this conclusion was a growing conviction that the use of the Negro as soldier was the only resource left to him to tip the scale of battle. And as a soldier, rather than a mere menial laborer for the army, the Negro could not only help to win the war and his own freedom, but also to prove his bravery and intelligence."[4]

Thomas's view of Lincoln's political methods is right on target. "So deft had been Lincoln's leadership that people often failed to recognize it. Few persons thought him great. His strength was flexible, like fine-spun wire, sensitive to every need and pressure, yielding but never breaking. Forced to adopt hard measures, he had tempered them with clemency. He exercised stern powers leniently, with regard for personal feelings and respect for human rights." Thomas sees in this book what many contemporaries often failed to see. Though people were unaware while he was doing so, Lincoln had a way of maneuvering people and winning them over. Thomas is right when he says, "But only with the slow march of time would it be given to most of his countrymen to understand the supreme meaning of his life. Only with that national soul-searching which is born of trial and challenge would they begin to share his vision of man's vast future, and to know their proper part in shaping it."[5] After reading passages like these, it is clear why Thomas's biography is so highly esteemed.

Abraham Lincoln: A Biography is Thomas's greatest book and an essential addition to a Lincoln bookshelf. Nobody has summed up Lincoln and his career as well as Thomas does in this single volume: "Tough, shrewd, and canny in his younger years, the man who was bringing the nation to victory had become strong, merciful, and wise. Success had come to him, and to the nation that he served, because he had lived and governed according to its ideals."[6]

NOTES

1. See Benjamin P. Thomas, *Portrait for Posterity: Lincoln and His Biographers* (New Brunswick: Rutgers University Press, 1947); Allen C. Guelzo, *Abraham Lincoln: Redeemer President* (Grand Rapids: Eerdmans, 1999), 469.
2. Benjamin P. Thomas, *Abraham Lincoln: A Biography* (New York: Modern Library, 1968), 11.
3. Ibid., 90–91.
4. Ibid., 192, 363.
5. Ibid., 497, 522.
6. Ibid., 498.

Lincoln and His Generals

AUTHOR: T. Harry Williams
PUBLISHED: 1952
GENRE: Presidency

*L*INCOLN AND HIS GENERALS is a book that argues for Lincoln's greatness as a military strategist and leader. T. Harry Williams puts Lincoln's actions as war president under a microscope and finds that Lincoln surpassed all other presidents in this regard. "Judged by modern standards, Lincoln stands out as a great war president, probably the greatest in our history, and a great natural strategist, a better one than any of his generals. He was in actuality as well as in title the commander in chief who, by his larger strategy, did more than Grant or any general to win the war for the Union." In fact, Williams sees U. S. Grant as following the ideas Lincoln had advocated for years. "He approved of Grant's strategy and let the General execute it because Grant conformed his plans to Lincoln's own strategic ideas. Fundamentally, Grant's strategy was Lincolnian."[1] In this assessment Williams overstates his case, yet he does mount an impressive argument for the importance of Lincoln's war leadership.

Williams sees Lincoln as an original thinker compared to his generals. Lincoln is given credit for seeing that the Confederate army was the true strategic objective of the Union army, rather than territory. When the Confederate army retreated across the Potomac after the defeat at Gettysburg, Lincoln wrote a letter to the Army of the Potomac commander, Maj. Gen. George Meade, expressing his disappointment that the enemy was allowed to escape. Though Lincoln never actually sent the letter, Williams thinks it offers an insight into Lincoln's military thinking: "It was an excellent essay in military art; and it demonstrated that Lincoln appreciated a strategic principle that Meade and many other generals seemed never to have heard of: the destruction of the enemy armies was the primary objective of Union armies." Lincoln also saw that the destruction of Lee's army required the Union army to use its numerical advantage. Williams recalls a conference held between Lincoln and Joseph Hooker before the battle of Chancellorsville. "Before he left for Washington, Lincoln sent for Hooker and Darius N. Couch, the senior corps commander. He said to them, possibly with the thought of failure of McClellan and Burnside to commit their reserves at Antietam and Fredericksburg: 'Gentlemen, in your next battle *put in all your men.*'"[2]

Lincoln's most controversial military decision during the war was to remove the Army of the Potomac from the Peninsula after the Seven Days' battles in the summer of 1862. Williams is critical of Lincoln for doing this. "Lincoln—and [Henry W.] Halleck and [Edwin M.] Stanton—would have done better to have left the army where it was. It was only twenty-five miles from Richmond and on a supply line that could always be kept open. It was closer to Richmond than it would be until 1864. Seldom if ever in military history has an army that near to an enemy capital retired without the enemy firing a shot at it. Lincoln would have made a wiser decision if he kept the army on the James and removed McClellan as its commander." Williams is even more critical of McClellan's actions during this period. He feels McClellan's constant demand for reinforcements suggested that he really was in a weak position and needed to be removed. "If Lincoln had known, as he would have, had McClellan possessed any ability to judge realities, that the Confederate army numbered not over 75,000, the President might have made a different decision about withdrawing the army. McClellan's weakness of magnifying the size of the enemy caught up with him at last. More than anybody, he was responsible for the collapse of the Peninsula campaign."[3] Williams is right not to blame either Lincoln or McClellan solely for the loss of the Peninsula campaign. There were enough mistakes to go around at that early stage of the war.

It is odd that there has not been a book-length study of Lincoln as commander in chief since this book was published fifty years ago. Williams himself says, "To the best of my knowledge, this book is the only work that treats of Lincoln as a war director—with him as the dominating figure—from the perspective of modern war." Questions about Lincoln and race/emancipation have dominated the field. Speaking of how history has remembered both Grant and William Tecumseh Sherman, Williams could see how the Lincoln legend has obscured his role as a strategist. "Grant had become the Great General, Lincoln the Great Emancipator. There was nothing in the Lincoln legend to recall that he had been a great war leader because he was also Lincoln the Great Strategist."[4]

Studies about emancipation are important, yet it could not have taken place without a Union victory in the field. The theme of Lincoln as war president has not been exhausted by any means. More scholarship in this area is needed; however, we are lucky to have this able study by T. Harry Williams.

NOTES

1. T. Harry Williams, *Lincoln and His Generals* (New York: Dorset Press, 1989), vii, 306; for another positive view of Lincoln as a military leader, see Colin R. Ballard, *The Military Genius of Abraham Lincoln* (Cleveland: World Publishing Co., 1952).
2. Williams, 269, 234.
3. Ibid., 145, 146.
4. Ibid., viii, 304.

The Collected Works of Abraham Lincoln

AUTHORS: Roy P. Basler, editor;
Marion Dolores Pratt and
Lloyd A. Dunlap,
assistant editors
PUBLISHED: 1953
GENRE: General

THIS EIGHT-VOLUME series is the bible of Lincoln scholarship. There is nothing that beats Lincoln's own words for getting an understanding of the man. In these volumes one can get Lincoln "unfiltered." The material comes from letters Lincoln wrote or speeches stenographers took down while he was giving them. There is no dispute whether Lincoln said something, as there is in people's recollections. Here it is in black and white. Lincoln's words are the basic building blocks for Lincoln scholarship, so every Lincoln author must refer at some point to these volumes.[1]

The material is arranged chronologically and starts with some doggerel that Lincoln wrote in an arithmetic copybook when he was fifteen years old in 1824. Lincoln wrote, "Abraham Lincoln his hand and his pen he will be good but god knows When." The last piece of Lincoln writing is a pass he wrote for George Ashmun before he left for Ford's Theatre on the night of April 14, 1865. "Allow Mr. Ashum & friend to come in at 9. A.M. to-morrow." There is something chilling about this pass, since it reminds one of how sudden and violent Lincoln's death was. In the last volume, there is material that is either undated or was discovered after the start of the project and could not be placed in chronological order. This in no way detracts from the overall quality of the project.[2]

Roy P. Basler and his assistant editors provide background information about each piece of Lincoln writing. This is helpful because one is not reading the letter or speech in a vacuum. It would have been easy for the editors to just string together all of Lincoln's writings, but instead they did the hard work of cross-referencing and sometimes reprinting a letter from someone else to whom Lincoln was responding. The editors do the same for the Lincoln-Douglas debates. They print what Douglas said, so the reader can understand what Lincoln is responding to.[3]

Lincoln's skill as a writer is unmatched by other presidents. It is easy to see this in things like the Gettysburg Address and the Second Inaugural Address, but his letters show a man who knew how to use words to their best advantage. When Salmon P. Chase resigned from the cabinet, Lincoln accepted the resignation and sent a letter to Chase explaining why: "Your resignation of the office of Secretary of Treasury, sent me yesterday is accepted. Of all I have said in commendation of your ability and fidelity, I have nothing to unsay; and yet you and I have reached a point of mutual embarrassment in our official relations which it seems can not be overcome, or longer sustained, consistently with the public service."[4] Lincoln would have been within his rights to write Chase a nasty letter, but he chose to write a letter that was firm without being vitriolic.

Lincoln also showed his great literary ability when writing to his generals. Most of them could be touchy, and Lincoln had to employ a soft touch to prod them along. Lincoln's letter to William S. Rosecrans before the battle of Chickamauga is a case in point: "You had informed me you were impressed, through Gen. Halleck, that I was dissatisfied with you; and I could not bluntly deny that I was, without unjustly implicating him. I therefore concluded to tell you the plain truth, being satisfied the matter would thus appear much smaller than it would if seen by mere glimpses. I repeat that my appreciation of you has not abated. I can never forget, whilst I remember anything, that about the end of last year, and the beginning of this, you gave us a hard earned victory which, had there been a defeat instead, the nation could scarcely have lived over. Neither can I forget the check you so opportunely gave to a dangerous sentiment which was spreading in the North." Lincoln could also be modest with his generals and admit when he was wrong. Remarking that he had once thought Grant's strategy at Vicksburg had been mistaken, "I now wish to make the personal acknowledgement that you were right, and I was wrong."[5]

The personal letters are also of significance for what they tell us of Lincoln's character and beliefs. Lincoln wrote to his best friend, Joshua Speed, about Speed's upcoming marriage. "I believe God made me one of the instruments of bringing your Fanny and you together, which union I have no doubt He had fore-ordained. Whatever he designs, he will do for *me* yet."[6] This letter to an intimate friend shows a Lincoln who believed God intervened in human affairs. In Lincoln's own handwriting, it is worth far more than hundreds of reminiscences from others of what Lincoln believed.

The Collected Works of Abraham Lincoln are going to be read by not only Lincoln scholars but by people everywhere who value democracy and freedom. They also will be read by those who want a glimpse into the heart and mind of this great man. The quantity of the material should not discourage those who seek to obtain these volumes; there are just too many wonderful insights to be gained by reading them.

NOTES

1. Roy P. Basler, Marion Dolores Pratt, and Lloyd A. Dunlap, eds., *The Collected Works of Abraham Lincoln,* 8 vols. and index (New Brunswick: Rutgers University Press, 1953), 1:ix. Two small supplements have appeared in 1974 and 1990. It should be noted that some of the material is questionable, such as the letter from Abraham Lincoln to William S. Wadsworth, January 1864, in ibid. 7:101–2.
2. Abraham Lincoln in Copybook Verses in Basler et al., 1:1; Abraham Lincoln in Card of Admission of George Ashmun in ibid., 8:413; ibid., 8:414–29.
3. See Basler et al., vol. 8.
4. Abraham Lincoln to Salmon P. Chase, June 30, 1864, in ibid., 7:419.
5. Abraham Lincoln to William S. Rosecrans, August 31, 1863, in ibid., 6:424–25; Abraham Lincoln to Ulysses S. Grant, July 13, 1863, in ibid., 6:326.
6. Abraham Lincoln to Joshua F. Speed, July 4, 1842, in ibid., 1:289.

Mary Lincoln: Biography of a Marriage

AUTHOR: Ruth Painter Randall
PUBLISHED: 1953
GENRE: Family and Genealogy

*M*ARY LINCOLN: *Biography of a Marriage* is the handbook for apologists of Mary Todd Lincoln. Ruth Painter Randall has written what is essentially a defense lawyer's brief for Mrs. Lincoln. She gives short shrift to Mary Todd's life outside the marriage, because she probably felt that Mary's marriage to Lincoln was the area subject to the most criticism. Since she is an advocate for Mrs. Lincoln, the book lacks objectivity. Like many advocates, Ruth Randall is selective in her evidence, uses double standards for proof, and engages in special pleading. Any reminiscence that casts a negative shadow on Mrs. Lincoln is immediately suspect, and the person is a liar or worse. Conversely, any reminiscence that is positive about Mrs. Lincoln is gospel truth. Unfortunately, Ruth Randall smears many people in order to defend Mary Todd Lincoln, her favorite target being William Herndon.

In order to discredit the many reminiscences critical of Mrs. Lincoln that Herndon collected, it is necessary to discredit Herndon himself. Ruth Randall uses some reminiscence material of her own to do this. "He made a pathetic picture when he walked the weary miles into town, so unkempt that little boys were told there was a bird's nest in his shaggy beard. . . . Neighbors had seen Herndon dead drunk, 'hauled home from town just like you would haul a hog on hay in the back end of the wagon.'" She uses Herndon's biographer, David Herbert Donald, to discredit him as well. Mrs. Lincoln once denied she had an interview with Herndon or objected to the way he recorded it. Ruth Randall quotes Donald as saying, "It was the signal for Herndon to loose up all his stored-up hate for Mary Lincoln." Whenever there is a quote that is negative from Donald, she will use it. However, she doesn't use the most relevant quote Donald made about the Lincoln marriage in his book. Donald thinks Herndon went too far in his denunciation of Mary, yet this quote is telling: "After a careful and sympathetic study of the Lincoln marriage, Paul M. Angle has concluded that 'no fair-minded student can disregard what Herndon wrote' on the subject. Herndon's own testimony and the reminiscences he collected as to Mrs. Lincoln's temper and to occasional 'flare ups' in the Lincoln home are supported by indisputable contemporary evidence."[1] Ruth Randall gives the impression that Donald supports her position, which is just not the case.

There is another major logical fallacy in this work. Ruth Randall feels that Herndon's material can't be trusted because he prompted people to tell negative things about Mary. She describes Herndon as "using lawyer's tricks of suggestion as to what he wished said, he began to collect all kinds of reminiscences." Thanks to Lincoln scholars Douglas Wilson and Rodney Davis, who published the Herndon interviews, we can see that this is not true. Herndon simply jotted down notes of what people told him. The height of inconsistency is reached when Ruth Randall selectively uses the very material she says is tainted by Herndon's bias when it suits her. The fact that there is some material sympathetic to Mary in the Herndon book undermines her contention that he was so biased he prodded people to say negative things about her. For example, she paraphrases Herndon's interview with James Gourley, who was a neighbor of the Lincolns. "The sum of James Gourley's testimony is that 'Mrs & Mr Lincoln were good neighbors.'"[2] While, predictably, Ruth Randall leaves out the negative things Gourley also said, she is still using the Herndon material she claims is so biased.

Ruth Randall reaches absurd levels when she defends Mrs. Lincoln's harsh berating of a servant girl. "Herndon's letter tells us that the severing of relations between Mrs. Lincoln and the girl took place as a result of Mrs. Lincoln getting very angry at the girl, but he fails to state what the girl had done to incur her anger." Ruth is sarcastic about Herndon's notion that the servant "'was a fine girl, industrious, neat, saving, and rather handsome, who would satisfy anybody on earth.' Maybe this was true, but such a paragon of among Springfield's domestic help would have been, by all accounts, a seven-day wonder!"[3] It is sad the way Ruth Randall must resort to smearing anyone who has any problems with Mary Todd Lincoln.

Since there is so much negative that can be said about the book, the question arises of why it is included here. The reason is simple. It is an important book to have because of its steadfast defense of Mary Todd Lincoln. If one wants to hear a counterargument to the literature critical of Mrs. Lincoln, this book will serve that purpose. Ruth Randall felt the need to defend Mary Todd Lincoln against the worst charges. One can admire her for that but must admit that she went too far and that her methods were often unfair and not altogether truthful. There are many things wrong with the book, but it is still the most thorough defense of Lincoln's wife one can find.

NOTES

1. Ruth Painter Randall, *Mary Lincoln: Biography of a Marriage* (Boston: Little, Brown and Co., 1953), 384, 383; David Herbert Donald, *Lincoln's Herndon* (New York: Da Capo, 1989), 359.
2. Randall, 356; see Douglas L. Wilson and Rodney O. Davis, eds., *Herndon's Informants: Letters, Interviews, and Statements About Abraham Lincoln* (Urbana: University of Illinois Press, 1998); Randall, 134; see Wilson and Davis, 451–53.
3. Randall, 109, 109.

Lincoln's Sons

AUTHOR: Ruth Painter Randall
PUBLISHED: 1955
GENRE: Family and Genealogy

THE SECOND book on the list by Ruth Painter Randall is *Lincoln's Sons*, an account of the lives of the four children of Abraham and Mary Todd Lincoln. Ostensibly, it is a biographical account of the four, but it is more than that. One of the leading topics of this book is Lincoln as a father. "When I adjusted the focus of my study on the Lincoln sons and attempted to relegate the father and mother to minor roles as mere parents, I found that Mr. Lincoln refused to take a back seat. His fatherhood was so basic a part of his life that he remained prominently in the picture." This is really, then, a study of the Lincoln family. It is a well-written book that does not have the apologetic agenda of *Mary Lincoln: Biography of a Marriage*.[1]

The book opens with an imaginary scene of the Lincoln household in 1857. This chapter reads like a novel. It has a style that usually only a novelist can provide. Randall describes Lincoln taking his time as he came home for dinner. "If he met a friend or neighbor, that was apt to prove even more delaying. They would stop and exchange small items of personal and public news, and then Mr. Lincoln was sure to be reminded of a story, and this meant that for Mrs. Lincoln and the children waiting at home supper was further postponed." One can forgive Ruth Randall's taking poetic license, since she does it so well, like Carl Sandburg.[2]

Randall entitles a chapter "Let the Children Have a Good Time." This is a quote from Lincoln that describes his parenting style. Randall writes: "One strongly suspects that the Lincoln sons would not have been so mischievous if their father had not laughed at their tricks and thought them smart. They adored him and he practically applauded every caper their inventive minds could think up. Even as early as 1847, when Robert was only four, annoyed fellow passengers on the train to Lexington had noted with amazement that the father 'aided and abetted' him in his mischief and beamed proudly, when what was called for, in the passenger's opinion was a good spanking." Lincoln was indeed an indulgent parent. Robert and William were able to do well under this style of parenting. We will never know about Edward, who died at three years of age; however, one wonders if a little firmness would have benefited the youngest son, Tad, who was the most rampant.[3]

Randall devotes considerable space to Robert Todd Lincoln. In the last part of the book, she analyzes his character. She feels that Robert was often estranged from his parents. "In the collected records he appears, as a boy, to have had an uncomfortable aloofness from the rest of the family, with perhaps a suggestion of antagonism." Robert seems never to have known his father well and perhaps secretly resented that fact. As the years passed, Robert's attitude changed. "What Allen Nevins has called 'the great, turbulent, confused experiment of living' is likely to bring to anyone a better comprehension of fundamental values. As Robert met the complications and afflictions of his own life, he could better understand the patient wisdom of his father in meeting the far more difficult problems of his." Robert became his father's staunchest defender, though he did it in his characteristically quiet way. He wrote letters and helped Lincoln's secretaries, Nicolay and Hay, write their ten-volume hagiographic biography of his father by letting them see the president's papers.[4]

It is to Randall's credit that she is sympathetic to Robert when he had his mother committed to an asylum in 1875. Randall's extremely defensive attitude toward Mary Todd Lincoln would have made it easy to blame the whole affair on Robert, as do some of Mary's modern-day defenders. Instead, she understands the difficulty Robert faced and the agony the decision caused him. She movingly describes his time on the witness stand at the trial to commit his mother. "To shed tears in public is an ordeal for any man, but to Robert, supersensitive to the public gaze, that being on the witness stand was pure torture."[5]

One criticism the book has faced is its "saccharine" nature. This is to be expected since Randall is writing about children, two of whom died before they reached adulthood and one who died shortly after becoming an adult. There is a lot of tragedy in the Lincoln family story. For Randall to focus solely on that would have been a mistake. She describes the children's antics in a charming fashion that gives balance to the story. Alternately sad and funny, the book is one of the definitive books on Lincoln's family.[6]

NOTES

1. Ruth Painter Randall, *Lincoln's Sons* (Boston: Little, Brown and Co., 1955), vii; see Ruth Painter Randall, *Mary Lincoln: Biography of a Marriage* (Boston: Little, Brown and Co., 1953).
2. Randall, *Lincoln's Sons,* 4; see Carl Sandburg, *Abraham Lincoln: The Prairie Years,* 2 vols. (New York: Harcourt, Brace & Co., 1926).
3. Randall, *Lincoln's Sons,* 71–83, 71–72.
4. Ibid., 8–9, 250, 244–45; John G. Nicolay and John Hay, *Abraham Lincoln: A History,* 10 vols. (New York: Century, 1890)
5. Randall, *Lincoln's Sons,* 221; for a critical look at Robert's role in the matter, see Jean H. Baker, *Mary Todd Lincoln: A Biography* (New York: W. W. Norton, 1987), 323.
6. Mark E. Neely Jr., *The Abraham Lincoln Encyclopedia* (New York: Da Capo, 1982), 189.

Lincoln and the
Tools of War

AUTHOR: Robert V. Bruce
PUBLISHED: 1956
GENRE: Presidency

*L*INCOLN AND THE TOOLS OF WAR takes a look at Lincoln's involvement in a little-known aspect of the war. The Civil War is usually seen as devoid of innovation, the rifled musket and frontal charges over and over again. This was not the case. Robert V. Bruce examines Lincoln's involvement in an attempt to gain a technological edge on the Confederates. His book reviews the technological innovations Lincoln was interested in implementing and the bureaucracy that stymied his efforts. Bruce's book is also important because it is the only book that truly highlights Lincoln's scientific mind.

Lincoln had lectured on inventions while in Illinois. The lecture was not a success, yet it was revealing of his mind. "The lecture fiasco notwithstanding, those who knew Abraham Lincoln at the closing of his prairie years acknowledged his knack for mathematics and machinery. In 1859, a generation after his junkets with compass and chain, Lincoln's opinion on a disputed point was sought by a convention of surveyors who met in Springfield."[1] If Lincoln did indeed have a "knack" for machinery, it stands to reason that he would look to technology to help the North win the war.

A partner in Lincoln's interest was Adm. John Dahlgren, the inventor of the Dahlgren cannon. Lincoln would often visit the naval yard to see Dahlgren. Bruce writes, "And why did Lincoln, for his part, seek Dahlgren's company? . . . Dahlgren was a man of intelligence and vigor; . . . and his unsurpassed knowledge of ordnance made him useful, as will be seen, to a President as busy in such matters as was Abraham Lincoln."[2]

If Dahlgren was Lincoln's ally in the cause of innovation, Brig. Gen. James A. Ripley was his nemesis. Ripley was an old soldier who was chief of army ordnance. He was no supporter of new technology. Bruce is critical of Ripley's actions early in the war. While praising his desire not to slow down production with too many changes, he still thinks Ripley could have done more. "If a new weapon promised to be valuable in battle and was not prohibitively expensive, the Chief of Ordinance, especially at the start of the war, should have racked his brains for ways to produce it outside the regular sources or to bring about a gradual change-over. Ripley did no such thing. Instead of seeking out better designs, he applied his ingenuity, which was considerable, to fighting them off."[3] Bruce is not altogether fair in this assertion; Ripley's position is defensible because the North needed as many guns produced early in the war as possible.

The one innovation Lincoln advocated that had the most potential was the breechloading rifle. Loading a rifle at the muzzle while not standing up was difficult. The ramrod would often be shot off in battle by accident, and guns were accidentally loaded more than once in the heat of battle. "The obvious solution was a gun which could be loaded at the breech. At a stroke, almost all the pitfalls and complexities of loading would be eliminated. The soldier with a breechloader could not, even if he tried, put in more than one load at a time." Lincoln rightly saw the potential the increased firepower could give the Union army, even if his chief of ordnance did not see it that way. Lincoln overruled Ripley and ordered twenty-five thousand of the breechloaders on October 14, 1861. Lincoln ordered more as the war went on. Bruce shows that the Union army benefited from these guns, and had Lincoln's advice been followed by the military professionals, the war might have ended sooner.[4]

Bruce tells the stories of some of the innovations Lincoln did not accept because of their bizarreness. Inventors often went to see the president himself in order to get a hearing for their inventions. "A venerable Bostonian named William Foster wrote Congressman Samuel Hooper to outline a plan for twenty small boats, each with a gun, all fixed together in an arc and so arranged to discharge all guns at once at the same point. As an engineer on the defenses of Boston Harbor in 1812, he had made the same suggestion without avail; but he was not easily discouraged. 'If what has been said do not find ears,' he wrote, 'I am willing to live ninty more years for a trial.'"[5] Lincoln was enough of a realist to see when an idea was impractical, but he was almost always willing to give it a hearing.

This book looks at a side of Lincoln not often discussed. Lincoln is most often seen as a humanitarian, yet the scientific nature of his thinking is also integral to his makeup. Lincoln was a practical thinker who saw the potential of technology to help win the war. Regrettably, his ideas were not carried out, due mainly to resistance from the military bureaucracy. Bruce's book rightfully shows a Lincoln ahead of his time.

NOTES

1. Robert V. Bruce, *Lincoln and the Tools of War* (Indianapolis: Bobbs-Merrill, 1956), 14.
2. Ibid., 21.
3. Ibid., 70.
4. Ibid., 100, 108, 288.
5. Ibid., 78.

Lincoln Reconsidered: Essays on the Civil War Era

AUTHOR: David Herbert Donald
PUBLISHED: 1956
GENRE: General

D AVID HERBERT DONALD collected some of his best essays up till 1956 and issued them here. The subjects of the essays are not exclusively Lincoln. Some deal with the Civil War in general. The essays on Lincoln, though, have been influential in the interpretation of Lincoln and his place in American history, so the book is important enough to include in a serious collection. *Lincoln Reconsidered* is also a quick and interesting read, due to Donald's ideas and literary style.

"The Radicals and Lincoln" is the most important of the essays. In it, Donald demolishes one of the major tenets of revisionism. The idea that the Radical Republicans were evil and thwarted Lincoln's humane policies was a staple of revisionism. Donald clearly shows this interpretation is wrong. Revisionists often assumed the Radicals' interest in ending slavery was not moral but economical. They wanted to wage the war to instill an industrial oligarchy in the North to rule over the South and saw the slave as a tool to reach this end. Donald writes, "Such then are the new villains of the piece. Civil War historians agree upon so few matters that one hesitates to start another controversy by questioning this universally held interpretation, but there seem to be valid reasons for challenging the stereotype of Lincoln-versus-the-Radicals."[1]

Donald sees a number of things factually wrong with the revisionist interpretation. "The charge they were spokesmen for the business interests of the North presupposes a degree of unity among the anti-slavery leaders which did not, in fact, exist." Donald shows they had diverse economic interests. For example, some were for looser credit and inflation while others favored hard money. It is true that the Radicals did criticize Lincoln, but so did the conservatives. The Northern Democrats were far harder on Lincoln than the Radicals. Donald rightfully states, "Far from breaking with the Radical Republicans, he tried to win their support. He worked with these men politically, and he got along with most of them personally. If antislavery zealots never gave Lincoln their full confidence, it was nevertheless the Radicals who stayed behind the administration, while Conservatives like Reverdy Johnson, [Horatio] Seymour, and O.H. Browning were in the Democratic opposition."[2] Donald's interpretation has won over most students of the Civil War, and coming from a former student of Randall was almost a deathblow to revisionism.

"Getting Right with Lincoln" is a humorous essay that traces the way politicians have used the name of Lincoln to further their own careers. While early on Lincoln was purely a Republican figure, over the years he became a national one. Donald can write, "In the 1948 election, everybody was for Lincoln. Dixiecrats remembered that Lincoln, as a fellow Southerner, preferred letting the race problem work itself out. Henry Wallace's Progressives asserted that they were heirs of Jefferson, Jackson, and Lincoln. Thomas E. Dewey, according to his running-mate, bore a striking resemblance to Lincoln—spiritual rather than physical, one judges—and President [Harry S.] Truman claimed that if Lincoln was alive, he would be a Democrat. Finally Lincoln has become a nonpartisan, nonsectional hero. It seems as Congressman Everett Dirkson solemnly assured his Republican colleagues, that these days the first task is "to get right with . . . Lincoln."[3] Donald wrote this over fifty years ago. It would be interesting to see how true this is today. Lincoln is still a national icon, but other figures, such as Martin Luther King Jr., have replaced him in the category of the national saint who represents freedom.

Donald also sees Lincoln as a "Whig in the White House." Lincoln had been a member of the Whig Party most of his adult life. When Lincoln formally joined the Republicans in 1856, he did not abandon all his previous views as a Whig. The Whig Party had preached the idea of a weak chief executive. They thought Congress should make the domestic policy for the nation. One must remember that the Whigs were often in opposition to strong Democratic presidents like Andrew Jackson. In times of war, they felt the president could be vigorous in the prosecution of war as commander in chief though. Donald argues convincingly that this is what Lincoln did. As president, he was active in the leadership of the war effort; however, in domestic politics, he simply deferred to Congress. It would have been hard for Lincoln to forget the years he spent fighting for the Whig philosophy.[4]

Donald's book is one of the few books in Lincoln scholarship that marked the end of an era. This book was the first from a serious historian to really question revisionism. It also looked at Lincoln's politics from a Whig perspective, something that had been downplayed before. Since *Lincoln Reconsidered* is a book of essays, there are some the reader may not agree with, but at the very least, Donald's book is a good look into the mind of one of the greatest Lincoln scholars of all time.[5]

NOTES

1. David Herbert Donald, *Lincoln Reconsidered: Essays on the Civil War Era* (New York: Vintage Books, 1989), 103–27, 109.
2. Ibid., 110, 127.
3. Ibid., 3–18, 17.
4. Ibid., 187–208.
5. For a book that minimizes Lincoln's Whig Party membership, see James G. Randall, *Lincoln the Liberal Statesman* (New York: Dodd, Mead & Co., 1947).

The Lincoln
Nobody Knows

AUTHOR: Richard N. Current
PUBLISHED: 1958
GENRE: General

THE PREMISE of *The Lincoln Nobody Knows* is simple. There are many areas of controversy in Lincoln's life and career where no definitive answers can be had. There is so much open to debate that the true Lincoln can never really be known by anyone. Richard N. Current puts it this way: "For my assumption is that, on issues where competent authorities differ, the questions cannot really be answered, no matter how positive individual experts may be." He also modestly states in his foreword, "On occasion, I advance conclusions of my own, but only on the understanding that they represent fallible opinion rather than incontrovertible fact."[1] Fortunately for the reader, Current's conclusions make a lot of sense.

Readers familiar to the Lincoln story are aware of the disputed areas in his life. The second chapter of the book, "The Son, Lover, Husband," covers the wide range of disputes about Lincoln's private life. Current gives both sides of a dispute and then tentatively comes down on one side or the other. For instance, the question of how Lincoln viewed his childhood is discussed at length. Current weighs all the evidence and concludes, "In looking back he saw more gloom than glamour in his boyhood years. After revisiting southern Indiana he said his home country was 'as unpoetical as any spot on earth.'" Despite the work of Louis Warren to portray Lincoln's childhood in a more positive light, Current feels that it was still a rough experience for the young Lincoln.[2]

A chapter on Lincoln's military ability is the most thought-provoking in the book. Current makes the often forgotten point that Lincoln as a war leader had to be aware of political implications of his decisions. Lincoln did not have the luxury of moving troops on a map around in a vacuum. Much of the criticism of Lincoln as a war leader forgets this important point. Lincoln is sometimes criticized for spreading the Union armies too thin in Virginia by insisting on maintaining a large force to defend the capital. Current defends Lincoln by stating, "In the widespread deployment of his armies, Lincoln violated the old and orthodox rule of concentration of force. But he had justification, both political and military. He could not and did not ignore politics in the broad (as distinct from the narrow, partisan) sense. He had to protect the Northern people against invasion, prevent the defection of wavering border states, and hold on to that priceless symbol, the capital of the Union. Only by spreading out his forces could he achieve these 'political' objectives."[3] This is one of the most cogent defenses of Lincoln's military thinking in print.

Current has a different take on Lincoln's supposed compassion. In the chapter "The Tenderhearted," Current views Lincoln as a tough-minded realist. "Mere breath, mere talk, killed no rebels, as Lincoln said. Squirts of rose water would not do the job. What would kill rebels was the muzzle-loader and Minié ball or, better yet, the repeating rifle, the mortar, or the machine gun. What would kill them was the exploding bullet or the incendiary shell. Hence Lincoln's personal interest in all this gadgetry of death." Lincoln may have been interested in the tools of war, but his motivation was to end the war as soon as possible. Current ends the chapter with the unanswerable question: "If, in the 1860s, Yankee ingenuity had been equal to producing such a weapon, would he have withheld the atom bomb? Or if, in the 1940s he had been in Harry Truman's place, would he have spared Hiroshima?" Current is right that Lincoln was intent on winning the war at all costs. Lincoln was willing for his country to suffer horrendous loss of life to maintain the Union and free the slaves. Is that compassion? As Current would say, this again is the Lincoln we cannot know.[4]

It is hard to accept Current's contention that Lincoln is unknowable. One wants definitive answers. "What is truth and what is falsehood? Are these contradictions unanswerable or may they be resolved? With regard to each of them, arguments can be made both pro and con." *The Lincoln Nobody Knows* is a book that gives the reader a lot to think about and challenges the reader to examine his or her own views of Lincoln. Any book that does that deserves to be studied and read. Not surprisingly, forty years after this book was published, Current still feels Lincoln is unknowable. He can say tongue-in-cheek, "I know—the correct answer to each of the questions I have raised. The only trouble is that, whatever side I pick, I face the tremendous weight of authority on the other side. This does not deter me from making up my mind, and it should not deter you from making up yours. Just as long as you agree with me!"[5]

NOTES

1. Richard N. Current, *The Lincoln Nobody Knows* (New York: Hill and Wang, 1995), vi, vi.
2. Current, 22–50, 31; see Louis A. Warren, *Lincoln's Youth: The Indiana Years, Seven to Twenty-one, 1816–1830* (Indianapolis: Century, 1991).
3. Current, 131–63, 161.
4. Ibid., 164–86, 185, 186.
5. Ibid., 21; Richard N. Current, "He's Still the Lincoln Nobody Knows," in John Y. Simon, Harold Holzer, and William D. Pederson, eds., *The Lincoln Forum: Abraham Lincoln, Gettysburg and the Civil War* (Mason City, Iowa: Savas Publishing, 1999), 18–31, 29.

Crisis of the House Divided: An Interpretation of the Issues in the Lincoln-Douglas Debates

AUTHOR: Harry V. Jaffa
PUBLISHED: 1959
GENRE: Prepresidential Years

O NE LINCOLN scholar said about this book, "Jaffa wrote what was incontestably the greatest Lincoln book of the century." Whether one agrees or not, Harry V. Jaffa's *Crisis of the House Divided: An Interpretation of the Issues in the Lincoln-Douglas Debates* has cast a long shadow in its interpretation of Lincoln and his thought. This book challenges many of the old assumptions of Lincoln and his views on slavery during the antebellum period. It also takes a fresh look at the issues leading up to the Civil War and puts the final nail in the coffin of revisionism.[1]

Jaffa's book draws a clear line of distinction between Lincoln and Stephen A. Douglas in their political philosophies. Revisionism had tried to downplay that difference. Jaffa speaks of revisionism chief supporter James Randall's contention that Lincoln and Douglas agreed on the most important points during their debates. "It is strange that Randall should so beg the question of why Lincoln, Douglas, and their contemporaries treated as real, fundamental, and important the differences he feels are illusionary, artificial, and slight. For the most superficial reading of the debates shows that the debaters themselves regarded the differences as radical and profound." Jaffa goes on to show that "Douglas's doctrine of popular sovereignty, with its self-proclaimed neutrality toward whether slavery was voted up or voted down, was a sheer absurdity on its face, according to Lincoln. How could anyone, he asked, at one and the same time advocate self-government and be indifferent to the denial of self-government?" Jaffa also points out, "When Douglas professed indifference as to whether slavery was voted up or down, he meant that not humanity or Christianity, or even the safety of society, but material self-interest was to determine Negro rights." It is absurd to think that Lincoln and Douglas were in basic agreement. Douglas refused to see any moral or ethical issue in slavery, while in Lincoln's mind these were the chief objections to the peculiar institution.[2]

Another tenet of revisionism was that slavery had reached its "natural limits." Climate would have prevented slavery from going any farther, so debate about laws designed to keep slavery out was pointless. The major proponent of this theory was Charles W. Ramsdell, whose 1929 essay on the subject heavily influenced revisionist thinking. Jaffa shows this argument is weak: "But Ramsdell's essay proves nothing whatever as to the possibility of slavery being extended into *other* occupations. Nor does it prove that any existing limitations were *permanent* limitations." If slavery had indeed reached its "natural limits," one could ask why the South would have been concerned about the issue. The obvious answer is, Jaffa is right and slavery was still a viable prospect in the territories and the states where it existed.[3]

Two early speeches are used in the book to illustrate Lincoln's political philosophy. The first is his 1838 speech "On the Perpetuation of Our Political Institutions." In this speech Lincoln sees the need for someone to act as a guardian against those who would tear down the laws of the land. The second speech is Lincoln's 1842 Temperance Address. Lincoln's topic here was the importance of moderation in reaching political goals. Denouncing tavern owners would not work; it would require persuasion. The ideas in the two speeches carried over into the debates with Douglas. Lincoln felt the nation needed to be saved from those who would deny its charter, the Declaration of Independence. He also felt this could be done only by recognizing human foibles and trying to move public opinion toward the right course. Of course, this is a gross simplification of what Jaffa writes; the two chapters on the two speeches are among the most thoughtful ever written about Lincoln.[4]

Since, in Jaffa's mind, Lincoln's opposition to slavery rested on his devotion to Jefferson and the Declaration of Independence, it is illustrative to see how the author thinks Lincoln's ideas compare to Jefferson's. "Lincoln's morality then extends the full length of Jefferson's, but it also goes further. Jefferson's horizon, with its grounding in Locke, saw all commands to respect the rights of others as fundamentally hypothetical imperatives: *if* you do not wish to be a slave, then refrain from being a master. Lincoln agreed, but he also said in substance: he who wills freedom for himself must simultaneously will freedom for others."[5] Lincoln took the declaration to its logical conclusion in regard to slavery.

Jaffa is one of the most philosophical and erudite of all the Lincoln writers. *Crisis of the House Divided* is not only about Lincoln but also about the ideals behind America. The importance of the idea of freedom to Lincoln separated him from Douglas. It was Lincoln's interpretation of what America is all about that ultimately won out. Lincoln saw America as being about more than self-interest. Jaffa shows the differences between Douglas and Lincoln were clear, and his work was a precursor to much of the scholarship that followed.

NOTES

1. Allen C. Guelzo, *Abraham Lincoln: Redeemer President* (Grand Rapids: Eerdmans, 1999), 468–69.
2. Harry V. Jaffa, *Crisis of the House Divided: An Interpretation of the Issues in the Lincoln-Douglas Debates* (Chicago: University of Chicago Press, 1982), 28, 31, 35.
3. Ibid., 392.
4. Ibid., 181–232, 233–72.
5. Ibid., 327.

Lincoln's Youth: The Indiana Years, Seven to Twenty-one, 1816–1830

AUTHOR: Louis A. Warren
PUBLISHED: 1959
GENRE: Family and Genealogy

L OUIS A. WARREN picks up where he left off in *Lincoln's Parentage and Childhood*. Warren last left Lincoln as he was moving from Kentucky to southern Indiana at the age of seven. In the first book, Warren attempted to rehabilitate Lincoln's father's image. In large part, he was successful. Thomas Lincoln lived a productive life in Kentucky. Warren was intent on making Lincoln's family noble and his early childhood a happy one. The problem with *Lincoln's Youth: The Indiana Years, Seven to Twenty-one, 1816–1830* is that it attempts to continue this interpretation into Indiana, where the circumstances were much different. Lincoln's years in Indiana were probably the toughest in his life and not at all like the romantic picture Warren attempts to paint in this book.[1]

Warren's book is divided into fourteen chapters, and each stands for one year in Lincoln's life. They have titles such as "Sorrow" for the 1818 chapter, since that is the year Lincoln's mother died, and "Independence" for the last chapter, when Lincoln turned twenty-one. Since it is impossible to know what Lincoln was doing for most of the time he was in Indiana, Warren chooses a theme for each chapter. The themes may not necessarily fit the year. For example, "Reverence" is the theme for Lincoln at age fourteen in 1823. The chapter is about Lincoln's early religious life. The year 1823 holds no special significance in that regard, but this chapter and others allow Warren to organize the book and focus on one aspect of Lincoln's life at a time.[2]

The best chapter is 1819's "Loyalty" because it tells the story of Thomas Lincoln's marriage to the widow Sarah Bush Johnston. Most scholars would agree she had a positive influence on Lincoln's life. Warren aptly describes the situation Lincoln's stepmother encountered when she first came to Indiana and saw the dirty and unkempt home Lincoln and his sister lived in: "Without casting any reflection on Nancy Lincoln as a house-keeper or on the domestic efforts of the twelve-year old Sarah, it can be said that there was plenty of work for Sally to do in the cabin. She had lived in a settled community all her life, and years later she recalled her arrival in Indiana: 'When we landed in Indiana Mr. Lincoln had erected a good log cabin, tolerably comfortable. . . . The country was wild and desolate.' Among Sally's innovations in the cabin life were improved facilities for 'cleaning up.' The habit of cleanliness is at a low ebb in a boy ten [years old] and no doubt Abraham needed considerable inducement to make use of his washstand and basin and gourd of soap which she set near the cabin door." Lincoln's new stepmother brought him love, yet she also brought opportunities for learning. "Abraham's new mother not only provided a refreshing new home life for him, but through her his world of books reached exciting new dimensions. Tucked among the furniture in the wagon from Kentucky were three volumes which the boy eagerly seized upon."[3]

Warren takes too romantic a view of the relationship between Lincoln and his father. He makes a puzzling assertion in 1821's "Admiration" chapter. He states, "According to Child Psychologists, when a boy is about twelve years old he enters a period of 'hero worship.'" Warren then draws the conclusion that Lincoln must have worshiped his father. "Thomas was the type of man to invite a boy's admiration. He was noted in the community for his unusual physical power, which must have brought pride to his son." This is nothing more than wishful thinking on Warren's part. It is possible that Lincoln idealized his father, yet the evidence seems to point in the opposite direction. As David Herbert Donald has remarked, "In all of his published writings, and, indeed, even in reports of hundreds of stories and conversations, he had not one favorable word to say about his father."[4]

It is important to remember that Lincoln spent fourteen years in Indiana, which is exactly one quarter of his life. Lincoln grew from a child to a man during those years, and *Lincoln's Youth* is the only book-length study of this time. The strength of the book lies in Warren's research about Indiana during the same period. A look at the notes section of the book shows Warren consulted local papers and documents that were not used before. Warren was a tireless researcher. He had shown that in his first book and continues the tradition in this book. The problem is not the facts but his interpretation. The tone of the book does not admit to the privations that were common on the Indiana frontier. Lincoln held no romantic view of his childhood there. In fact, a campaign biographer once related Lincoln's views of his youth: "He seemed to be painfully impressed with the extreme poverty of his early surroundings—the utter absence of all romantic and heroic elements."[5] Warren's book is a good one but might have been even better had he taken this into consideration while writing it.

NOTES

1. See Louis A. Warren, *Lincoln's Parentage and Childhood: A History of the Kentucky Lincolns Supported by Documentary Evidence* (New York: Century, 1926).
2. Louis A. Warren, *Lincoln's Youth: The Indiana Years, Seven to Twenty-one, 1816–1830* (Indianapolis: Indiana Historical Society, 1991), 43–57, 203–15, 112–24.
3. Ibid., 58–70, 65, 66.
4. Ibid., 84–95, 84, 85; David Herbert Donald, *Lincoln* (New York: Simon & Schuster, 1995), 33 .
5. John L. Scripps to William Herndon, June 24, 1865, in Douglas L. Wilson and Rodney O. Davis, eds., *Herndon's Informants: Letters, Interviews and Statements About Abraham Lincoln* (Urbana: University of Illinois Press, 1998), 57.

The Almost Chosen People: A Study of the Religion of Abraham Lincoln

AUTHOR: William J. Wolf
PUBLISHED: 1959
GENRE: Psychology and Religion

WHAT EXACTLY was Lincoln's religion? Was he a Christian? Was he an infidel? These are the questions William J. Wolf seeks to answer in *The Almost Chosen People*. The title comes from a speech Lincoln made on his way to Washington in 1861. Lincoln addressed the New Jersey State Legislature and said that he wished to be "a humble instrument in the hands of the Almighty, and of this, his almost chosen people, for perpetuating the object of that great struggle." Wolf has assembled a good deal of the information obtainable about Lincoln's religious views. He argues that Lincoln was in essence a Christian. His argument might not be totally convincing, yet his position has a certain logic that makes it a possibility. In any case, Wolf has written one of the best books on Lincoln's theology and personal beliefs.[1]

The book opens with Lincoln meeting his cabinet as he prepared to issue his Emancipation Proclamation. Wolf uses two contemporary diary entries from Gideon Welles and Samuel P. Chase to show that Lincoln believed God had chosen the time for him to go forward with the proclamation. Chase quotes Lincoln as saying, "When the Rebel Army was at Frederick, I determined, as soon as it should be driven out of Maryland, to issue a Proclamation of Emancipation, such as I thought most likely to be useful. I said nothing to anyone, but I made a promise to myself, and (hesitating a little) to my Maker."[2] While not illustrative of Lincoln's Christianity, this passage is proof that, at the very least, Lincoln was not an atheist.

Wolf argues that Lincoln's Christianity was unorthodox, so others thought of him as an infidel. Lincoln apparently did not believe in the concept of hell. Wolf quotes a conversation Isaac Cogdal, an old friend from New Salem, had with Lincoln in 1859. Cogdal states, "He did not nor could not believe in the endless punishment of any one of the human race. He understood punishment for sin to be a Bible doctrine; that the punishment was parental in its object, aim, and design, and intended for the good of the offender; hence it must cease when justice is satisfied. He added that all that was lost by the transgression of Adam was made good by the atonement: all that was lost by the fall was made good by the sacrifice, and he added this remark, that punishment being a 'provision of the gospel system,' he was not sure but the world be better off if a little more punishment was preached by our ministers and not so much pardon of sin."[3]

The above paragraph contains many theological concepts. Lincoln seems to have believed that Christ's death was atonement for all sins, which is an integral part of Christian doctrine. He differs widely from it, though, in his belief that Christ's death was atonement for everyone. This is not "justification by faith." Orthodox Christianity would insist someone must believe Christ's death was atonement in order for it to be so for them. If this truly represents Lincoln's religious views, he was not a Christian in the technical sense of the term. Lincoln's problems with orthodox Christian values are also attested to by his intimate friend Joshua Speed. "'When I knew him in early life,' said Speed in a lecture after Lincoln's death, 'he was a skeptic. He had tried hard to be a believer, but his reason could not grasp and solve the great problem of redemption as taught.'"[4] Some would say Lincoln's belief system can be called Christian; if so, it would be of a very liberal stripe.

Wolf insists Lincoln's belief system can rightfully be called Christian and refers to Lincoln's supposed quoting of the apostle Paul's first letter to the Corinthians, "For just as in Adam all die, so too in Christ shall all be brought to life." The problem is, the essay in which Lincoln supposedly wrote this no longer exists. We only have

Mentor Graham, a friend of Lincoln, quoting the essay some forty years later.[5]

Wolf includes *The Creed of Abraham Lincoln in His Own Words* by William E. Barton. It is a series of statements by Abraham Lincoln stitched together to make a coherent Christian confession of faith. It is interesting, but hardly admissible. Barton's taking statements out of context and putting them together cannot be said to be Lincoln's belief system. Its value comes in that it highlights Lincoln's profound religiosity whether it is Christian or not.[6]

The subject of Lincoln's religion is such a difficult one because of the problem of defining terms. *The Almost Chosen People* is a well-argued book that advocates the position of Lincoln's basic Christianity. There are counterpoints to much of what Wolf says, but his position cannot be easily dismissed and needs to be taken into account in discussions on Lincoln's religion.

NOTES

1. Abraham Lincoln to New Jersey legislature, February 1861, in William J. Wolf, *The Almost Chosen People: A Study of the Religion of Abraham Lincoln* (Garden City, N.Y.: Doubleday & Co., 1959), 117.
2. Wolf, 18; Salmon P. Chase as quoted in ibid., 19.
3. Isaac Cogdal as quoted in ibid., 104.
4. Joshua Speed as quoted in ibid., 56.
5. 1 Corinthians 15:22; Wolf, 46–47.
6. William E. Barton, "The Creed of Abraham Lincoln in His Own Words" in Wolf, 195–96; for an excellent collection of many of Lincoln's statements on God, see Gordon Leidner, *Lincoln on God and Country* (Shippensburg: White Mane Publishers, 2000).

Lincoln As a Lawyer

AUTHOR: John P. Frank
PUBLISHED: 1961
GENRE: Prepresidential Years

LINCOLN SPENT the years 1837–60 as a lawyer, which was most of his adult life. True, he did practice politics during that time and held elective office, but he earned his living almost solely through law fees. Because this is not considered an exciting or glamorous aspect of Lincoln's life, it has been neglected by most biographers. John P. Frank's *Lincoln As a Lawyer* is a good corrective of this. Frank rightfully states, "To say that Lincoln practiced law for twenty-five years is to use a phrase so shorthand it may conceal meaning. One may hear the words, but the quantity of the thing escapes whole perception, as one refers to a billion dollars. The finest and most compendious of Lincoln's biographies devote only a chapter or two to his law practice. . . . Yet this was Lincoln's life." Frank does not offer a narrative of Lincoln's legal career. Instead, he focuses on some major themes and aspects of Lincoln's law practice that put it in proper perspective. This is helpful to those who want an overview of Lincoln as a lawyer without getting bogged down in reading about case after case.[1]

The rules for becoming a lawyer were much less stringent in the early nineteenth century. Frank still believes, though, that Lincoln came at a disadvantage to the practice of law: "Lincoln's lack of all formal education set him apart more severely from his fellow practitioners than did his lack of formal legal education, for this was the era of the office-taught lawyer." Lincoln was essentially self-taught.

He read law by himself at New Salem. Lincoln's early success had mostly to do with his partnership with John T. Stuart, who was a distinguished politician and lawyer.[2]

Lincoln overcame his lack of formal education with his innate intelligence and hard work. As Frank states, "Lincoln was capable of very careful workmanship. The turbulence of his rapid-fire practice might sometimes preclude that care, but I suspect that this was not a matter of taste, and that he preferred to be careful when he could." By today's standards Lincoln's preparation was not great, but as Frank points out, the sheer volume of cases Lincoln handled precluded this.[3]

Frank stresses that a major component of Lincoln's success as a lawyer came from the techniques he used in court: "Lincoln was extremely effective both on direct and cross-examination and had a major talent for jury appeal. He was gifted far above the average in putting his case into simple focus and in organizing his facts for clarity. His manner was appealing, and his occasional bursts of eloquence extremely effective. He was blessed with a capacity to ask questions clearly and with a pertinacity in keeping after evasions."[4] This all goes back to Lincoln's basic personality. He was a magnetic figure to many, and this carried over into the courtroom.

Lincoln was relatively successful professionally. As Frank points out, "Lincoln made a thoroughly comfortable living at the law. We have no sufficient data to be able to compare him with other Springfield lawyers in this respect, principally because while others may have been wealthier, their income in at least some known instances came from nonprofessional sources. His fees were modest, even by the standard of his own generation, and he had an outright moral revulsion against being overpaid."[5] While Lincoln was not rich from his law practice, he might have been had it been his sole focus in life. One gets the impression that Lincoln treated law as a job while his passion was politics. He must have lost quite a bit of income during periods such as his senatorial campaign in 1858, but that was the price of his ambition.

Frank does not argue Lincoln was one of the great lawyers of his day. "By way of comparison with the lawyers in the rest of the country, it is fair to conclude that if Lincoln had died in 1860 no one would ever have heard from him again as an attorney. This is not very significant datum, since the same could be said for more than 99 per cent of the rest of the bar. However, for what it is worth, his reputation was not such that a list of the greatest lawyers of America of that period would, except for his political prominence, have included him."[6] Frank's assessment in this regard is honest and fair. One should not be tempted to overstate Lincoln's success at the bar.

It is fortunate that *Lincoln As a Lawyer* was written by a lawyer. Frank brings a lawyer's perspective to Lincoln's legal practice and understands the nuances of it better than an academic historian would. Frank's book is written in a clear and concise way that is evidence of his own legal experience. After reading this book, Lincoln's law practice is better understood not just in his life but in the context of his time. As the best book on Lincoln's legal career, this book is essential to a Lincoln library.[7]

NOTES

1. John P. Frank, *Lincoln As a Lawyer* (Chicago: Americana House, 1991), 4; for those wanting more of a narrative of Lincoln's law career, see John J. Duff, *A. Lincoln: Prairie Lawyer* (New York: Rinehart & Co., 1960). Lincoln's complete law papers are now available on DVD format, so a reappraisal of his law career is inevitable.
2. Frank, 11.
3. Ibid., 79, 169.
4. Ibid., 170.
5. Ibid., 170.
6. Ibid., 171.
7. Cullom Davis in introduction to Frank, xii.

Prelude to Greatness: Lincoln in the 1850's

AUTHOR: Don E. Fehrenbacher
PUBLISHED: 1962
GENRE: Prepresidential Years

THIS BOOK is the one all modern biographers refer to when discussing Lincoln's political activities during the decade before the Civil War. *Prelude to Greatness* is a series of essays Don E. Fehrenbacher wrote to clarify some of the controversial issues historians grapple with in dealing with the 1850s. Some of the issues he covers are Lincoln's role in the early Republican Party in Illinois, his nomination for senator, his House Divided speech, and his use of the Freeport Question during the Lincoln-Douglas debates. Fehrenbacher answers the questions raised in such an authoritative and logical way that his book, while forty years old, remains the standard study of Lincoln for this time period.

Fehrenbacher believes that the House Divided speech has been persistently misunderstood by most historians. The usual view is that the speech was aimed at the South. Fehrenbacher disagrees. He feels it had more to do with the unique political situation that Lincoln faced in challenging Douglas. Douglas had taken a stand against the proslavery Lecompton Constitution in Kansas. He had broken with President James Buchanan and the Southern Democrats because he believed it did not reflect the true will of the citizens of Kansas. He probably also recognized that most Illinois voters would not support what looked like an attempt to force slavery on Kansas. Douglas wasn't a fool and was in no hurry to commit political suicide. The problem Lincoln faced was how to convince voters that Douglas's principle of popular sovereignty would still lead to slavery expanding. Lincoln feared Republicans might go over to Douglas. Fehrenbacher states, "Remote as it may seem in retrospect, the possibility that the Republican party—or a considerable portion of it—might become a tail fastened to the Douglas kite loomed before Lincoln's eyes as a real and imminent danger in the spring of 1858. The Lecompton controversy, besides making Douglas a hero to many antislavery leaders, had also softened opposition to his 'great principle.'"[1]

Lincoln needed a clarion call to his party. He had to show that Douglas's doctrine of not caring whether slavery was accepted or rejected by the voters could lead to the nationalization of slavery. Lincoln stressed the moral indifference Douglas had toward slavery. "The House Divided speech represents one of those moments of synthesis which embody the past and illuminate the future. Lincoln, who revered his country's historical tradition, believed that the cause he embraced pointed the way to a fuller realization of the ideals upon which the republic had been built." Lincoln had to have a forceful speech to rally the faithful to his banner, and he obviously got it with the House Divided speech.[2]

Along these same lines was Lincoln's senatorial nomination. At the time, senators were not nominated by party conventions. Lincoln's nomination was an anomaly. While historian Albert Beveridge thought the nomination of Lincoln had to do with stopping a potential rivalry in the Republican ranks, Fehrenbacher shows it really was a display of solidarity aimed at the eastern Republican leaders who were flirting with Douglas because of his anti-Lecompton stand.[3]

Another myth Fehrenbacher tackles is the famous Freeport Question. Lincoln had asked Douglas in their debate at Freeport how the people of a territory could keep slavery out if the Dred Scott decision stated that slavery couldn't legally be excluded by Congress from the territories. Douglas replied, in what would be called the Freeport Doctrine, that slavery could be kept out locally by a territorial legislature's refusal to enact local laws to protect slavery. He believed these laws would keep slavery out as effectively as an actual congressional ban. Some would suggest that while this answer helped Douglas in the Illinois senatorial race, it ensured Lincoln's election to the presidency in 1860 because it cost Douglas Southern support. Fehrenbacher dispels this interpretation of the question: "In summary, it seems reasonable to suggest that the famous exchange at Freeport is not the key to the historical significance of the great debates . . . that Douglas's opposition to the Lecompton constitution was the principal reason for his loss of standing in the South; and the Freeport doctrine, for all the talk about it, was only a superficial factor in the disruption of the Democratic party." Fehrenbacher is convincing in his argument. Historians may have been too quick to point to the Freeport Question as a turning point because it supposedly showed Lincoln's great political skill and foresight.[4]

Prelude to Greatness is one of those Lincoln books that overturned long-held interpretations. The Lincoln who emerges in this book is a man of consummate political skill as well as strong moral convictions. Fehrenbacher's title could have left out the *Prelude,* since in his interpretation Lincoln is already great.

NOTES

1. Don E. Fehrenbacher, *Prelude to Greatness: Lincoln in the 1850's* (Stanford: Stanford University Press, 1991), 85, 78.
2. Ibid., 94.
3. Ibid., 50, 62–63.
4. Ibid., 121–22, 142.

Lincoln and the Negro

AUTHOR: Benjamin Quarles
PUBLISHED: 1962
GENRE: General

BENJAMIN QUARLES was one of the most distinguished African-American historians of the twentieth century. It is only natural that he would look at Lincoln and his connection with black history. Quarles is generally admiring of Lincoln. He sees Lincoln growing in the years he was president in his support of the rights of former slaves. It should be noted that Quarles is not without his reservations about Lincoln, yet he can still write warmly about African Americans' devotion to Lincoln's memory nearly a century after his death. "They have not bothered to claim any superior devotion to his memory, yet it is a matter of historical record that they loved him first and loved him longest."[1]

Lincoln's racial attitudes have been a source of controversy for some time. His statements made during the debates with Douglas are certainly racist when looked at today. Quarles agrees with that assessment: "It must be noted that while Lincoln supported Negro freedom, he was no advocate of Negro equality. 'I have no purpose,' wrote he in 1858, 'to introduce political and social equality between the white and black races.' Lincoln did not believe the Negro was on par with the white man in mental endowment. . . . Lincoln believed in the equality of opportunity for all Americans, but he did not fully sense that a denial of any basic right was, in effect, a denial of equal opportunity for advancement." Quarles does not engage in "presentism" though. He admires Lincoln's attitude as compared to his contemporaries'. He states, "Lincoln was not anti-Negro, however, despite the strong racial prejudices so prevalent where he lived." As an authority on black history in America, Quarles's assessment is fair and carries a lot of weight.[2]

Quarles includes a chapter about Lincoln's relationship with the black troops in the Union army. Black soldiers faced serious danger if they were captured by the Confederates. Both the Confederate president and Congress saw them as insurrectionists subject to the death penalty. Lincoln believed his government was responsible for the welfare of all the troops in the field, regardless of color. Quarles recounts a remarkable order Lincoln gave after the battle of Fort Wagner when there was fear the Confederates were going to carry out their threats: "Lincoln knew some action by the White House was necessary. One week after Fort Wagner, he sent for General Halleck and told him to prepare an order for the protection of Negro prisoners. The draft submitted by the War Department reflected Lincoln's views, ordering that, for every Union soldier killed in violation of the laws of war, a rebel soldier would be put to death, and that, for every Union soldier sold into slavery, a rebel soldier would be put at hard labor on the public works." It would be hard to say Lincoln was indifferent to the fate of black soldiers when he was willing to engage in an "eye for an eye" policy in regard to them. Lincoln's order probably saved many soldiers' lives. There were still massacres of black soldiers, such as the one at Fort Pillow in 1864, but the Confederate government never implemented its official policy, possibly out of fear of retaliation from Lincoln's government.[3]

The most touching part of the book is Quarles's description of the reaction to Lincoln's death among former slaves. It is easy to be cynical today, yet this book conveys the enormous sense of admiration former slaves had for the man they saw as being responsible for freeing them. Quarles writes, "Typical of the Lincoln funeral exercises in the coastal regions was that held at Beaufort, South Carolina. In a schoolroom draped in black, the mourners assembled. Everyone wore some emblem of sorrow—a black headband or a black bow or topknot. One man had turned his coat inside out in order to achieve the proper color. . . . Wearing their black 'sacredly,' and hence sensing nothing ludicrous in their appearance, the solemn-faced Negroes listened to prayers and chants, one leader calling Lincoln by every endearing name he could think of. Many gave way to low sobs and moans, which seemed to deepen the general fervor."[4] These were people who had nothing because of the brutality that had been their existence, and yet they could still muster whatever small amount of resources they had to remember the man they considered their liberator.

Lincoln and the Negro remains the best book written by a black historian on Lincoln. Biographers of Lincoln tend to write with a certain detachment about the slaves. They are players in the Lincoln story, yet Lincoln's thoughts and actions remain the focus. Quarles's book redresses that imbalance. Here is the story of what blacks thought and what their actions toward Lincoln were. Quarles's judgment is keen when he writes, "Doubtless the Negro's attitude was tinged by wish-fulfillment, seeing him as they wanted him to be. . . . Yet the Negro of his day saw him as a man growing in knowledge and wisdom, and to them he was 'emancipator, benefactor, friend and leader.'"[5]

NOTES

1. Benjamin Quarles, *Lincoln and the Negro* (New York: Da Capo, 1990), foreword; see Benjamin Quarles, *The Negro in the Making of America* (New York: Macmillan, 1973).
2. Quarles, *Lincoln and the Negro*, 36, 36.
3. Ibid., 153–83, 175.
4. Ibid., 239–49, 245.
5. Ibid., foreword.

Twenty Days

AUTHORS: Dorothy Meserve Kunhardt
and Philip B. Kunhardt Jr.
PUBLISHED: 1965
GENRE: Assassination

TWENTY DAYS was the period of time between Lincoln's last day alive and his burial in his hometown of Springfield. Dorothy Meserve Kunhardt and Philip B. Kunhardt Jr. cover the momentous events of those days in a collection of photographs. They also provide explanatory material to help the reader understand what the country underwent from April 14 to May 3, 1865. This book was published exactly one hundred years after Lincoln's death. It was also two short years after Kennedy's assassination. The authors call the similarities between the two events "uncanny." Regardless of the truth of that assessment, *Twenty Days* provides a unique and emotional look at the tragedy of Lincoln's death.[1]

The authors have quite a pedigree in Lincoln photography. They are descendants of Fredrick Hill Meserve, who was one of the all-time great collectors of Lincoln photographs. The authors dedicate the work to Meserve and can say because of him, "The photographic records of the twelve funerals in twelve cities westward were sought out from the archives and historical collections, along the actual funeral route, and the full picture of that incredible trip is shown here for the very first time."[2] It was indeed an incredible trip, and its record is not lost to us due to the invention of photography and the work of Meserve and others to collect this material.

It would be impossible to cover all the photographs in this book, so only some of the highlights will be mentioned. The single most striking image is the two-page spread "HE IS GONE: HE IS DEAD." On a black background, a life mask of Lincoln, made two months before his death, is placed. It looks so peaceful that many have incorrectly assumed it was his death mask. The next page shows the bed Lincoln died in shortly after his body was removed. One of the white pillows is saturated with the president's blood. The title of this page is the simple but haunting "LINCOLN DIED HERE TWO HOURS AGO." The authors also have taken a photograph of Lincoln and the derringer Booth used and arranged them to show exactly the angle of Lincoln's head when it was struck by the bullet and how far away the gun was. It is frightening to look at how close Booth approached Lincoln before firing.[3]

Extensive coverage is given to the trial and fate of Booth's conspirators. Of the four to be hanged, there are drawings of them in their cells during their last few hours. One almost feels sorry for Lewis Paine, the appointed assassin of William Seward, as he sits alone and dejected in his cell awaiting his fate. Photographs are shown of the four conspirators being prepared to hang. Their corpses are also shown hanging lifeless and still. On a wider shot of the gallows, freshly dug graves are shown. These photographs might not be to everyone's taste, but they do give a sense of how terrible the punishment was for some of the people who worked with Booth. Mere text would not have given the same effect.[4]

The bulk of the book covers the massive funerals Lincoln was given at each city his coffin stopped on its way back to Springfield to be buried. The amount of grief shown is amazing. In Buffalo they had a huge funeral attended by thousands, without even having the real Lincoln coffin. The city did not know the funeral train was going to include them, so they had a funeral anyway with a mock coffin. When the real coffin arrived, the city had to have another funeral. In Philadelphia there was almost a riot as the Lincoln train arrived in the station. More than three hundred thousand people attended the funeral and filed past the coffin as it lay in Independence Hall. Titles to photographs of some of the other Lincoln funerals are "IN

COLUMBUS—A FUNERAL OF FLOWERS," "INDIANAPOLIS SAYS GOOD-BY TO INDIANA'S FARM-BOY," and "ALMOST HOME— CHICAGO HONORS THE RAIL-SPLITTER."[5]

Near the end of the book the authors compile some Lincoln photographs in chronological order. The first being when Lincoln was only thirty-seven years old. However, most of the photographs are from Lincoln's days as president, and they show a marked deterioration in his appearance. Lincoln's health suffered under the strain of the presidency, but it has never been shown as effectively as it is in *Twenty Days*. By 1865 Lincoln looks like a haggard old man, when only a few years before he looked healthy and vibrant.[6]

This book is easy to pick up and hard to put down. The text is well written, but it is the photographs that make *Twenty Days* the essential book it is. There is much to look at and ponder on page after page. The authors have skillfully arranged the material to give its best possible effect. If a good picture can tell a thousand words, this book tells millions.

NOTES

1. Dorothy Meserve Kunhardt and Philip B. Kunhardt Jr., *Twenty Days* (New York: Harper & Row, 1965), 3.
2. Ibid., 6.
3. Ibid., 80–81, 82–83, 38–39.
4. Ibid., 206–9, 206, 210–13, 214–15, 204–5.
5. Ibid., 218–19, 146–51, 222–23, 224–25, 232–33.
6. Ibid., 293–99.

Lincoln's Preparation for Greatness: The Illinois Legislative Years

AUTHOR: Paul Simon
PUBLISHED: 1965
GENRE: Prepresidential Years

*L*INCOLN'S *PREPARATION FOR GREATNESS* is the most complete account of Lincoln's career as an Illinois state representative. Written by an Illinois politician, it looks at Lincoln as a legislator and seeks to analyze his effectiveness. Simon also dispels some of the myths of Lincoln's years in the legislature that are remnants of Albert Beveridge's look at Lincoln's Illinois political career. This book contains many facts and records of votes that are rarely covered in Lincoln biography. It is also insightful and remains the most important secondary work about Lincoln's early political officeholding.

Beveridge's work had accused Lincoln of "logrolling" to get the state capital moved from Vandalia to Springfield. Beveridge believed that Lincoln and the Sangamon delegation traded votes for internal improvements in exchange for votes for Springfield as the capital. While this charge did not originate with Beveridge, he was its most able advocate. Simon shows that many of the assumptions behind this interpretation are wrong. First of all, for the logrolling charge to be true, the Sangamon delegation would have had to vote as a block nearly always in order to make the trade of its support for internal-improvement measures worth anything to those who would trade their vote for Springfield as capital. Simon shows that this was not the case. In the twenty-five cases where logrolling was possible, members of the Sangamon delegation were often absent. "It is of much greater significance that on fifteen of the twenty-five roll calls there was division within the Sangamon delegation." The Sangamon delegation would be expected to vote together more often than most since they were all Whigs, yet this didn't happen. Simon also notices that the charge of logrolling was not made at the time by the people who would be expected to make it. "Another minor piece of evidence is the fact that logrolling would be common knowledge among politicians and could hardly fail becoming a major election issue, but it did not." Vandalia would be expected to make much out of the issue, but instead there is a contemporary silence. Simon admits the case against the logrolling charge is not airtight. He reasonably concludes, though, "Every session of the legislature has some trading, but there is no evidence that Lincoln supported any measure with which he was in basic disagreement in order to secure votes for Springfield." The fact that Lincoln voted for almost every internal improvement has more to do with his Whig philosophy than his desire to see Springfield become the capital.[1]

Despite the title of the book, Simon does find that Lincoln erred much in his career as a legislator. Lincoln scholar Gabor Boritt put it this way: "Although Simon entitled his book *Lincoln's Preparation for Greatness,* and he rescued Lincoln from many a Beveridge excess, he failed to reach much beyond Stephen Vincent Benét's 'crude small-time politician.' He thus failed to make the title of the book meaningful." In particular, Lincoln's unwavering support of internal improvements is seen as foolish when it was bankrupting the state. Simon writes, "But sensible Lincoln actions on internal improvements were few. Some of the votes are difficult to understand. For example, a resolution disapproving payments of interest by the state, until the state received the money, carried overwhelmingly, 76–8, but Lincoln was one of the eight against it." Lincoln's Whig philosophy led him to support internal improvements, but Simon is right to point out that when the system started to fail, Lincoln should have backed off in his support of it as others had done.[2]

What, then, is the final assessment made of Lincoln as a state legislator in this book? Simon writes, "He was an above-average legislator, but if you were to pick *one* legislator for distinguished service award for each session, at no time would the award have gone to Lincoln. If you had been a spectator trying to determine which legislator might become the leader of the nation, it is not likely you would have chosen Lincoln. Only when a moral issue like slavery came up did any hint of future greatness appear." This is unfair, since judging the young Lincoln in relation to his greatness as president is a flawed comparison. The job of a state representative is much different from that of a president. The concerns are much more parochial, and national issues like slavery and union would rarely come up.[3]

Some might be tempted to dismiss the years Lincoln spent as a legislator, and thus this book, as unimportant. That would be a mistake. Simon rightfully asserts, "When he entered the Illinois House of Representatives in 1834, he knew little about the complexities of practical politics. When he left the House of Representatives eight years later, he had acquired not only a broad knowledge of the many issues on which a legislator must vote, but also an effective working knowledge of how the political world runs."[4]

NOTES

1. Paul Simon, *Lincoln's Preparation for Greatness: The Illinois Legislative Years* (Urbana: University of Illinois Press, 1971), 76–105, 83, 101, 104; see Albert J. Beveridge, *Abraham Lincoln: 1809–1858*, 2 vols. (Boston: Houghton Mifflin Co., 1928).
2. Gabor S. Boritt, *Abraham Lincoln and the Economics of the American Dream* (Urbana: University of Illinois Press, 1994), 308; Simon, 186.
3. Simon, 292.
4. Ibid., 289–90.

Robert Todd Lincoln: A Man in His Own Right

AUTHOR: John S. Goff
PUBLISHED: 1969
GENRE: Family and Genealogy

THERE HAS rarely been a subtitle to a book truer than *Robert Todd Lincoln: A Man in His Own Right*. John S. Goff provides a solid biography of Lincoln's eldest son with this book. It is often said that Abraham Lincoln's father's reputation suffered because of his being compared to his son. This is just as true with Robert Todd Lincoln. He lived a long and distinguished life, but because his father was so successful, this is often forgotten. Goff's book seeks to correct this by giving a truer picture of Robert's life.

Lincoln was often absent from home while on the circuit as a lawyer, and Robert was off in college when Lincoln was president. As a result, Robert did not know him as well as he might have. Goff articulates it this way: "A question which logically presents itself at this point is, to what extent was Robert Lincoln involved in the affairs of the government during the war period? Did his father confide in him regarding matters of state? Young Lincoln once wrote of the war years, 'I was a boy occupied by my studies at Harvard College, very seldom in Washington, and having no exceptional opportunity of knowing what was going on.'" Robert served on the staff of U. S. Grant late in the war, and was visiting home when his father was shot. Robert's deep feelings for his father are attested to by Goff. "On the bed lay the dying Abraham Lincoln, surrounded by officials of government and his friends. Throughout the long night, as life ebbed, Robert Lincoln stood at the bedside; at intervals he wept upon the shoulder of Charles Sumner." Robert is pictured as cold, but scenes like this point to his deep sense of loss at his father's death.[1]

It should be remembered that the young twenty-two-year-old Robert had enormous responsibility thrust upon him by his father's death. He was now responsible for a mother who was showing signs of mental illness and a brother who was ten years his junior. It is a testament to the strength of character that he weathered these trials along with the death of his own young son while continuing to lead a public life.[2]

Goff covers the enormous accomplishments of Robert in the world of business and politics. He was a successful lawyer, president of the Pullman Company, U.S. Secretary of War, and minister to Great Britain. At one point he was even talked about as a candidate for president himself. Goff quotes an editorial from the *New York Times* in which they endorsed Lincoln: "Mr. Lincoln is an energetic and capable Secretary of War. His successful administration of that department gives the assurance of a credible discharge of the duties of the Presidency." Robert's candidacy never got beyond this, but it is telling that he was mentioned as a legitimate candidate.[3]

In politics, Robert was much more conservative than his father. He did not like the progressivism of Theodore Roosevelt, who he thought was misrepresenting himself as a follower of the ideas of Lincoln. "In the bitter 1912 presidential campaign Lincoln wrote a strongly worded letter to Theodore Roosevelt condemning his use of the name of Abraham Lincoln to support his 'New Nationalism' policies." He apparently did not share his father's sympathy toward labor. When the Pullman Company cut the wages of its employees, there was a strike. Robert made no public utterances on the matter, but Goff thinks it is clear where he stood. "One may presume that he was in agreement with Pullman's stand since he was close to Pullman during the time." Robert's politics, while not popular today, were common in the Gilded Age.[4]

Robert had a negative effect on the writing of history. He controlled his father's papers and only gave Lincoln's secretaries the chance to see them while writing their biography of Lincoln. Robert did this because he had editorial control of what they wrote. Others, such as Albert Beveridge, sought to gain access to the papers but were denied. Robert stipulated in his will that the papers would be sealed for twenty-one years after his death. They were not available to scholars until 1947. Robert erred in his judgment here; there was nothing in the papers embarrassing to Lincoln.[5]

Goff labored under a disadvantage when writing this biography. Robert was a private person who did not leave a diary and late in life largely kept to himself. Goff's book is still a credible effort. Goff realizes the impossibility of separating Robert from his father: "In any attempt to assess the worth of the younger Lincoln in relation to the political, legal, and economic record of his own age, there is always present the shadow of the preceding generation." While this is true to an extent, it is possible to see Robert as a unique individual. Goff has left a record of Robert's accomplishments that shows he was worthy of a biography, regardless of his father.[6]

NOTES

1. John S. Goff, *Robert Todd Lincoln: A Man in His Own Right* (Norman: University of Oklahoma Press, 1969), 53, 65, 70.
2. Ibid., 195.
3. Ibid., 91–105, 125–41, 222–23, 192–208; *New York Times,* June 2, 1884, as quoted in ibid., 144.
4. Goff, 240, 220.
5. Ibid., 179–80, 191, 255.
6. Ibid., 265.

Mary Todd Lincoln: Her Life and Letters

AUTHORS: Justin G. Turner and
Linda Levitt Turner

PUBLISHED: 1972

GENRE: Family and Genealogy

THE AUTHORS of this volume have compiled every existing letter Mary Todd Lincoln wrote. Justin G. Turner and Linda Levitt Turner have also written a biography they place between the letters. This blending is very effective, since it gives context to the letters. Unfortunately, most of the letters date to after Lincoln's death. The letters that have survived before that time are an invaluable source on the Lincoln marriage. The letters Mary wrote from 1865 to 1882 are important, too, but lack the immediacy the others have regarding Lincoln. Also, they do not paint a positive picture of Mrs. Lincoln. They are concerned mainly with acquiring money. Be that as it may, *Mary Todd Lincoln: Her Life and Letters* remains an essential book. Just as Lincoln's own words are the best source for understanding him, Mary's are for understanding her as well.[1]

The most important surviving letter from the period of the Lincoln marriage is the one Mary wrote to her husband while he was in Congress. It shows the warm relationship they enjoyed at times. Mary wrote, "It is growing late, these summer eves are short, I expect my long scrawls, for truly such they are, weary you greatly. . . . I must bid you good-night—Do not fear the children have forgotten you, I was only jesting—Even E[ddy's] eyes brighten at the mention of your name." It is a shame that more letters such as this have not survived.[2]

There is a very telling letter Mary wrote in 1856 to her half sister, Emile Todd Helm. Those who argue that Mary was a political partner to Lincoln in the same way Eleanor Roosevelt was to her husband have to explain this letter. By 1856 Lincoln had joined the Republican Party and left the Whigs behind. This is probably the most important political decision he ever made and led to his becoming president. In her letter Mary shows she was not on the same page as her husband. Mary supported the anti-immigrant Know Nothing Party in 1856. She wrote, "My weak woman's heart was too Southern in feeling to sympathize with any but [Millard] Fillmore, I have always been a great admirer of his, he made so good a President & is so just a man & feels the necessity of keeping foreigners, within bounds. If some of you Kentuckians, had to deal with the 'wild Irish,' as we housekeepers are sometimes called to do, the south would certainly elect Mr Fillmore next time." Compare this with a letter Lincoln wrote to his friend Joshua Speed a short time before. In explaining why he wasn't a Know Nothing, he said, "How can I be? How can one who abhors the oppression of negroes, be in favor of degrading classes of white people?"[3]

Turner and Turner include a touching letter Mary wrote to Queen Victoria. Both women had lost their husbands. Queen Victoria had written Mary a consoling letter about her loss. Mary responded, "I have received the letter which Your Majesty has had the kindness to write, & am deeply grateful for the expressions of tender sympathy, coming as they do, from a heart which from its own sorrow, can appreciate the intense grief I now endure. Accept, Madam, the assurance of my heartfelt thanks & believe me in the deepest sorrow, Your Majesty's sincere and grateful friend."[4] It is a shame that Mrs. Lincoln did keep this exchange of letters to herself. They would have shown the public the grace and eloquence of which the first lady was capable.

As stated above, the majority of the letters written after Lincoln's death are not complimentary to Mrs. Lincoln. Mary shows signs of mental imbalance in some of the letters. Turner and Turner, who are sympathetic toward Mary, are forced to admit, "It cannot be denied that Mary Lincoln was in some ways mentally disturbed even before her husband's death." In her defense, though, they argue, "Yet whatever else she has, interestingly, and ironically enough, refused to testify to her own madness." Here they overstate their case. When Mary was released from the sanatorium to which she was forced to go by law for her insanity, she wrote her only surviving son, "Two prominent clergy men, have written me, since I saw you—and mention in their letters, that they think it advisable to offer up prayers for you in Church, on account of your wickedness against me and High Heaven. In reference to Chicago you have the enemies & I chance to have the friends there. Send me all that I have written for, you have tried your game of robbery long enough." Mary blamed her son for putting her in the sanatorium, but her letter reveals a malice and childishness that are striking.[5]

The letters of Mary Todd Lincoln are an important primary source for looking at her life. In the letters in this volume, Mary is allowed to speak unfiltered by any biographer with an agenda. Ultimately, one has to judge for oneself how Mary fares in this test.

NOTES

1. For a typical letter concerning money, see Mary Todd Lincoln to Noyes W. Miner, February 24, 1882, in Justin G. Turner and Linda Levitt Turner, *Mary Todd Lincoln: Her Life and Letters* (New York: Knopf, 1972), 715.
2. Mary Todd Lincoln to Abraham Lincoln, May 1848, in ibid., 38.
3. Mary Todd Lincoln to Emile Todd Helm, November 23, 1856, in ibid., 46; Abraham Lincoln to Joshua Speed, August, 24, 1855, in *The Collected Works of Abraham Lincoln*, ed. Roy P. Basler, 8 vols. (New Brunswick: Rutgers University Press, 1953), 2:323; for the argument for Mary's political partnership see Jean H. Baker, "Mary and Abraham: A Marriage" in *The Lincoln Enigma: The Changing Face of an American Icon*, ed. Gabor Boritt (New York: Oxford University Press, 2001), 36–55.
4. Mary Todd Lincoln to Queen Victoria, May, 21, 1865, in Turner and Turner, 230–31.
5. Turner and Turner, 614, 614; Mary Todd Lincoln to Robert Todd Lincoln, June 19, 1876, in ibid., 615.

A True History of the Assassination of Abraham Lincoln and the Conspiracy of 1865

AUTHOR: Louis J. Weichmann
PUBLISHED: 1975
GENRE: Assassination

O NE OF the unsung heroes of the aftermath of the Lincoln assassination is Louis J. Weichmann. Over the years he has been the repeated target of smears and character assassination by the defenders of Mary Surratt and Dr. Samuel Mudd. His testimony helped convict both of them, and their supporters have never forgiven him. However, as hard as they try, they cannot destroy his credibility. The story he tells in *A True History of the Assassination of Abraham Lincoln and the Conspiracy of 1865* is a compelling view of the conspiracy from someone who saw much of it firsthand.[1]

Weichmann was studying to be a Catholic priest when he met John Surratt. He befriended Surratt and stayed as a boarder in John's mother's boarding house during the war. While he was there, he witnessed meetings Booth had with his fellow conspirators. After the assassination, he was a suspect for a time but eventually became the star witness for the prosecution. Because he was so instrumental in convicting Mary Surratt, her son John attempted to portray Weichmann as a liar in a lecture that he gave shortly after his own trial. Others followed suit, and Weichmann was often a target for the rest of his life. Weichmann, who was a deeply religious man, resented these attacks, and on his deathbed signed a statement that he had told the truth in the trial and was ready to meet his God.[2]

This book was written late in Weichmann's life and almost never saw the light of day. It was acquired by the editor of the volume,

Floyd E. Risvold, from the niece of Weichmann. Risvold edited the manuscript and added other material, such as Surratt's 1870 lecture and letters that Weichmann wrote over the years. In doing so, he preserved an essential account of the conspiracy against Lincoln.[3]

The most controversial parts of the book concern Mary Surratt. Weichmann drove Mary to her tavern in Maryland to drop off a package Booth had given her on the day of the assassination. The package contained a field glass. She told John Lloyd, who rented the place, that Booth would be there later that night for the package and also told him to have the "shooting irons" ready. She was referring to guns the conspirators had previously stored at the tavern. Weichmann can rightly ask at this point in the narrative, "What was John Wilkes Booth doing at Mrs. Surratt's house at the time? How did he happen to know that she was going into the country just then? What interest could he have in her visit to Surrattsville that afternoon? Can Mrs. Surratt's apologists and defenders explain it? It looks to me as if the whole thing had been planned before hand." Weichmann lays out a strong case for Mary's knowledge and involvement in the plot. Those who would argue otherwise have a strong witness to contend with in Weichmann.[4]

Weichmann also places Dr. Mudd firmly in the Booth conspiracy. He was present with John Surratt when Mudd introduced Booth to Surratt in Washington in December 1864. The four men met on the street and went into a hotel room. Weichmann describes the scene in the room: "Dr. Mudd arose, went out into the entry that led past the door, and called Boone (Booth) out after him. They did not take their hats with them nor did they go downstairs; had they done so I could easily have heard their retreating footsteps. In the course of five or six minutes both returned to the door and called out, 'Surratt.' Then these men remained in the hall for several minutes longer before returning." It is beyond belief that Mudd would not remember this meeting during his trial. He related it only on the way to prison, but then quickly said the meeting was accidental. It is obvious Mudd was being less than truthful.[5]

The lecture John Surratt gave in 1870 highlights the desperation of those who wished to impeach Weichmann. When accusers don't have the facts on their side, engaging in ad hominem is a useful tactic. "Give me a man who can strike his victim dead, but save me a man who, through perjury, will cause the death of an innocent person. Double Murderer!!! Hell possesses no worse fiend than a character of that kind." Surratt conveniently leaves out where exactly Weichmann committed perjury in his testimony.[6]

It is providential that Risvold published this book. Had he not done so, a valuable record of the assassination would have been lost. In addition to the above mentioned parts of the book, it contains a descriptive narrative of the people and events leading up to the assassination. Weichmann will never have the professional defenders that Mudd and Surratt have, yet justice demands that his story be told and the smears on his character end.

NOTES

1. Floyd E. Risvold in editor's introduction to Louis J. Weichmann, *A True History of the Assassination of Abraham Lincoln and the Conspiracy of 1865* (New York: Knopf, 1975), xvii.
2. Risvold in ibid., xiv–xv, xvii, xvi.
3. Ibid., xviii–xix.
4. Weichmann, 165, 166.
5. Ibid., 33, 257–58.
6. John Surratt in Rockville Lecture in ibid., 435.

Lincoln and the Economics of the American Dream

AUTHOR: Gabor S. Boritt
PUBLISHED: 1978
GENRE: General

ABRAHAM LINCOLN spent most of his political life as a Whig. The Whig Party is sometimes scoffed at as being a bunch of aristocrats and bankers. It is almost as if Lincoln's Whiggery needed to be explained away. Gabor S. Boritt takes the opposite tack. He celebrates Lincoln's early Whig political beliefs and believes Lincoln carried them with him to the White House. Boritt is the first to take Lincoln's economic views seriously, and *Lincoln and the Economics of the American Dream* is the first in-depth look at them.

Boritt feels Lincoln's main economic principle was that everyone has the "right to rise." It was Lincoln's early experience in life that led him to this belief. Boritt writes, "It had all begun long ago with a poor boy's conviction—in a time and at a place which nurtured such convictions—that a man should receive the whole fruit of his labor so that he might get ahead in life." The poverty of Lincoln's youth led him to not romanticize the agricultural life the way someone like Thomas Jefferson, who never did any of the work himself, did. As Boritt writes, "Thus he showed more down-to-earth realism, perhaps even more honesty than most of his countrymen. His regard for the laboring man was deep. But America's longing for rustic simplicity, like her hero-building, her guilt over chasing after riches, her indulgence in a sometimes unprogressive outlook, and her Democratic politics could claim him not." Lincoln saw the city and commerce as offering more opportunities for a man wanting to rise in life.[1]

177

Lincoln admired the Whig leader Henry Clay because he felt his "American System" offered the best means for the development of the nation. The system called for protective tariffs to encourage manufacturing and using the money collected to finance internal improvements within the country. Lincoln saw many farmers losing the fruit of their labor through an antiquated transportation system. Canals and roads would help the farmer bring his goods to market much easier. As a young Illinois state legislator, Lincoln ardently supported internal improvements, perhaps too much so, for the state was not ready for the amount he wanted.[2]

Banks were another part of the Whig program for development. The Illinois State Bank had no stauncher defender than Lincoln. In fact, to prevent a quorum, he tried to escape out the window in a legislative session that would have hurt the bank. Lincoln felt the need for a frontier economy to have a sound medium for exchange. The idea of the "rail-splitter" on the side of banks is counterintuitive to many, but Lincoln saw credit as a way of improving the lot of laborers by inviting development. Historians have been too simplistic in painting the banks as evil and the Jacksonians as the champions of the common man for defeating them. Lincoln shows one can favor the banks as well as the laboring class. According to Lincoln, Jacksonian politics, for all its talk of helping the common man, kept him in an underdeveloped economy and prevented him from enjoying the full fruits of his labor.[3]

Boritt sees that some of Lincoln's antislavery views were rooted in his economic ideas. Lincoln's idea that all had the "right to rise" was contradicted by slavery. Boritt quotes Lincoln on his belief that blacks have this right: "And I believe a black man is entitled to it—in which he *can* better his condition—when he may look forward and hope to be a hired laborer this year and the next, work for himself afterward, and finally to hire men to work for him! That is the true system." It is true Lincoln's main objections to slavery were moral and political, but Boritt points out the economic aspect was important as well.[4]

Lincoln's economic ideas did not change when he entered the White House. The war and the slavery issue forced the ideas to the side, but they were there, all the same. Boritt writes, "It is worth noting again that although at times the vast problem of war finance distressed Lincoln, and he deplored inflation, he also maintained a very large measure of confidence in the ability of the United States, both the government and the economy, to underwrite improvement works while engaged in a great war." He kept up the idea of internal improvements, like the transcontinental railroad, because he felt the future welfare of the nation depended on it. Lincoln was no longer a member of the Whig Party as president, but his economic views never left that party.[5]

Boritt's book has been influential. His thesis of the "right to rise" being the most important part of Lincoln's economic philosophy has entered into the mainstream of Lincoln scholarship. Boritt sees Lincoln as personally embodying that philosophy. "The Lincoln mythos, with all its religious symbolism is the living evidence for the common man that the American Dream of the right to rise is true."[6]

NOTES

1. Gabor S. Boritt, *Lincoln and the Economics of the American Dream* (Urbana: University of Illinois Press, 1994), 284, 80.
2. Ibid., 281, 25–39; for an in-depth view of Henry Clay and his American System, see Robert V. Remini, *Henry Clay: Statesman for the Union* (New York: W. W. Norton, 1991).
3. Boritt, 55; for a highly sympathetic view of Jacksonian politics, see Arthur M. Schlesinger Jr., *The Age of Jackson* (Boston: Little, Brown & Co., 1953).
4. Abraham Lincoln as quoted in Boritt, 173.
5. Boritt, 214.
6. See Allen C. Guelzo, *Abraham Lincoln: Redeemer President* (Grand Rapids: Eerdmans, 1999); Boritt, 311.

A. Lincoln: The Crucible of Congress

AUTHOR: Paul Findley
PUBLISHED: 1979
GENRE: Prepresidential Years

L INCOLN'S TWO years spent in Congress are the subject of Paul Findley's book. Findley was a congressman himself and brings his enthusiasm for Washington and the institution to *A. Lincoln: The Crucible of Congress.* This book is well illustrated with many pictures and drawings from the time period. It is the story not just of Lincoln as a congressman but also of Washington in 1847–49.

Lincoln as a congressman has never won rave reviews. He is usually seen as being narrowly partisan and ineffective. This is true to some extent. Lincoln was hardly the most influential member of Congress, yet any freshman congressman hardly ever is. It is also true that he was a regular Whig who supported his party. Findley sees nothing wrong in this. He writes, "A politician who articulates the sentiments of the party to which he belongs frequently acquires the label 'party hack.' A cynicism toward partisan politics prompts this response, and it is often unjustified. Surely there are occasions when party consensus honestly reflects the deeply held convictions of individual party members." Findley is right on this point. Lincoln supported the Whig Party because it did reflect his political views, and there is no need for censure in the matter.[1]

As a Whig, Lincoln was a persistent critic of Democratic president James K. Polk. He introduced his famous "Spot Resolutions," which demanded to know if the war started on American or Mexican territory. There is no reason to believe Lincoln did this on purely partisan grounds. Findley shows as evidence private letters Lincoln wrote to his law partner, William Herndon. In these letters, he argues that Polk's idea of the president's war powers was unconstitutional. Findley concludes the chapter with the astute statement: "Lincoln in the 1840s was as thoroughly principled in his opposition to the Mexican War as he was in the 1860s in opposition to slavery."[2]

Lincoln did introduce a series of resolutions dealing with slavery in the District of Columbia. They are important because they show Lincoln's thinking on slavery at the time. With the help of antislavery congressman Joshua Giddings, Lincoln crafted an eight-part bill. The bill called for compensated emancipation for slaveholders in the district, and any child born to a slave after 1850 would be free. There was a provision to make sure fugitive slaves could not use Washington as a means to escape. The bill also called for a referendum by the citizens of Washington on the bill; it would go into effect only if they approved. Judged by later events, this bill seems very conservative. However, at the time, it was too far advanced to even be put to a vote. The bill did catch the ire of arch-defender of slavery John C. Calhoun though. He wrote back to his state of South Carolina that there were ominous bills in Congress, including one introduced by "a Member from Illinois."[3]

Since 1848 was a presidential election year, Lincoln was heavily involved in the move to nominate Zachary Taylor as the Whig candidate. After Taylor's nomination, he worked hard for his election. Findley covers this well and quotes the humorous speech Lincoln made on the floor of Congress concerning the Democratic candidate, Lewis Cass. The Democrats were trying to make Cass into a military hero of the War of 1812. Lincoln responded to this with some sarcastic self-mockery: "By the way Mr. Speaker, did you know I am a military hero? Yes, sir; in the days of the Black Hawk war I fought, bled and came away. Speaking of General Cass's career reminds me of my own. . . . It is quite certain that I did not break my sword, for I had none to break; but I bent a musket pretty badly on one occasion. If Cass broke his sword, the idea is he broke it in desperation; I bent the musket by accident." This is one of the greatest examples of political humor ever heard in Washington.[4]

The pictures in the book are interesting, particularly the ones showing Washington in the late 1840s. It was hardly the grand capital it is today. The photographs and drawings show a muddy village with only a few impressive buildings. Findley also includes photographs of some of the famous men of the day with whom Congressman Lincoln dealt.[5]

This book corrects a fault in Lincoln scholarship. Findley decries how scholars have been blind to Lincoln's accomplishments as a congressman. He states, "They simply closed their eyes to the facts. By the end of his term Lincoln had become one of the two leading Whigs in the entire state of Illinois. His role as a national campaigner for the Whig presidential ticket had spread his reputation far beyond the borders of Illinois." Findley goes on to say, "The purpose of this volume is to set the record straight and produce a better understanding of Lincoln the Congressman." After reading this book, one would have to say that Findley succeeded in his quest.[6]

NOTES

1. Paul Findley, *A. Lincoln: The Crucible of Congress* (New York: Crown Publishers, 1979), 153–54; for a generally negative view of Lincoln's years in Congress, see Donald W. Riddle, *Congressman Abraham Lincoln* (Westport, Conn.: Greenwood Press, 1957).
2. Findley, 151–52, 154–55, 158.
3. Ibid., 138; John C. Calhoun as quoted in ibid., 139.
4. Abraham Lincoln as quoted in ibid., 187.
5. Findley, 70–73, 76–77, 79–82; e.g., see ibid., 121.
6. Ibid., x, xi.

Lincoln and Black Freedom: A Study in Presidential Leadership

AUTHOR: LaWanda Cox
PUBLISHED: 1981
GENRE: Presidency

I T HAD long been assumed that Lincoln's successor, Andrew Johnson, was carrying out Lincoln's plans for Reconstruction during his presidency. This was one of the main tenets of revisionism. The assumption was that Lincoln wanted to readmit the Confederate states to the Union with little or no change as far as the former slaves were concerned. While the school of revisionism was on the wane by the early 1980s, the orthodoxy of Lincoln's similarity to Johnson in the area of Reconstruction had not yet been sufficiently challenged. LaWanda Cox's *Lincoln and Black Freedom: A Study of Presidential Leadership* does challenge it and does so most effectively.[1]

Cox feels that Lincoln worked consistently for the rights of former slaves during his administration. As she writes, "Lincoln's effort to extend freedom and insure its future safety was varied and persistent. Beginning quietly behind the scenes in the spring of 1863, he moved to obtain emancipation in occupied states through state action, a piecemeal but constitutionally unchallengeable solution." Cox is right to point out the constitutional limitations the president faced. What is remarkable is the way Lincoln manipulated the legal avenues he had to ensure freedom.[2]

The Reconstruction of Louisiana is the main topic of study in this book. It is where Lincoln was most involved in creating a reconstructed state government. His "Ten Percent Plan" was attempted in Louisiana. He wanted at least 10 percent of the voters who had voted in the 1860 election to swear allegiance to the Union and abolish slavery in their state. Cox covers the often behind-the-scenes actions by Lincoln to create a Free State and to ensure suffrage for the former black soldiers. Lincoln sent a private letter to the first Free State governor of Louisiana, Michael Hahn, stating, "Now you are about to have a Convention which, among other things, will probably define the elective franchise. I barely suggest for your private consideration, whether some of the colored people may not be let in—as for instance, the very intelligent, and especially those who have fought gallantly in our ranks. They would probably help, in some trying time to come, to keep the jewel of liberty within the family of freedom." Cox maintains, "On the surface, this appears a weak, tentative expression of a preference. In fact, it represented a presidential directive, tactfully stated but not to be taken lightly." Lincoln was playing a dangerous political game, and if the Democratic Party saw that he was pushing for black suffrage in the South, it would have made political hay out of it.[3]

Writers often assume Lincoln's Ten Percent Plan was an attempt to lure the Southern states back with lenient terms. If it was, it failed miserably because the war lasted one and a half years after it was proposed in 1863. Cox sees it instead as an antislavery measure. She concludes, "From the Louisiana perspective, Lincoln's 'Ten Percent Plan' can be recognized for what it was, not a policy of leniency but one of expediency, a means to precipitate an antislavery minority government. It reflected a first priority not, as generally assumed, for restoring an errant state as quickly as possible but priority for insuring freedom."[4] Lincoln would have liked to have lured the Southern states back with his Ten Percent Plan, but at the point in the war it was issued, he was not going to allow the freedmen to be enslaved again.

The best chapter in the book is titled "Reflections on the Limits of the Possible." Cox makes a strong case for judging what Lincoln accomplished on the criteria of what was possible as opposed to what was ideal. Those who would argue Lincoln and others missed a golden opportunity to achieve full racial justice in the 1860s are misjudging the times. There just wasn't the political will in the North to fight for civil rights. Cox writes, "The years of political Reconstructions, to borrow an apt phrase from Thomas B. Alexander's study of Tennessee, offered no 'narrowly missed opportunities to leap a century forward in reform.' Not even a Lincoln could have wrought such a miracle."[5] Cox shows that Lincoln's political skill advanced the rights of the freedman about as far as was possible at the time.

Cox's work is a groundbreaking book on Lincoln and Reconstruction. It places Lincoln with the Radicals on the issue, and it makes a convincing argument for this position. A possible criticism of the book is that it can be hard to read. Cox had to cover the intricacies of Louisiana politics during the war to make her case, and it is sometimes difficult to follow all the different leaders and factions. However, this does not take away from the overall importance of this book in showing the leadership Lincoln gave to the issue of black freedom and his desire for a just Reconstruction policy.

NOTES

1. For the most extreme and racist view of the supposed continuity between Lincoln and Johnson, see Claude G. Bowers, *The Tragic Era: The Revolution After Lincoln* (Cambridge, Mass.: Riverside Press, 1929).
2. LaWanda Cox, *Lincoln and Black Freedom: A Study in Presidential Leadership* (Columbia: University of South Carolina Press, 1981), 15.
3. Abraham Lincoln to Michael Hahn as quoted in ibid., 94; Cox, 94.
4. Cox, 142.
5. Ibid., 142–84, 183.

The Abraham Lincoln Encyclopedia

AUTHOR: Mark E. Neely Jr.
PUBLISHED: 1982
GENRE: General

REFERENCE WORKS are usually dry and do not make for easy reading. *The Abraham Lincoln Encyclopedia* is an exception to the rule. It not only provides a wealth of information in an easily accessible format, it is also a good read. Mark E. Neely Jr. has become one of the premier Lincoln scholars in the field, and this encyclopedia is an example of why. The breadth of knowledge on display is remarkable. The encyclopedia covers prominent topics like the Lincoln-Douglas debates and the Emancipation Proclamation. However, it also covers such esoteric topics as biographies of Lincoln collectors and sculptors.[1]

Neely had been director of the Louis A. Warren Lincoln Library and Museum. He gives his reason for writing this book: "I was faced with a steady stream of inquiries about Lincoln. They came to my office every day by mail and telephone. Puzzled scholars, students, buffs, collectors walked into my office holding questionnaires, fragments of term papers, old letters, newspaper clippings with curious allegations about Lincoln, or odd artifacts. I had a vast library at my disposal from which to respond to them, but I was less pleasantly surprised by the difficulties encountered in finding answers." Neely's book is wonderful because he did exactly what he set out to do; he created a resource that could answer almost any question about Lincoln or at least point a person in the right direction.[2]

It should not be assumed that the book has no overall ideology or theme. Neely writes, "The picture of Lincoln that emerges from an encyclopedia is necessarily fragmented but not necessarily self-contradictory or conventional." Neely's Lincoln is one who values the Declaration of Independence over the Constitution instead of the other way around. Under the topic of "Nationalism," Neely writes, "The Constitution never figured in Lincoln's thought as *the* fundamental American document. The Declaration of Independence held that place in his thought. Therefore, he did not hesitate to violate the Constitution, especially for the sake of the precious principles of the Declaration of Independence and the Union which embodied those principles." The older school of thought was apologetic about Lincoln's loose constitutional thinking, but Neely believes it was not as important as thought. Lincoln did revere the Constitution, but he revered it because it allowed the declaration to become a reality.[3]

Neely was right to include Lincoln haters in his encyclopedia. These people are rarely mentioned in Lincoln scholarship, and this book is the first time many ever hear of them. The most prominent is Edgar Lee Masters. Masters wrote an epitaph for Ann Rutledge but later came to hate Lincoln. His book *Lincoln: The Man* reflected Masters's own political prejudices. Neely explains, "He was a Democrat and thought that Thomas Jefferson was America's greatest statesman. He loathed the Republican party, war (which made 'brutes of those who practice it') and the Christian religion." The encyclopedia also includes the son of President John Tyler, Lyon Gardner Tyler. His hatred of Lincoln knew no bounds. Neely quotes Tyler as saying, "But Lincoln by freeing the negro 'was the true parent of reconstruction, legislative robbery, negro supremacy, cheating at the polls, rapes of white women, lynching, and the acts of the Ku Klux Klan.' The black man, barely raised from being 'a barbarian and a cannibal,' was not ready for freedom." These interpretations are not popular today, but they are valuable historically, for they show Lincoln was never universally admired.[4]

The book is also fair to Lincoln's opponents in his own lifetime. It does not claim George B. McClellan was a complete military failure as do many books. McClellan is also portrayed as a strong Union man, even when he ran against Lincoln in 1864. Stephen A. Douglas also is given a fairly positive entry in the encyclopedia. Neely can write, "Douglas has always suffered by association with Lincoln's fame. It is hard to remember that, when Lincoln debated Douglas in 1858, he was essentially attempting to share the limelight that Douglas, the most famous politician in America at the time, naturally attracted." Douglas is sometimes portrayed as a simple demagogue, but Neely gives his political views a full hearing.[5]

The best entries are the short ones dealing with each Lincoln-Douglas debate. Neely gives some local flavor and explains the highlights of each debate. He can be critical in describing a debate, such as his entry of the last one at Alton: "The moderate size of the crowd was an index of the somewhat anticlimactic nature of the debate. As a consequence of the substantial press coverage of the preceding six debates, the people were not as curious to hear what the candidates had to say. In truth, the candidates themselves did not have much to say that was new."[6] The debates have such a high reputation in American life that it is refreshing to be reminded they were not always high-minded affairs.

The Abraham Lincoln Encyclopedia is twenty years old and could use some revision in a few areas. For the most part it has held up, but thinking on entries such as Thomas Lincoln and Ann Rutledge has changed. The book naturally missed the Lincoln renaissance of the 1990s. Be that as it may, it is not likely to be replaced soon as the Lincoln reference book of record.[7]

NOTES

1. Mark E. Neely Jr., *The Abraham Lincoln Encyclopedia* (New York: Da Capo, 1982), 79–81; see, e.g., ibid., 226, 36.
2. Ibid., v.
3. Ibid., viii, 215–16, 216.
4. Ibid., 206–7, 206, 315; Lyon Gardner Tyler quoted in ibid., 315.
5. Ibid., 199–202, 84–88, 88.
6. Ibid., 5.
7. Ibid., 265, 187–88.

Lincoln's Quest for Union: Public and Private Meanings

AUTHOR: Charles B. Strozier
PUBLISHED: 1982
GENRE: Psychology and Religion

PSYCHOBIOGRAPHY IS a wonderful and dangerous discipline. When it is done well it can be illuminating and insightful, but when done poorly it can be a disaster. Lincoln's psyche has been looked at in the past, but Charles B. Strozier is the first to do it both successfully and persuasively. His *Lincoln's Quest for Union: Public and Private Meanings* represents a watershed in the psychobiography of Lincoln. Using primary sources, particularly those from William Herndon, he creates a vivid picture of Lincoln's psyche. While the picture he creates may not be convincing to all, at the very least it is credible and cannot be ignored.[1]

Strozier's insights into Lincoln's sexuality are original and noteworthy. He ties Lincoln's forebodings about marriage to Mary Todd to his sexual inexperience. In order for Lincoln to overcome his fears, he uses his best friend, Joshua Speed, as an emotional proxy. Strozier writes, "Lincoln projected his own attitude and conflicted feelings onto Speed. . . . Lincoln related to Speed's difficulties in courtship with an intensity and involvement that suggests he saw Speed as a mirror of his own inner experience." The two were unusually close, and both were probably sexually inexperienced. They shared the same bed at the time of their respective courtships. Strozier believes it is no coincidence Lincoln broke his engagement to Mary Todd on the same day Speed left Springfield for Kentucky. He writes, "This separation threw Lincoln into a panic that shook his fragile sexual

189

identity. In this state his fear of intimacy with a woman was revived, and he broke his engagement with Mary. One point is worth stressing, namely, that Lincoln's conflicts and fears operated at an unconscious level. He was only dimly aware of his conflicts as he struggled to define his identity." When Speed was married, Lincoln wrote him a very personal letter: "Are you now, in *feeling* as well as *judgment* glad you are married as you are? From any body but me, this would be an impudent question not to be tolerated, but I know you will pardon me. Please answer quickly as I feel impatient to know."[2] Speed must have been happy, for Lincoln did overcome his fear of intimacy by marrying Mary Todd.

Strozier sees many conflicts in Lincoln's life. He moves away from the Ruth Painter Randall version of the Lincoln marriage and sees it as a tempestuous affair. He does not blame Mary entirely for this; he sees Lincoln's emotional distance as being partially responsible. There is also conflict between Lincoln and his father. Strozier believes, "Lincoln's style of intellectuality and his interest in books created frequent conflict with his father. Dennis Hanks noted that Thomas sometimes had 'to slash him for neglecting his work by reading.' His inquisitiveness also irritated Thomas: 'When strangers would ride along and up to his father's fence, Abe always, through pride and to tease his father, would be sure to ask the first question, for which his father would sometimes knock him a rod.'"[3] While there is little consensus about the nature of Lincoln's relationship with these two family members, Strozier is on solid ground maintaining there were periods of conflict between Lincoln and them.

In the chapter titled "The Group Self and the Crisis of the 1850s," Strozier broadens his analysis from Lincoln to the country. He doesn't seem to be as persuasive here as he is in other chapters. He says, "The basis for a cohesive group self, however, was being forged. A firm idealization of the Constitution and Declaration of Independence fed on idealizing cultural needs after the Revolution." While this is probably true, Strozier's explanation of the roots of the war in a breakup of this "group self" psychologically is too far-ranging a conclusion from the data. Lincoln scholar Herman Belz once wrote of this chapter: "I concur with the judgment of the *Journal of American*

History that this chapter, which may be described as warmed-over revisionism dressed up in the language of psychohistory, is 'perverse.'"[4] However, this chapter does not take away from the overall value of the book.

Ultimately, Strozier believes Lincoln's conflicts in his private life helped shape his public career. He concludes, "After 1854 Lincoln discovered, remarkably enough, that his private concerns found reflection in the country as a whole. His own ambivalent quest for union—with his dead mother, his bride, his alienated father—gave meaning to the nation's turbulence as it headed for the civil war. It took time for Lincoln to bridge the two exactly. He needed the right metaphor. In the idea of a house divided, Lincoln found a way of creatively enlarging his private concerns to fill the public space. When he found it, there was a resonance."[5] Is Strozier right about this or is he overstating his case? It is impossible to say one way or the other with certainty, and that is one of the reasons psychobiography is so engaging and frustrating at the same time.

NOTES

1. For a less successful psychobiography, see Dwight G. Anderson, *Abraham Lincoln: The Quest for Immortality* (New York: Knopf, 1982).
2. Charles B. Strozier, *Lincoln's Quest for Union: Public and Private Meanings* (New York: Basic Books, 1982), 47, 44; Abraham Lincoln to Joshua Speed, as quoted in ibid., 48–49.
3. See Ruth Painter Randall, *Mary Todd Lincoln: Biography of a Marriage* (Boston: Little, Brown and Co., 1953); Strozier, 67–108, 15.
4. Strozier, 182–203, 195; Herman Belz, "Commentary on Lincoln's Quest for Union" in *The Historian's Lincoln: Pseudohistory, Psychohistory and History*, ed. Gabor S. Boritt (Urbana: University of Illinois Press, 1996), 247.
5. Strozier, 233.

Beware the People Weeping: Public Opinion and the Assassination of Abraham Lincoln

AUTHOR: Thomas Reed Turner
PUBLISHED: 1982
GENRE: Assassination

S TUDY OF the assassination of Lincoln has suffered from a case of "historical malpractice," according to authority Edward Steers Jr. Professional historians had always refused to treat it in detail. James G. Randall and Richard N. Current refused to even mention it in their massive *Lincoln the President*. Unfortunately, this has allowed amateurs to dominate the field. They have written uncritically about some of the more outlandish stories, such as the alleged Jesuit involvement in Lincoln's death. It has also led to personal and familial crusades, like the Mudds' efforts to clear Dr. Samuel Mudd, being viewed as legitimate history. Thomas Reed Turner's *Beware the People Weeping: Public Opinion and the Assassination of Abraham Lincoln* is the first book about the assassination to be written by an academic historian. He brings the tools of his professional craft to the topic and has written an essential book on the assassination and many of its related issues.[1]

Turner puts the assassination in the larger context of history. He does not view it as an isolated event in Civil War history. He writes, "No serious student of the [John F.] Kennedy assassination would think of writing about the event without attempting to place it in its historical context. Yet before this occurrence, assassinations were apparently so remote from the experience of historians that there was a tendency to view them in a vacuum. Only by combining what is valid in the views of contemporaries with what is valid in recently discovered materials will the assassination of Lincoln once again be placed in its proper historical setting." Turner is right; John Wilkes Booth had serious political motives to kill Lincoln, and those motives must be viewed in the context of the war. He notes sermons preached right after the assassination were just as likely to blame slavery and the Confederacy as they were Booth himself.[2]

Many Civil War histories assume once Robert E. Lee surrendered, the country was ready to be reunited and the feelings of rancor were gone. Lincoln's assassination is seen as creating bitterness in the North when its people were in the process of forgiving the South. Turner views this explanation as too simplistic. He concludes, "On the surface one might get the impression that with this era of renewed brotherhood at hand, the assassination was the major, if not the only, reason that this feeling was dispelled. Many historians have completely forgotten the bitterness engendered by four years of war, as well as the events leading up to the war. . . . However, it seems much more realistic to view such conciliatory expressions as merely a first exuberant outbreak, with the understanding that the nation would have been faced with harsher realities before long, even if the assassination had not occurred." Conflicts over Reconstruction would have arisen under Lincoln just as they did under Andrew Johnson.[3]

Turner takes a more benign view of the military commission that tried the conspirators than many writers have before him. It was usually seen as a "kangaroo court." While the common view today is the military trial was illegal because it had no jurisdiction in the matter, Turner sees it as being a logical decision to make at the time. It is also commonly asserted that Secretary of War Edwin Stanton is the real villain in the trial. Turner writes, "Although Stanton is usually charged with leading a witch-hunt and rounding up innocent persons indiscriminately, there is evidence that he was more moderate . . . in many instances, it was Stanton who took a hand in releasing prisoners or allowing them to reclaim their property from Ford's Theatre and other locations."[4]

Mary Surratt is often thought of as being the main victim of the military tribunal, but Turner shows this was not the majority view at the time. "The many attempts to vindicate Mrs. Surratt have been almost entirely by later writers. To contemporaries, the evidence brought out seemed strongly to indicate her guilt. Even the opposition press, on the whole, agreed with this appraisal."[5] The evidence does indeed point to her guilt in Booth's conspiracy, and professional historians would have likely found it had they bothered to look.

Turner responded to a review of his work by agreeing with the reviewer, Harold Hyman. Turner wrote, "He notes that professional historians have often looked with disdain at research into areas such as assassinations. And assassinations hardly stand alone for if one researches the Dracula legend and its historical roots, the Lizzie Borden murder trial, or the life of Jesse James, one can experience similar condensation. These topics are surrounded by so much sensationalism that one needs to convince professional colleagues about the value of scholarly endeavor in these areas."[6] It is a good thing Turner did not shy away from the topic of the assassination because of this. By not doing so, he has opened the door for further study by professional historians.

NOTES

1. Edward Steers Jr. in speech at Chambersburg Lincoln Symposium, February 2002; James G. Randall and Richard N. Current, *Lincoln the President,* 4 vols. (New York: Dodd, Mead & Co., 1945–55).
2. Thomas Reed Turner, *Beware the Public Weeping: Public Opinion and the Assassination of Abraham Lincoln* (Baton Rouge: Louisiana State University Press, 1991), xiii, 80.
3. Ibid., 21.
4. Ibid., 154, 147–48.
5. Ibid., 166.
6. Thomas Reed Turner, "The Assassination" in The *Historian's Lincoln: Pseudohistory, Psychohistory and History,* ed. Gabor S. Boritt (Urbana: University of Illinois Press, 1996), 414.

Abe Lincoln Laughing: Humorous Anecdotes from Original Sources by and About Abraham Lincoln

AUTHOR: P. M. Zall, editor
PUBLISHED: 1982
GENRE: General

THE PURPOSE of P. M. Zall's *Abe Lincoln Laughing: Humorous Anecdotes from Original Sources by and About Abraham Lincoln* is to present the definitive collection of Lincoln's jokes and humorous stories. Many jokes and stories commonly attributed to Lincoln are left out because they are not absolutely certain to have been said by Lincoln. As Ray Allen Billington states in the foreword, "For this is no uncritical, helter-skelter assembling of Lincoln yarns, selected indiscriminately from the thousands that have been attributed to the Great Emancipator. It is, true, rich in humor, invaluable for its insights into the life of nineteenth-century America, and an uproarious delight to read. But it's also a work of impeccable scholarship, designed with one basic purpose: to separate the authentic from the apocryphal Lincoln stories."[1]

Lincoln's humor has helped make him continually popular with most Americans. Mark Neely puts it this way: "In the twentieth century, Lincoln's humor became one of his most endearing qualities. Along with his democratic manners, it made Lincoln an approachable and loveable national saint."[2] Having all of Lincoln's authentic humor in one volume is a wonderful idea and puts this book on the list.

Zall includes two indexes in this book to help the reader locate particular jokes or stories. The topical index covers the broad range of themes in Lincoln's humor, while the subject index covers each story individually. This is valuable to the reader because often one knows a joke but doesn't remember all the details. Zall also offers the probable origins of a joke or story Lincoln told. Lincoln is not credited with creating all the humor in this book. In fact, he once said, "You speak of Lincoln stories. I don't think that is the correct phrase. I don't make the stories mine by telling them." Zall finds about 60 percent of Lincoln's jokes have traceable origins, some of which were contemporary with him.[3]

The frontier contributed an earthiness to Lincoln's humor that still may shock some readers. There are a number of stories under the topical category of "Sex and Scatology." Zall records this story of Lincoln's told by one of his friends: "In the morning after my marriage Lincoln met me and said—'Brown why is a woman like a barrel'—C.C.B. could not answer. 'Well,' said Lincoln—'You have to raise the hoops before you put the head in.'" Zall also records when Lincoln once laid into a man on the witness stand who portrayed himself as a great ladies' man. Lincoln said, "There's Busey—he pretends to be a great heart smasher—does wonderful things with the girls—but I'll venture that he never entered his flesh but once & that is when he fell down and stuck his finger in his —."[4]

The humor itself is arranged in chronological order of when it was first published. For example, the first of the 325 pieces comes from a speech he made in 1839 reported by a local paper. Lincoln compares the Democrats who ran off with public funds to "a witty Irish soldier, who was always boasting of his bravery, when no danger was near, but who invariably retreated without orders at the first charge of an engagement [who], being asked by his Captain why he did so, replied: 'Captain I have as brave a heart as Julius Caesar ever had; but some how or other, whenever danger approaches, my cowardly legs will run away with it.'"[5] Sadly, we are not able to witness Lincoln's delivery of this joke or others. No doubt, his timing or the way he stressed a word was crucial to his success and reputation as a humorist.

As this early example shows, Lincoln could use humor with devastating political effect. Even the formidable Stephen Douglas once said, "Every one of his stories seems like a whack upon my back." While it is true Lincoln's humor was a weapon, it could also be directed against him. Neely reminds us, "In the Victorian era people were supposed to be earnest rather than jocular, fun-loving, pleasure-seeking, or easy-going. . . . Much respectable cultural opinion saw Lincoln as a jokester too small for his office, a trifling Nero who fiddled with funny stories while the Constitution and the Republic burned." Neely is right when he states Zall and others have placed too much emphasis on Lincoln's use of humor for political effect. It could be Lincoln was humorous because it was his nature to be so. James G. Randall once said, "Humor was no mere technique but a habit of [Lincoln's] mind."[6]

If Randall is right, this book is essential in understanding Lincoln's personality. Zall's book has the fine quality of being both a serious scholarly work and a collection of some very humorous stories, so having it on a Lincoln bookshelf is not only important but fun.

NOTES

1. Ray Allen Billington, foreword to *Abe Lincoln Laughing: Humorous Anecdotes from Original Sources by and About Abraham Lincoln,* ed. P. M. Zall (Knoxville: University of Tennessee Press, 1997), x; for a collection of more dubious Lincoln stories, see Emmanuel Hertz, ed., *Lincoln Talks: An Oral Biography* (New York: Viking Press, 1939).
2. Mark E. Neely Jr., *The Abraham Lincoln Encyclopedia* (New York: Da Capo, 1982), 155.
3. Zall, 177–79, 181–93; Abraham Lincoln as quoted in ibid., 3, 3.
4. Zall, 179; C. C. Brown as quoted in ibid., 61; Abraham Lincoln as quoted in ibid., 98.
5. Abraham Lincoln as quoted in Zall, 13–14.
6. Stephen A. Douglas as quoted in P. M. Zall, "Abe Lincoln Laughing" in *The Historian's Lincoln: Pseudohistory, Psychohistory and History,* ed. Gabor S. Boritt (Urbana: University of Illinois Press, 1996), 10; Mark E. Neely Jr., "Commentary on 'Abraham Lincoln Laughing'" in Boritt, 28.

The Lincoln
Murder Conspiracies

AUTHOR: William Hanchett
PUBLISHED: 1983
GENRE: Assassination

BEFORE THOMAS TURNER'S *Beware the People Weeping,* the assassination was a topic left to the amateurs. There were some fine works like George Bryan's *The Great American Myth* and Lloyd Lewis's *Myths After Lincoln,* but the public's attention was taken up by more sensational fare, and many outlandish theories have been proposed. William Hanchett's *The Lincoln Murder Conspiracies* is an attempt to survey those theories of Lincoln's assassination and to examine the evidence, or lack thereof, that underpins them.[1]

The most controversial and, sadly, influential theory is the Eisenschiml thesis. The originator of this theory, Otto Eisenschiml, was a chemist by trade. His theory rested on the notion that Secretary of War Edwin Stanton was behind Lincoln's murder. John Wilkes Booth was simply a hired gun. In his book *Why Was Lincoln Murdered?* he offered a series of questions that in his mind cast suspicion on Stanton. Why had the telegraph suspiciously malfunctioned on the night of the assassination? Why was every road barred out of Washington except the one Booth used to escape? Why didn't U. S. Grant go to the theater that night with Lincoln? Was it possible Booth was ordered murdered to silence him? Eisenschiml is quick to say at the end of his book that he cannot prove his case against Stanton but is merely asking questions. What he was really doing was pulling off one of the most successful smears in history.[2]

Eisenschiml's book is full of innuendoes, and many of its "facts" are simply not true. For example, only the commercial telegraph malfunctioned; the military telegraph continued to work all through the night. Hanchett spends the bulk of the book destroying this theory and can rightfully say, "When scrutinized point by point, Eisenschiml's grand conspiracy thus falls apart, and one wonders how Eisenschiml, professing scientific objectivity all the while, could present it as a work of honest scholarship. Perhaps he justified his misrepresentations to himself by so often citing and even discussing the evidence that exposed them, and by observing that he was, after all only raising questions ignored by historians." Hanchett refutes Eisenschiml's ideas until there is nothing left of his theory. It is a shame it took so long for a professional historian to do this because the theory was and still is widely believed. Filmmakers and others have taken the Eisenschiml thesis to ludicrous heights with conspiracies so byzantine that they defy any rational explanation.[3]

The major reason Eisenschiml's book was originally well received was because it was written during the heyday of revisionism. Revisionism gave Stanton a motive for having Lincoln killed. In revisionism, Lincoln would have given the South a just and mild peace. The Radical Republicans, including Stanton, were not going to allow that to happen. They wanted a vindictive peace. Eisenschiml implied the best way to do that was to have Lincoln killed. Hanchett points out that Eisenschiml went even further. He accused Stanton of prolonging the Civil War to make himself an attractive presidential candidate by becoming an indispensable war leader. In his best passage, Hanchett states, "Lincoln would not have enjoyed the extravagant and pseudoreligous praise being offered in his name by so many Americans. Possibly he would have been reminded of some anecdote by which to deflate the absurdities of such exaggerations. But one suspects that if he could learn the slush written about the suggested involvement of his secretary of war in his own death he would simply become angry."[4]

Hanchett also takes a look at the original idea that the conspiracy was the work of Jefferson Davis and the Confederate government. Hanchett looks at this conspiracy with a skeptical eye. He believes

Stanton and Judge Advocate General Joseph Holt both came to finally see it wouldn't hold up after they had pursued the idea with such force after the assassination. He writes, "While it is unlikely that Holt doubted for a moment that Davis and the others were guilty as charged, he and Stanton were far too able and experienced to fail to recognize that the evidence presented at the conspiracy trial was not proof of guilt but only hearsay and that it was only as credible as the witness who gave it." *The Lincoln Murder Conspiracies* was written before the book *Come Retribution* breathed new life into the idea of a Confederate grand conspiracy. Hanchett has since come to the conclusion there might have been truth to that conspiracy. His conclusions in this book, though, are reasonable, and the idea is far from settled.[5]

The Lincoln Murder Conspiracies is an essential book on the assassination because it clears up so many misconceptions that have worked their way into the public consciousness. Hanchett has also written a lively narrative that shows why the assassination continues to fascinate so many. The public will continue to believe much of the misinformation about the assassination, but owning this book is the perfect antidote.

NOTES

1. See Thomas Reed Turner, *Beware the People Weeping: Public Opinion and the Assassination of Abraham Lincoln* (Baton Rouge: Louisiana State University, 1991); George S. Bryan, *The Great American Myth: The True Story of Lincoln's Murder* (Chicago: Americana House, 1990); Lloyd Lewis, *Myths After Lincoln* (New York: Press of the Reader's Club, 1941).
2. William Hanchett, *The Lincoln Murder Conspiracies* (Urbana: University of Illinois Press, 1986), 158–84; see also Otto Eisenschiml, *Why Was Lincoln Murdered?* (Boston: Little, Brown, 1937).
3. Ibid., 174, 181, 226–28.
4. Ibid., 181–83, 248.
5. Ibid., 73; see William A. Tidwell, James O. Hall, and David W. Gaddy, *Come Retribution: The Confederate Secret Service and the Assassination of Abraham Lincoln* (Jackson: University of Mississippi, 1988); Hanchett gives the Confederate Grand Conspiracy another look in Bryan, xxiv.

Mary Todd Lincoln: A Biography

AUTHOR: Jean H. Baker
PUBLISHED: 1987
GENRE: Family and Genealogy

MARY TODD LINCOLN had lacked a full-scale scholarly biography until Jean H. Baker's *Mary Todd Lincoln: A Biography*. Ruth Painter Randall's biography focused on Mary's relationship with Lincoln and didn't devote much space to Mary's life before or after the marriage. Baker's book is more expansive in its scope. While it is not as apologetic as Randall's, she has written a sympathetic life of the troubled woman. Using the sociology of the nineteenth century to view Mary Todd Lincoln, she has created an original portrait that fills in many of the gaps in her story.[1]

Baker's approach to the "Fatal First of January" in which Lincoln and Mary Todd broke their engagement is novel. Baker thinks the breakup was probably mutual. She believes Lincoln was late to an engagement, and Mary flirted with an older man named Edwin Webb to get back at Lincoln. Had Lincoln, as most biographers assume, or Mary unilaterally broken the engagement, the reconciliation the following year would have been much harder to attain. Baker writes, "In view of the personalities of the principals, the romance would never have revived unless both had shared in its destruction. A unilateral wound to such sensitive psyches would have been beyond healing, whereas a misunderstanding over a phantom lover could be resolved."[2] This may be too speculative for most, but with the confusing nature of the evidence surrounding the breakup, it is as plausible as many other explanations.

The most engaging and informative part of the book deals with the Springfield years of Mary. Her daily chores are cataloged. "Her workday began early in the tiny kitchen at the back of the cottage at Eighth and Jackson. There on the cast-iron Thompson range—the type with the flat top permitting kettles to sit on the surface—she started the soup. Some days the coals were out, and it was her husband's job to start them again, though when he was away she did this herself. She used a dry sink for cleaning dishes and preparing fresh produce." Many scholars forget this part of the Lincoln story because it seems tedious, but it is an accurate picture of what went on in their home. Mary had servants, too, but because of economic difficulties and her own abrasive personality, she was unable to keep them for any length of time.[3]

Baker's knowledge of women's history allows her an insight into the Lincolns' birthing patterns. "Years before the emergence of any organized birth control movement in the United States, thousands of American couples like the Lincolns were not fooled by the obscure title of Charles Knowlton's 1832 handbook of contraceptive information, *Fruits of Philosophy: The Private Companion of Young Married People*. While this volume had only a small underground circulation, its methods circulated by word of mouth. In Springfield married women sent away for similar pamphlets about reproduction, the contents of which, disguised in brown wrappers, remained a mystery even to nosy mailmen." The even patterns between the birth of the Lincolns' sons and the long time Mary took to wean them suggest the Lincolns used some form of birth control.[4]

Because of her generally apologetic tone, Baker explains away many ambiguities in Mary too easily. Mary probably engaged in outright fraud with John Watt, the White House gardener, involving kickbacks. Baker dismisses the whole matter in a few paragraphs and never explores what should be an important issue. Likewise, she quickly dismisses the Ann Rutledge affair by calling it a "Gothic romance of Herndon's imagination." Lincoln's law partner, Herndon, who brought the romance to light, is described this way: "Cranky, alcoholic Herndon was often wrong about things." The book would have given a clearer picture of Mary had Baker not been so dismissive of Herndon and other parts of the Mary story that are not so attractive.[5]

Baker gives a good description of Mary's life at Bellevue, the asylum to which she was committed. "Mary Lincoln had one of the shortest incarcerations in Bellevue's history. She was in the asylum exactly three months and three weeks, during which time, in prudent advertisement of her sanity, she was a model patient who required no chloral hydrate, cannabis indica, hypodermics of morphine, or even the physical restraints exercised by Mrs. Ruggles, Bellevue's uniformed matron and her staff of attendants." Unfortunately, Baker is unfair to Robert. She blames him for committing his mother and implies he was disappointed when she showed signs of improvement.[6]

This is the best biography of Mary Todd Lincoln. Its scope is wide and emphasizes things that a male historian might not have. Baker's book is too apologetic in places, but it is still an essential book. Mary Todd Lincoln, for better or worse, was an integral part of the Lincoln story, and *Mary Todd Lincoln: A Biography* gives Mary's complete history as no other book does.

NOTES

1. See Ruth Painter Randall, *Mary Lincoln: Biography of a Marriage* (Boston: Little, Brown & Co., 1953).
2. Jean H. Baker, *Mary Todd Lincoln: A Biography* (New York: W. W. Norton, 1987), 90–91, 94.
3. Ibid., 99–129, 110, 106.
4. Ibid., 128–29.
5. Ibid., 19, 268, 267; for other listings of bias in the work, see Michael Burlingame, *The Inner World of Abraham Lincoln* (Urbana: University of Illinois Press, 1994), 326.
6. Baker, 336, 336; for a fuller look at the whole episode that exonerates Robert of the worst charges, see Mark E. Neely Jr. and R. Gerald McMurtry, *The Insanity File: The Case of Mary Todd Lincoln* (Carbondale: Southern Illinois University Press, 1986).

Lincoln in Text and Context: Selected Essays

AUTHOR: Don E. Fehrenbacher
PUBLISHED: 1987
GENRE: General

D ON E. FEHRENBACHER had been an admired student of Lincoln for decades. His essays have been both thought-provoking and influential. *Lincoln in Text and Context: Selected Essays* is a collection of some of his best essays. They range in topic from Lincoln's stand in opposition to the Mexican War to his assassination. Fehrenbacher provides introductory remarks before each essay to explain when and why he wrote it and how his conclusions might have changed since then. Taken as a whole, these essays show why Fehrenbacher has been such an admired Lincoln scholar.[1]

The most important essay in the book is "Only His Stepchildren." The title refers to a passage in a speech Frederick Douglass gave to commemorate a statue of Lincoln paid for by freedmen. When mentioning Lincoln and the freed slaves, Douglass said they were "only his stepchildren." Fehrenbacher shows that while Lincoln was adamant in his opposition to slavery, he was less interested in the welfare of free blacks. As Fehrenbacher states, "Yet if his plans for reconstruction are an accurate indication, Lincoln at the time of his death had given too little consideration to the problem of racial adjustment and to the needs of four million freedman. . . . Certainly his policies by 1865 no longer reflected all the views expressed in 1858, when he had repudiated both Negro citizenship and Negro suffrage." Lincoln had grown, but it is hard to say how much political capital he would have used in the cause of the freed slave.

Fehrenbacher does not think he would have done much: "For several reasons Lincoln's role was likely to be more subdued than we might expect from the Great Emancipator. First, during peacetime, with his powers and responsibilities as commander in chief greatly reduced, he probably would have yielded more leadership to Congress in the old Whig tradition. Second, at the time of his death, he still regarded race relations as primarily a local matter."[2] Fehrenbacher is too harsh. Emancipation was hard enough politically. The Thirteenth Amendment abolishing slavery had not even gone into effect when Lincoln died. It shouldn't be a surprise Lincoln does not have much to say about the freed slave.

There is a good chapter on the post offices of the day. Postmasterships were political jobs handed out by the administration in power. This is an unfamiliar practice in the twenty-first century, and its abuse led to civil service reform. Fehrenbacher shows Lincoln used the postmasterships as his predecessors had. He writes, "Republicans were naturally the loudest complainers about [James] Buchanan's use of the Post Office as a political instrument, but on gaining power in 1861, they rivaled their enemies in the energy in which they wielded the patronage. About 80 percent of the 'presidential-class' postmasterships were replaced during the first year of the Lincoln administration, and within two years some seven thousand lesser postmasters were removed."[3] Lincoln knew the importance of patronage, and it was one of the keys to his success.

Fehrenbacher has some insightful things to say about psychobiography in one essay: "Sound historical interpretation cannot be founded on conjecture—often learned and technical and emphatically stated, but conjecture nonetheless. . . . That Lincoln suffered from oedipal guilt associated with his mother's death, that he projected himself into the role of a dictator—these are possibilities to be borne speculatively in mind as one struggles to construct the true story of his life out of better-verified materials. Psychohistorical possibility is in a sense a wilderness of history, a twilight region with treacherous footing that nevertheless invites adventurous exploration because of the profound truths it is rumored to conceal—and probably does."[4]

That is one of the best summations of the promises and perils of psychohistory ever written.

There is a humorous essay about the Minor forgery. This was when love letters were supposedly found between Lincoln and Ann Rutledge. The letters, produced in the 1920s by Wilma Frances Minor, were originally well received. However, Lincoln scholars eventually saw through the ruse. What is humorous is how Minor tried to explain her behavior. Fehrenbacher quotes her confession as follows: "I would die on the gallows that the spirits of Ann and Abe were speaking through my Mother to me so that my gifts as a writer combined with her gifts as a medium could hand in something worthwhile to the world." In other words, she had written the letters, but the spirits of Lincoln and Ann had dictated them. Fehrenbacher does hold out hope, though, that someday real letters may be found: "Yet perhaps somewhere in a battered trunk pushed into the darkest recesses of an old attic there are documents—authentic documents—waiting to tell us the whole truth."[5]

There is so much to ponder in this book. It touches on almost every aspect of Lincoln scholarship. Fehrenbacher's research is thorough and his conclusions are sound. Don E. Fehrenbacher was one of the great Lincoln scholars, and *Lincoln in Text and Context* shows just why he will be missed.

NOTES

1. Don E. Fehrenbacher, *Lincoln in Text and Context: Selected Essays* (Stanford, Calif.: Stanford University Press, 1987), 3–15, 164–77.
2. Ibid., 95–112; Frederick Douglass as quoted in ibid., 112; Fehrenbacher, 111, 112.
3. Fehrenbacher, 24–32, 31–32.
4. Ibid., 214–27, 227.
5. Ibid., 246–69; Wilma Frances Minor as quoted in ibid., 268; Fehrenbacher, 269.

The Historian's Lincoln: Pseudohistory, Psychohistory and History

AUTHOR: Gabor S. Boritt, editor
PUBLISHED: 1988
GENRE: Historiography

THIS BOOK is a forerunner to the renaissance Lincoln scholarship underwent in the 1990s. Lincoln's 175th birthday was celebrated in 1984, and a conference of the top scholars took place at Gettysburg College. Gabor Boritt has collected the essays presented and added critiques from various scholars. In a later edition he added an appendix with replies to the critiques from some authors. What he has created is a lively running debate on such important topics as Lincoln's ideology, economic ideas, psychohistory, and assassination. It is the back-and-forth that makes *The Historian's Lincoln: Pseudohistory, Psychohistory and History* so unique.[1]

The scholars present at the conference were not all admirers of Lincoln. Dwight G. Anderson's essay, "Quest for Immortality: A Theory of Abraham Lincoln's Political Psychology," attempts to show that Lincoln yearned for power from an early age, that his main ambition was fame and the immortality it brings. Anderson writes, "Lincoln and Macbeth: both were fascinating characters, capable of great goodness but driven by ambition to defy the gods; men entrapped by 'necessity' in a process of violence, but who had the intelligence to foresee the consequences of their acts, and the sensitivity to accept the burden of guilt lesser men might have ignored." In a somewhat mocking response, Robert V. Bruce writes, "What sort of tyrant would so meekly resign himself to being deposed by popular vote in a wartime election, for example?" Boritt also includes

M. E. Bradford, who is even more skeptical of Lincoln than Anderson. He offers a neo-Confederate viewpoint on Lincoln's efforts to save the Union and free the slaves. Regarding the Union, he writes, "Rather, as the scholarship tends to agree, he played the central role in transforming it forever into a unitary structure based on a claim to power in its own right, a teleocratic instrument which, in the name of any cause that attracts a following, might easily threaten the liberties of those for whose sake it existed."[2] Neither Anderson's nor Bradford's views have had much of a following in the field of Lincoln scholarship, but Boritt was right to include their essays for the sake of diversity.

Richard Current contributes a thoughtful essay on LaWanda Cox and Stephen B. Oates, both of whom believe Lincoln's plan of Reconstruction was in line with the Radical Republicans. Current had collaborated with the great revisionist historian James G. Randall on his Lincoln biography. Revisionism is the antithesis of what Oates and Cox believe. Current now places himself in the middle. He has moved away from his literary partner, Randall, but has not gone as far as Cox and Oates. He concludes, "Oates and other recent writers who emphasize Lincoln's growing radicalism are much closer to the truth than were the earlier historians who portrayed him as a reluctant destroyer of slavery but the willing preserver of a caste system. There can be no doubt as to the direction in which he was moving during the presidential years. Under the pressure of events he tended to advocate the more and more immediate realization of the promise of equality." However, "Oates and like-minded writers make him appear to have been further advanced than the evidence warrants." Boritt allows Cox to respond, "He has no quarrel with us as to the direction Lincoln was moving nor as to his accelerating pace during the presidential years. Current and I . . . seem to differ on the question of whether Lincoln's pace quickened because he was *pressured* by events or because he was *freed* by events." Cox's observation is on target and underlines differences of attitude in regard to Lincoln's motives.[3]

James M. McPherson asked a trenchant question in reaction to William Hanchett's essay on the assassination conspiracy theories. After admitting they are ludicrous, he states, "The question I want to focus on is not the truth or falsity of these theories, but rather what has made them so popular among so many people. The myths of a people can tell us a great deal about their culture. Conspiracy theories are a form of a myth." He rightfully asks, "What was CBS's motivation in putting on the television docudrama in 1972 called *They've Killed Lincoln*? Who went to the movie or read the book *The Lincoln Conspiracy* in 1977? Was there a pattern? If so, what does it tell us about popular culture?"[4] The psychology of conspiracy theories is a question too big for any Lincoln scholar to answer, but it would be helpful to know why so much nonsense about Lincoln's assassination is believed.

Boritt assembled some of the best of what Lincoln scholarship has to offer in this volume. The quality and diversity of Lincoln scholars are rarely on display as they are in this book. Lincoln scholarship was about to enter a golden age in the 1990s, and *The Historian's Lincoln* is a wonderful sampling of what was to come.

NOTES

1. Gabor S. Boritt, ed., *The Historian's Lincoln: Pseudohistory, Psychohistory and History* (Urbana: University of Illinois Press, 1996), ix, 393–419.
2. Dwight G. Anderson, "Quest for Immortality: A Theory of Abraham Lincoln's Political Psychology" in ibid., 253–74, 270; Robert V. Bruce, "Commentary on 'Quest for Immortality'" in ibid., 277; M. E. Bradford, "Commentary on 'Lincoln's Economics'" in ibid., 113.
3. Richard N. Current, "Oates and the Handlins" in ibid., 383–84, 384; LaWanda Cox, "Lincoln and Black Freedom" in ibid., 402; for Stephen Oates's view on Lincoln's relationship to black freedom, see Stephen B. Oates, *With Malice Toward None: A Life of Abraham Lincoln* (New York: HarperPerennial, 1994); for LaWanda Cox's view, see LaWanda Cox, *Lincoln and Black Freedom: A Study in Presidential Leadership* (Columbia: University of South Carolina Press, 1981); see also James G. Randall and Richard N. Current, *Lincoln the President*, 4 vols. (New York: Dodd, Mead & Co., 1945–55).
4. James A. McPherson, "Commentary on 'The Lincoln Murder Conspiracies'" in Boritt, 342, 343.

Building the Myth: Selected Speeches Memorializing Abraham Lincoln

AUTHOR: Waldo W. Braden, editor
PUBLISHED: 1990
GENRE: Historiography

THIS VOLUME collects some of the greatest commemorative speeches about Lincoln. They range in time from shortly after the assassination to a speech New York governor Mario Cuomo gave in 1986. The editor of this volume, Waldo W. Braden, was a professor of speech communication, so he knew what makes a great speech. He has also included introductory material before each speech to help the reader understand the context in which a speech was given. Each speech in itself is a treasure, and reading *Building the Myth: Selected Speeches Memorializing Abraham Lincoln* is a real delight that gives the reader a greater appreciation of what Lincoln has meant to America and the world.[1]

Braden has broken the speeches into several categories. Among them are eulogies shortly after the assassination, speeches celebrating emancipation, Republican partisan speeches, speeches international in tone, and speeches that seek to shape the Lincoln image. By classifying the speeches into genres, Braden allows a certain variety to the speeches and highlights what the different orators thought was important and how this has changed over time.[2]

Of the speeches eulogizing Lincoln, the best one is by Bishop Matthew Simpson at Lincoln's grave in Springfield. As Lincoln's body was being put in the temporary tomb, he spoke of no peace being possible with Rebels. However, he did make an appeal for mercy using Lincoln's own words. He closed with, "But to the deluded masses we shall extend arms of forgiveness. We will take them to our hearts. We will walk with them side by side, as we go forward to work out a glorious destiny. The time will come when, in the beautiful words of him whose lips are now forever sealed, 'the mystic cords of memory, which stretch from every patriot's grave shall yield a sweeter music when touched by the angels of our better nature.'" Henry Ward Beecher also rose to heights of eloquence when he said at the memorial service in his church, "There has not been a poor drummer-boy in all this war that has fallen for whom the great heart of Lincoln would not have bled; there has not been one private soldier, without note or name, slain among thousands and hid in the pit among hundreds, without even the memorial of a separate burial, for whom the President would not have wept."[3]

Frederick Douglass's speech commemorating the Freedmen's Monument in 1876 has long been considered a classic. Douglass is bitter because of the failure of Reconstruction to lead to a lasting change in the South and wishes Lincoln would have done more. He can still comment favorably on Lincoln's character: "He had not been schooled in the ethics of slavery; his plain life had favored his love of truth. He had not been taught that treason and perjury were the proof of honor and honesty. His moral training was against his saying one thing when he meant another. The trust which Abraham Lincoln had in himself and in the people was surprising and grand, but it was also enlightened and well founded. He knew the American people better than they knew themselves, and his truth was based upon this knowledge."[4] Only Douglass could have this level of insight and be able to put it so beautifully.

British statesman David Lloyd George made Lincoln not just an American icon but a symbol of international liberalism. George stated in 1923, "All I know about him is that he was one of those rare men whom you do not associate with any particular creed, party, and, if you will forgive me for saying so, not even with any country, for he belongs to mankind in every race, in every clime, and in every age."[5] By the twentieth century, Lincoln was well on his way to becoming an international symbol.

While for a time Lincoln was used exclusively by the Republican Party, Braden shows that by the turn of the century such Democrats as William Jennings Bryan and Woodrow Wilson were able to make Lincoln nonpartisan. This book contains a 1986 speech by the Democratic governor of New York, Mario Cuomo. In this speech, Cuomo all but turns Lincoln into a liberal Democrat. He states, "In Lincoln's time, one of every seven Americans was a slave. Today, for all our affluence and might, despite what every day is described as our continuing economic recovery, nearly one in every seven Americans lives in poverty, not in chains—because Lincoln saved us from that—but trapped in a cycle of despair that is its own enslavement."[6]

It is hard to pick one speech in this volume and say it is the best because they have so many different objectives. The wide variety in purpose shows the Lincoln theme has been a magnet for orators. There is obviously something about the sixteenth president that brings out the best efforts of our greatest speechmakers.

NOTES

1. For the specific criteria Braden used to pick speeches of quality, see Waldo W. Braden, *Building the Myth: Selected Speeches Memorializing Abraham Lincoln* (Urbana: University of Illinois Press, 1990), 7; Braden also wrote of Lincoln's own speechmaking in Waldo W. Braden, *Abraham Lincoln: Public Speaker* (Baton Rouge: Louisiana State University Press, 1988).
2. Braden, *Building the Myth*, v–vi.
3. Matthew Simpson, May 4, 1865, in ibid., 86; Henry Ward Beecher, April 23, 1865, in ibid., 41.
4. Frederick Douglass, April 14, 1876, in ibid., 101–2.
5. David Lloyd George, October 18, 1923, in ibid., 204.
6. Braden, *Building the Myth*, 137–44, 176–81; Mario M. Cuomo, February 12, 1986, in ibid., 242.

The Lincoln Family Album

AUTHORS: Mark E. Neely Jr. and
Harold Holzer
PUBLISHED: 1990
GENRE: Family and Genealogy

A REVOLUTION in camera technology shortly before the Civil War made the family photograph album a common requirement for the middle class. "The carte de visite, which, according to an 1861 issue of the *American Journal of Photography,* 'swept everything before it,' caused a small parlor revolution. This paper photographic print was about two by four inches in size, and backed with a stiff card, it could be slipped into the empty windows framed by the thick cardboard pages of a parlor album. . . . When family or friends called or when someone wanted to reminisce quietly about relatives in distant places or husbands and sons on battlefields, their pages provided convenient and orderly access to photographs."[1] These albums are valuable today for the wonderful glimpse they give of the past, and the Lincoln family album is no exception.

It should come as no surprise the Lincoln family kept such an album. It was handed down from Mary Todd Lincoln to eventually her great-grandchildren. Along the way, photographs of family members were added. This treasure was not available to the public until 1985 upon the death of the last Lincoln descendant, Robert Todd Lincoln Beckwith. Mark E. Neely Jr. and Harold Holzer bring together some of the best of this material in *The Lincoln Family Album.* There is everything from photographs of friends and political associates to famous sites around Washington.[2]

This book contains many photographs of Lincoln's in-laws. That is hardly surprising for a family album. What is surprising is how most of the Todds opposed Lincoln's election to the presidency yet wanted political office from him, as the text makes clear. Margaret Todd Kellogg is typical. She was the half sister of Mary Todd Lincoln. The authors write, "Like other Todds, Margaret expected an Administration patronage plum for her husband, preferably a foreign assignment, where Charles could be closer to his brother, the painter Miner Kilbourne Kellogg, then working in Europe. That autumn, Mary expressed indignation that 'Kellogg . . . did not know why he had not received his appointment as Consul,' adding snidely: 'Is not the idea preposterous?' Lincoln consoled him with an army job." The book also contains a photograph of Lockwood Todd and Willie and Tad Lincoln. Todd was another Democrat who expected a job, and Lincoln did appoint him a "Drayman of the Port" in San Francisco. As the authors explain, "A petition protesting Todd's worthiness to receive the patronage job arrived at the White House from San Francisco Republicans, who pointed out that he was a Democrat who had vigorously stumped for Lincoln's rival Stephen A. Douglas, in California in 1860." It is easy to see that Lincoln's reputation for forgiveness was not exaggerated. A less magnanimous man would have turned his back on his unworthy in-laws.[3]

The photographs of Robert Todd Lincoln's children are numerous in this collection. Robert had three children: two daughters, Mary and Jessie, and a son. The son was named Abraham but was called Jack. Like many of the stories in the Lincoln family, his does not end happily. He was a handsome boy from the photographs provided. The authors praise him. "As the boy's Chicago professor conceded, Jack was 'up in athletics, and used to lead the boys in the playground.' His father's law partner thought the boy was 'unusually well developed for his age . . . a large, strong fellow, with good muscles . . . the manliest boy, I think I may say without exception, I ever knew.'" While in England with his father, he died at age sixteen from an infection. A devastated Robert wrote, "Jack was to us all that any father and mother could wish and beyond that, he seemed to realize that he had special duties before him. . . . I did not realize until he was gone how deeply my thoughts of the future were in him."[4]

The last generation of Lincolns included Robert's grandson from his daughter Mary, Lincoln Isham, and a grandson and granddaughter from Jessie named Robert and Peggy. None of the three had any children, and the direct line of descent from Lincoln died with them. The book includes a picture of Robert and Peggy in old age. The two siblings look remarkably like their great-grandparents, Abraham and Mary, yet they claimed no special insight into Lincoln. The authors conclude, "Peggy Beckwith spoke volumes with but nine words that neatly summed up the enormous gap between the generations in this famous family. Said one of the last Lincolns: 'I'm as far away from him as anyone else.'"[5]

The reason *The Lincoln Family Album* is such a great addition to a Lincoln bookshelf is that most of the pictures are unavailable elsewhere. It also shows the Lincoln story did not end with Robert Todd Lincoln but continued for two more generations. This precious photograph album was saved for years, and through the efforts of Neely and Holzer is here for us lucky viewers.

NOTES

1. Mark E. Neely Jr. and Harold Holzer, *The Lincoln Family Album* (New York: Doubleday, 1990), viii.
2. Ibid., ix, 58–59, 17, 19.
3. Ibid., 57, 73, 9, 9.
4. Ibid., 142–45, 145; Robert Todd Lincoln to John Hay, as quoted in ibid., 147.
5. Neely and Holzer, 154.

Lincoln, Douglas, and Slavery: In the Crucible of Public Debate

AUTHOR: David Zarefsky
PUBLISHED: 1990
GENRE: Prepresidential Years

W HAT TYPE of arguments did Lincoln and Douglas use during their debates? It is often assumed the arguments and the skill of the debaters were of the highest quality, and they were to a large degree. These were two experienced politicians at the top of their game. Henry Jaffa has written about the deeper meaning of the debates in *Crisis of the House Divided,* and scholars have analyzed who won or lost and what the debates meant for the country. Until David Zarefsky, it seems nobody had really looked at the rhetoric and arguments used in the debates themselves.[1]

David Zarefsky shows in *Lincoln, Douglas, and Slavery: In the Crucible of Public Debate* the arguments used were often proxy arguments for the real issue on which the candidates had no common ground. In order to debate any issue, some agreement is necessary. For example, if one is to debate educational policy, both debaters have to agree that quality education is the desired end result. The one issue that ultimately divided the debaters in 1858 was the humanity of African Americans. Lincoln believed in it; Douglas did not. They were coming from such divergent positions that real debate was impossible. Zarefsky argues persuasively, "These two moral positions did not directly engage each other, and each candidate could dismiss the other's challenges as beside the point. If Lincoln insisted slavery was evil, Douglas could reply that the views of those present did not really matter; the real question was who had the power to decide whether to admit the institution into a community."[2] The two debaters were essentially arguing past each other.

Each candidate accused the other of engaging in conspiracies. Douglas charged Lincoln with "abolitionizing" the old Whig Party in order to gain a Senate seat, while Lincoln believed Douglas had conspired with Presidents Franklin Pierce and James Buchanan, as well as Chief Justice Roger Taney. Both charges were false, but since they were so far apart about the humanity of African Americans, this was one of the few ways they could meaningfully engage each other. Zarefsky thinks politically these were the best arguments each made. He quotes a correspondent who thought Douglas's men had been "staggered" by Lincoln's charge. He also states, "As for Douglas, his charge that Lincoln was part of an abolitionist plot, coupled with his historical argument that he would develop later, was his strongest and most successful appeal in the campaign." Conspiracies had been a staple of nineteenth-century political campaigns, and they found a believing audience in the uncertain 1850s.[3]

Another proxy argument used was the historical. Both candidates tried to stress their policy toward slavery was carrying out the desires of the Founding Fathers. Since the Revolutionary War generation was all but worshiped, this was a politically wise thing to do. Zarefsky writes, "Each man portrayed his vision as the wave of the future and yet portrayed the vision as being in danger of defeat if the threat were not arrested and the country returned to the vision of the Fathers. Both men's historical argument was an appeal for restoration of a lost sense of united purpose. . . . Hence, an appeal to the spirit and vision of the Fathers was both a surrogate for future policy and the means to achieve fundamental change." In order to make the historical argument, each candidate had to assume the Founding Fathers held the same political sentiments as himself. Both had evidence to back up their respective positions, but it was in large part inference and a selective reading of the facts.[4]

Since both men were lawyers, it is no surprise they engaged in legal arguments. They harked back to the Constitution, but this was dangerous. As Zarefsky writes, "What made reliance on the Constitution both predictable and troublesome was the great document was fundamentally ambiguous. Written by one generation for future generations, it was necessarily general in its language so that it might uncover unforeseen situations. Embodying ideals and hopes as well as describing a pragmatic structure of government, it contained conflicting values within the same text."[5] Both had made history fit their preconceived notions; now they made the Constitution into their own image.

The Lincoln-Douglas debates will always fascinate Americans. Zarefsky's book is the first to look at the arguments used by the debaters themselves. There has been a large amount of writing on the debates, but a true and full understanding is not possible without Zarefsky's book. As a speech professor himself, Zarefsky's final analysis of the debates is hard to argue with: "If not the epitome of eloquence and statesmanship, the Lincoln-Douglas debates were an outstanding case of argumentative artistry. The skills they reflect are not always present in contemporary public debate. They are valuable skills about which we may be both enlightened and inspired by the great forensic clash on the Illinois prairies in the fall of 1858."[6]

NOTES

1. See Henry V. Jaffa, *Crisis of the House Divided: An Interpretation of the Issues in the Lincoln-Douglas Debates* (Chicago: University of Chicago Press, 1982).
2. David Zarefsky, *Lincoln, Douglas, and Slavery: In the Crucible of Public Debate* (Chicago: University of Chicago Press, 1990), 245, 225.
3. Ibid., 69, 110, 110, 110.
4. Ibid., 146, 164–65, 163.
5. Ibid., 139.
6. Ibid., 246.

Abraham Lincoln and the Second American Revolution

AUTHOR: James M. McPherson
PUBLISHED: 1991
GENRE: Presidency

THE CIVIL WAR was just as much a revolution as the American War of Independence, according to historian James M. McPherson. His *Abraham Lincoln and the Second American Revolution* defends that position and argues for Lincoln's role as being crucial in making it happen. In the preface he states why Lincoln scholarship is so popular: "The issues that Lincoln grappled with will never become obsolete: the meaning of freedom; the limits of government power and individual liberty in time of crisis; the dimensions of democracy; the nature of nationalism; the problems of leadership in war and peace; the tragedies and triumphs of a revolutionary civil war."[1] McPherson deals with all these issues ably in this book. In a series of essays he surveys Lincoln's actions during the war and finds much to admire. He believes Lincoln did not just win the Civil War but transformed the nation as well.

In the first essay, "The Second American Revolution," McPherson takes aim at those who would argue the Civil War and Reconstruction were essentially meaningless, since the civil rights of African Americans were ignored shortly after. While he agrees somewhat with this assessment by acknowledging the "counterrevolution" launched by former Confederates, he still feels the view is too pessimistic. "The counterrevolution overthrew the fledgling experiment in racial equality. But it did not fully restore the old order. Slavery was not reinstated. The Fourteenth and Fifteenth Amendments were not repealed. Blacks continued to own land and to go to school. The counterrevolution was not as successful as the revolution had been." McPherson is convincing in his argument that historians have failed to notice the radical changes effected even if they were not all that could be wished for.[2]

In the second essay, "Abraham Lincoln and the American Revolution," McPherson rebuts revisionist scholars like James Randall who see Lincoln as a conservative. He quotes Randall on Lincoln's supposed conservatism: "caution, prudent adherence to tested values, avoidance of rashness, and reliance upon unhurried, peaceable evolution." According to McPherson, Randall is mistaking the situation Lincoln inherited as the one he favored. He writes, "For it was his own superb leadership, strategy, and a sense of timing as president, commander in chief, and head of the Republican party that determined the pace of the revolution and ensured its success. With a less able man as president, the North might have lost the war or ended it under the leadership of Democrats who would have given its outcome a different shape. Thus in accepting 'the need of dealing with things as they were,' Lincoln was not a conservative statesman but a revolutionary one."[3]

McPherson shows that Lincoln and the South had two different views of liberty. The South viewed the white man as being the only person capable of truly enjoying the benefits of liberty. Lincoln in turn believed everyone was entitled to liberty regardless of color. McPherson concludes, "It was Lincoln's eloquent definition—or redefinition—of liberty that the South most feared." Lincoln got his views from the most famous revolutionary document, the Declaration of Independence. His Gettysburg Address harkens back to Thomas Jefferson when he talks about saving a nation "conceived in liberty and dedicated to the proposition that all men are created equal."[4]

In a strangely titled essay, "The Hedgehog and the Foxes," McPherson makes a comparison of the two animals and concludes Lincoln was much more like the hedgehog. The two animals come from a saying by a Greek philosopher: "The fox knows many things, but the hedgehog knows one big thing." According to McPherson, the deeper meaning would be the hedgehog is fixed on one goal and pursues it relentlessly, while the fox is too scattered and winds up accomplishing nothing. He states, "The Union—with or without slavery—had become the one big thing, the 'single central vision' of Lincoln the hedgehog." He writes that, eventually, "Liberty and Union became 'the one big thing' instead of two big things, enabling Lincoln to become a true hedgehog." It was Lincoln's fusing of the two that made his leadership so focused. A fox would have kept the issues separate, and neither would have come to fruition. In another context, McPherson states, "After skillfully steering a course between proslavery Democrats and antislavery Republicans during the first eighteen months of the war, Lincoln guided a new majority coalition of Republicans and converted Democrats through the uncharted waters of total war and emancipation . . . emerging triumphant into a second term on a platform of unconditional surrender that gave the nation a new birth of freedom."[5] Once again, it is Lincoln's own actions that shaped the outcome of the war.

McPherson is one of the leading historians of the Civil War era. He is also one of the most popular, and reading this book shows why. His writing style is scholarly yet accessible. There have always been a few cynical historians who wish to downplay Lincoln's importance; this book refutes them perfectly.[6]

NOTES

1. James M. McPherson, *Abraham Lincoln and the Second American Revolution* (New York: Oxford University Press, 1991), x.
2. Ibid., 3–22, 21, 22.
3. Ibid., 23–42; James G. Randall as quoted in ibid., 23; McPherson, 42.
4. McPherson, 50–52, 55; Abraham Lincoln as quoted in ibid., 56.
5. McPherson, 113–30, 113–14, 130, 91.
6. See James M. McPherson, *Battle Cry of Freedom: The Civil War Era* (New York: Oxford University Press, 1988); for an overview of some of the New Left that has seen Lincoln in this light, see Merrill D. Peterson, *Lincoln in American Memory* (New York: Oxford University Press, 1994), 357–58.

The Fate of Liberty: Abraham Lincoln and Civil Liberties

74

AUTHOR: Mark E. Neely Jr.
PUBLISHED: 1991
GENRE: Presidency

I T IS a truism in Civil War studies that Lincoln had to usurp the Constitution to save the Union. Southern apologists have often pointed this out. What exactly is the real story? Mark E. Neely Jr., a man with impeccable Lincoln credentials, looks at the documentary record to see what did happen in *The Fate of Liberty: Abraham Lincoln and Civil Liberties*. His study is so original it won the Pulitzer Prize for History in 1992.

Neely makes clear there was little precedent for Lincoln to rely on after the fall of Fort Sumter. Various generals in the past had imposed martial law at specific places, but none had faced a problem as vast as his. Lincoln moved quickly to save Maryland for the Union after troops on their way to Washington were attacked in Baltimore. Congress was not in session to deal with the problem, and if Maryland fell, so would the nation's capital. By making a few arrests, the policy worked. Neely writes, "In these early months of the Civil War, the Lincoln Administration overcame its fears of public reaction to restrictions on civil liberties, instituted a novel internal security system, and came to believe that it worked. Not every historian today would credit it with saving Maryland for the Union, but that conclusion became a truism in Lincoln's day." Again and again Neely points out the Lincoln administration was working in uncharted territory and showed remarkable strength and decisiveness in those early days of the war.[1]

The worst time for civil liberty in the North followed the draft. It was Secretary of War Edwin M. Stanton who was toughest in this respect. He had an army to raise and could be ruthlessly efficient. An order came from the War Department on August 8, 1862, calling for the arrest of anyone who interfered in the recruitment of the army. Democrats and subsequent historians have assumed that the order was issued to stifle opposition to the coming Emancipation Proclamation. Neely shows why this is wrong: "The orders of August 8, 1862, were aimed at enforcing the first national conscription in American history. Their issuance was unrelated to the Emancipation Proclamation, the timing of which was premised on the unpredictable: a military victory. . . . [T]he best proof of that is the 54 percent of arrests that netted young men (and their accessories) heading for Canada or other areas to escape conscription." Proof the order was given to help recruiting, as opposed to silencing the Democratic opposition, is that it was lifted one month later while the fall elections had yet to occur.[2]

Neely looks at the actual numbers of arrests and the supposed crimes the suspects committed in the old records. He admits the records are incomplete, but he does draw some pertinent observations. Chief of the Record and Pension Office, F. C. Ainsworth, had come up with a figure of 13,535 civilians imprisoned due to Lincoln's suspending of the writ of habeas corpus. Neely finds no real support for that number. He actually feels the number is probably higher, but the arrests themselves are less significant for the question of civil liberties. He concludes, "Precise figures are not available, but historians can nevertheless be precise about what the available figures mean. They indicate that after 1862 a majority of citizens arrested were citizens of the Confederacy. They suggest a variety of causes for arrest of Northerners, among which speaking, writing, and gathering in political groups was rare. . . . There were more arrests, but they had less significance for traditional civil liberty than anyone realized." Most of those arrested in the North were in areas of battle in the Border States. Any attempt to prove a systematic effort by the Lincoln administration to destroy its political enemies this way will flounder on these statistics.[3]

In a telling aside, Neely laments the fact that so much literature on this subject has focused on Lincoln's mercy and goodwill. Neely says of Lincoln, "He was by nearly universal testimony a man of compassion, but he was not ubiquitous." The fact is, Lincoln did not intervene often in these cases. Even had he wanted to, it would have been impossible to sort through all the arrests made by officers in the field and elsewhere.[4]

It is disconcerting that Neely feels no real historical lesson can be learned from Lincoln's actions during the Civil War. Neely closes the book with, "If a situation were to arise again in the United States when the writ of habeas corpus were suspended, government would probably be as ill-prepared to define the legal situation as it was in 1861. The clearest lesson is there is no clear lesson in the Civil War—no neat precedents, no ground rules, no map. War and its effect on civil liberties remain a frightening unknown." The rhetorical question Lincoln asked in 1863, "Must I shoot a simple-minded boy who deserts, while I must not touch a hair of a wiley agitator who induces him to desert?" remains an unanswerable one.[5]

NOTES

1. Mark E. Neely Jr., *The Fate of Liberty: Abraham Lincoln and Civil Liberties* (New York: Oxford University Press, 1991), 5, 29.
2. Ibid., 56, 64, 63.
3. Ibid., 115, 137–38, 32–50.
4. Ibid., 118.
5. Ibid., 235; Abraham Lincoln, 1863, as quoted in ibid., 68.

Lincoln the War President: The Gettysburg Lectures

AUTHOR: Gabor S. Boritt, editor
PUBLISHED: 1992
GENRE: Presidency

I N THIS volume Gabor Boritt has once again compiled a series of essays from some of the best in the field. *Lincoln the War President: The Gettysburg Lectures* contains essays from such scholars as Robert V. Bruce, Carl N. Degler, Arthur Schlesinger Jr., Kenneth M. Stampp, and Boritt himself. These essays examine different aspects of Lincoln's wartime leadership and are thought-provoking and original.[1]

Robert V. Bruce's essay deals with a blunder Lincoln and most of the country committed. Hardly anyone actually thought there was going to be a Civil War. As Bruce writes, "Generations of lurid warnings had also made civil war a more familiar and hence less frightening idea. Notwithstanding all those years of rhetorical hemorrhaging, it may be doubted that many people comprehended the reality of war, or that anyone can without experiencing it." Threats of disunion had been made so many times, they were disregarded by most. One wonders how Lincoln would have acted if he had known the South was in earnest about secession. Bruce reasonably concludes Lincoln would have acted largely as he did, because he believed that both the Union and stopping the expansion of slavery were principles worth the enormous cost of the war.[2]

The strength of the current United States may be due to the fact it was tested on the battlefield, according to Carl Degler. He compares Canada with the United States and finds Canada lacking in the strength of national unity. The reason is that the United States sealed its Union in blood. Canada never had that war. In the most original passage in the book, Degler compares Lincoln's actions to Otto von Bismarck's in Germany: "The way in which Lincoln fought the war also reminds us at times of Bismarck's willingness to use iron, as well as shed blood, in order to build a nation."[3]

Kenneth Stampp points out a dilemma in American political philosophy Lincoln faced and never quite resolved. America has long favored "self-determination" in its foreign policy. Woodrow Wilson even made it official. However, as Stampp writes, "I wonder what the public response would be if the question of self-determination should arise as an American internal issue as it now presents itself in many other nations." Lincoln was presented with that very issue and decided the Union was more important than the "self-determination" of the Southern states. Earlier in his career, Lincoln seemed to favor self-determination in regard to Latin American countries overthrowing their colonial governments. This shows the concept of self-determination is perhaps one America needs to refine.[4]

Arthur Schlesinger Jr. compares Lincoln to Franklin Roosevelt. He feels both men faced a war that threatened the survival of the nation and sees a lot of similarity in the steps they took. He writes, "Roosevelt in 1941, like Lincoln in 1861, did what he did under what appeared to be a popular demand and a public necessity. Both Presidents took their actions in light of day and to the accompaniment of uninhibited political debate. They did what they thought they had to do to save the republic. They threw themselves in the end on the justice of the country and the rectitude of their motives. Whatever Lincoln and Roosevelt felt compelled to do under the pressure of crisis did not corrupt their essential commitment to constitutional ways and democratic processes."[5] Schlesinger is quite right to point out the country was fortunate to have such levelheaded and strong leaders during those two difficult periods.

Boritt contributes a thoughtful essay on how Lincoln the "war opponent" became Lincoln the "war president." He writes, "The man who took the oath of the presidential office in the spring of 1861 was not a pacifist but he was a pacific man. . . . He prized the 'Reign of Reason,' the 'mind, all conquering mind.' He tried to hold on to antimilitaristic feelings, succeeding most of the time, and he harbored a resentment of military intrusion into political life." Lincoln was a strong opponent of the Mexican War. To him it was a war fought for the political advantage of President James K. Polk. When Lincoln was president his attitude toward war changed. Boritt shows how far Lincoln had come toward the end of the war: "By 1864 Lincoln unleashed [William Tecumseh] Sherman in Georgia, [Philip H.] Sheridan in the Shenandoah Valley, and made war, some said, again barbaric." It is not as if Boritt sees Lincoln himself as barbaric. At one point he asks, "Can this nation, or any nation, hope for a better, more decent leader?"[6] Boritt doesn't draw any conclusions about Lincoln's transformation but instead leaves it to the reader to ponder.

Boritt has an eye for selection. Every essay in this book is of the highest quality. The nature of Lincoln's wartime leadership is a subject that has strangely been neglected in relation to other aspects of his presidency. These essays raise questions for further study and show the topic is far from exhausted.

NOTES

1. Gabor S. Boritt, ed., *Lincoln the War President: The Gettysburg Lectures* (New York: Oxford University Press, 1992), 121–44, 89–120, 1–28, 145–78, 179–211; the subtitle refers to the fact these were originally lectures presented at Gettysburg College.
2. Robert V. Bruce, "The Shadow of a Coming War" in ibid., 21.
3. Carl N. Degler, "One Among Many: The United States and National Unification" in ibid., 119, 108.
4. Kenneth M. Stampp, "One Alone? The United States and National Self-Determination" in ibid., 124, 125.
5. Arthur M. Schlesinger Jr., "War and the Constitution: Abraham Lincoln and Franklin D. Roosevelt" in ibid., 174.
6. Gabor S. Boritt, "War Opponent and War President" in ibid., 200, 205, 211.

Lincoln: An Illustrated Biography

AUTHORS: Philip B. Kunhardt Jr.,
Philip B. Kunhardt III, and
Peter W. Kunhardt
PUBLISHED: 1992
GENRE: The Lincoln Image

THE TORCH of Lincoln photographs has been passed to a new generation of Kunhardts. One of the authors of *Twenty Days* and his two sons have put together this exquisite book of Lincoln photographs. *Lincoln: An Illustrated Biography* is a fine biography, but it is the beautiful, clear, and crisp images that make it an essential Lincoln book. Lincoln scholar David Herbert Donald summed it up well in the foreword: "But the heart of the Kunhardts' *Lincoln* is, of course the pictures. They present a complete photographic record of Lincoln, from his earliest, awkward daguerreotype to that final, careworn, and almost saintly portrait made by Alexander Gardner just a few weeks before his assassination. Here, too, are the faces of Mary Lincoln, as proud wife and tragic widow, and the portraits of Lincoln's children. So comprehensive is the Kunhardts' coverage that they show us Lincoln's office and his books, his house and even his outhouse." An endorsement from Donald is a coveted honor in the Lincoln field and is well deserved here.[1]

The authors discuss Lincoln's homely appearance in detail: "Lincoln could appear handsome at one time, homely at another. When his hair was too long or too short, when it shot out every which way like brown wheat or stood up in spikes, Lincoln looked odd indeed. When his weak right eye wandered, or his beak of a nose was caught in a sharp profile, or his thick lower lip hung down, when his hollow cheeks seemed sucked in more than usual, when his massive jaw took on a mulish set, or sadness and melancholy deadened his eyes, then his visage was construed as heavy and unpleasant." There also seems to be a consensus, though, among those who knew Lincoln that his ugliness disappeared when he spoke. The photographs in this book can't capture those moments, but the authors do quote Lincoln's law partner, Herndon, to that effect. He once said, "When those little gray eyes and face lighted up by the inward soul on fires of emotion . . . then it was that all those apparently ugly or homely features sprang into organs of beauty. . . . Sometimes it did appear to me that Lincoln was just fresh from the hands of his Creator."[2]

The best reproductions of Lincoln in this book are the two Alexander Hesler photographs made in 1860. Lincoln himself thought these were the best ever taken. One is of Lincoln's profile. The lines and weathering on his face are clear to see. In the other, Lincoln is looking forward into the distance. His lips are pursed tightly, and his expression is almost one of sadness. These striking images are so clear and powerful that they would warrant framing if not bound in the book.[3]

There is a unique photograph of Lincoln's final burial in 1901 in his permanent tomb. A group of men from Springfield had come to witness the event. Attempts had been made to steal Lincoln's corpse, so to remove all doubt of the identity of the burial, Lincoln's body was viewed for the last time. The authors relate, "At the final burial ceremony, a plumber cut a little window in the lead of the coffin just over Lincoln's face. A pungent odor arose. There was the face, still white with the chalk applied by the undertaker on the funeral trip west back in 1865. There were his nose and chin, as prominent as in life. There was the little black bow tie in place, and the suit of black cloth Lincoln had worn at his second inauguration, now whitened with mildew. There was the head, fallen to one side on the sunken pillow."[4] Never again would human eyes view the great man, and the story of his final burial has a poignancy that makes it worth telling.

The book contains a number of photographs of Lincoln's family. The first photograph of his wife, Mary, taken in 1846, reveals why she was attractive to men. Her features are pretty, and she is dressed fashionably. The last photograph of Mary is a tragic one. Mary had been taken in by a "spirit photographer" who added a ghostly image of Lincoln to Mary. The photograph is an obvious forgery, but Mary wanted to believe Lincoln's spirit was hovering around her so badly that she accepted the photograph as real.[5]

There has been no shortage of Lincoln picture books. There are a good number of Lincoln photographs that can easily be reproduced and placed between hard covers. This book does not fit the typical "cut and paste" pattern of many of these books. The subjects of the photographs are many and varied, too varied to be discussed in detail here. The Kunhardt family had images handed down through the family that were not available to other authors. Most important, the quality of the reproductions is so superb, one could stare at some of these photographs for hours.

NOTES

1. See Dorothy Meserve Kunhardt and Philip B. Kunhardt Jr., *Twenty Days* (New York: Harper & Row, 1965); David Herbert Donald, foreword to Philip B. Kunhardt Jr., Philip B. Kunhardt III, and Peter W. Kunhardt, *Lincoln: An Illustrated Biography* (New York: Random House, 1992), vi.
2. Kunhardt et al., *Lincoln*, 9; William H. Herndon as quoted in ibid., 9.
3. Kunhardt et al., *Lincoln*, 10, 10–11.
4. Ibid., 398–99, 399; for an account of the attempt to steal Lincoln's body, see Lloyd Lewis, *Myths After Lincoln* (New York: Press of the Readers Club, 1941), 266–81.
5. Kunhardt et al., *Lincoln*, 66, 397.

Lincoln at Gettysburg: The Words That Remade America

AUTHOR: Gary Wills
PUBLISHED: 1992
GENRE: Presidency

THE GETTYSBURG ADDRESS is one of the most recited documents in America. It has become so familiar it has lost most of its original force. Gary Wills examines the address line by line in *Lincoln at Gettysburg: The Words That Remade America*. The interpretation he gives to the speech is fresh and original and causes one to see it in a new light. He reminds the reader, "By accepting the Gettysburg Address, its concept of a single people dedicated to a proposition, we have been changed. Because of it, we live in a different America."[1]

In the most original chapter, Wills compares the Gettysburg Address to the great funeral oratory of Pericles. Wills points out the many parallels in style between the two. Edward Everett, who gave the long speech before Lincoln's, also used the Greek model for his speech yet did not do it in such a powerful way as Lincoln. The central point Lincoln and Pericles made was that the dead were to be an inspiration for the living. Both praised the dead but reminded the audiences the cause for which they died had not yet been won.[2]

There was a "culture of death" in the nineteenth century that is hard for modern-day Americans to understand. Death was something dwelled on, and excessive mourning was not seen as unusual. Wills observes of Lincoln, "He was part of his age, at home in its culture of death. He went to Gettysburg as alert to all the resonances of the rural cemetery as any of those who would listen to him." Lincoln had known death at an early age and wrote melancholy poetry about

231

it. The pathos necessary for the occasion was easy for Lincoln to summon, for it was part of his psyche.[3]

For a speech associated with a particular battle, there is very little reference to the actual event. This no doubt contributed to its timeless quality. Wills contrasts Everett to Lincoln in this regard: "Everett succeeded with his audience by being thoroughly immersed in the details of what he was celebrating. Lincoln eschews all local emphasis. His speech hovers far above the carnage. He lifts the battle to a level of abstraction that purges it of grosser matter."[4] Lincoln had a much larger purpose in mind. He was seeking to not just commemorate a particular battle but to change the direction of American thought.

Lincoln's greatest accomplishment in the speech was making the Declaration of Independence the central document of American history. As Wills writes, "The Gettysburg Address has become an authoritative expression of the American spirit—as authoritative as the Declaration itself, and perhaps even more influential, since it determines how we read the Declaration. For most people now, the Declaration means what Lincoln told us it means, as a way of correcting the Constitution without overthrowing it. It is this correction of the spirit, this intellectual revolution, that makes attempts to go back beyond Lincoln to some earlier version so feckless." Many Americans would be surprised today to learn the phrase "All men are created equal" is not in the Constitution. Lincoln, in effect, put it there through the power of his oratory. Wills rightly points out that attempts by die-hard conservatives to read the Constitution as not having the phrase as its intent are doomed to failure. Lincoln was just that successful.[5]

By changing the meaning of the declaration, Lincoln also changed both the meaning and the goals of the war. Wills states, "Both North and South strove to win the battle of *interpreting* Gettysburg as soon as the physical battle had ended. Lincoln is after even larger game— he means to 'win' the whole Civil War in ideological terms as well as military ones. And he will succeed: the Civil War *is* to most Americans what Lincoln wanted it to *mean*. Words had to complete the work of guns." The prescient Democrats in the North saw what Lincoln had done, and they were not happy. He was moving the war away from a simple upholding of the Constitution. Influenced by Wills's interpretation, David Herbert Donald wrote of the Democratic Party's reaction to the speech: "The bitterness of these protests was evidence that Lincoln had succeeded in broadening the aims of the war from Union to Equality and Union."[6]

The speech Lincoln gave at Gettysburg is one of the classics of American prose. The strength of this book is that it takes a familiar speech and makes it fresh. Wills's book shows how this speech changed the fundamental beliefs of the nation. In the past too much emphasis has been placed on the minutiae and details of the event at Gettysburg and not on the deeper meanings of the address.[7] Wills rectifies this oversight and produces an essential Lincoln book in the process.

NOTES

1. Gary Wills, *Lincoln at Gettysburg: The Words That Remade America* (New York: Touchstone, 1992), 147.
2. Ibid., 41–62, 46, 62.
3. Ibid., 63–89, 75, 76.
4. Ibid., 37.
5. Ibid., 146–47.
6. Ibid., 37–38; David Herbert Donald, *Lincoln* (New York: Simon & Schuster, 1995), 466.
7. See, e.g., William E. Barton, *Lincoln at Gettysburg: What He Intended to Say; What He Said; What He Was Reported to Have Said; What He Wished He Had Said* (Indianapolis: Bobbs-Merrill, 1930).

Dear Mr. Lincoln: Letters to the President

AUTHOR: Harold Holzer, editor
PUBLISHED: 1993
GENRE: Presidency

THE ABRAHAM LINCOLN PAPERS are in the Library of Congress. They include drafts of letters and speeches, official state papers, and incoming correspondence. The amount of the material is so great it takes up ninety-seven reels of microfilm. This material was not available to the general public until 1947. Robert Todd Lincoln, who controlled the material, stipulated that it would not be open until twenty-one years after his death. It is now available to scholars but is inaccessible to the average reader. Harold Holzer has taken some of the more interesting letters sent to Lincoln included in the papers and reprinted them in *Dear Mr. Lincoln: Letters to the President*. Anytime generally unseen primary-source material is made available, it is usually an essential Lincoln book.[1]

Holzer organizes the letters into different chapters, which include "Requests and Demands," "Family Matters," "Complaints and Criticism," and "Threats and Warnings" among others. Holzer picks some letters serious in tone, others angry, and some just plain funny.[2]

Holzer includes a touching and pathetic letter from a daughter with a plea for her father's life in the "Requests and Demands" chapter. She writes with a speed and emotion that did not allow for careful wording: "O Mr Lincoln have you got no little girls and suppose you was in papa place and your little girl was to be a man for mercy and he to grant it. O would not you love him; O how papa would would [sic] love you. O how can i stand it. O pardon, O pardon my

234

papa Mr Lincoln, O if I could see you, I would kiss your feet."[3] Holzer can find no record of the case or a reply from Lincoln, but the fact the letter was saved indicates Lincoln probably acted on the girl's request.

The nicest letter Lincoln received was from a Springfield friend, William Florville. The letter is in the chapter "Family Matters." Florville was a black barber Lincoln had known and liked in his hometown. The letter does not beg for money or a job. It is just a friendly letter to tell Lincoln what was going on in Springfield. He writes, "My family is well. My son William is married and in business for himself. I am occupying the same place in which I was at the time you left. Tell Taddy that his (and Willys) Dog is alive and Kicking doing well he stays mostly at John E. Roll with his Boys Who are about the size now that Tad and Willy ware when they left for Washington."[4] It must have been a relief for Lincoln to hear from an old friend who was not coming hat in hand to him.

Lincoln received a good deal of cheap advice from the general public, some of which is available in the chapter "Complaints and Criticism." One woman used his name to try to influence him: "You stand on the hearts of widows and orphans and childless mothers to be, and the voice of their wailing goes up to God this day. It is written of Abraham [?] that though he loved not God, he found favor with the Angel because he loved his fellow-men. Where think you is there favor for him who places the interests of any party high above the life & liberty of his fellow men? . . . The wail of lost souls slain in faith makes mournful music to live and die by." The letter is signed, "One who loves our country North & South."[5] Lincoln apparently didn't reply to this missive.

In the scariest chapter, "Threats and Warnings," Holzer collects some truly terrifying letters to Lincoln. Since it is known what Lincoln's ultimate fate was, the letters are even scarier because we know the writers were in earnest. In an obscenity-laden screed, a barely literate Mr. A. G. Frick tells Lincoln to resign or be killed. He then let Lincoln have it: "You g-d or mighty g-d dam sundde of a bitch go to hell and buss my A— . . . and call my Bolics your uncle Dick g-d dam a fool and g-ddam Abe Lincoln who would like you g-ddam you excuse me for using such hard words with you but you need it you are nothing but a g-ddam n-gger."[6]

The Lincoln Papers are an invaluable source for the study of Lincoln, and because of Holzer more are able to see samples of this material than before. One must remember that the letters in the papers are the ones Lincoln's secretaries deemed worthy of saving. This was only a fraction of the total letters, of which this book contains only a fraction. The Abraham Lincoln Papers are too massive a collection to be put in book form. Holzer has done all Lincoln readers a favor by putting some of the best of this material between two hard covers.[7]

NOTES

1. David Herbert Donald, *Lincoln* (New York: Simon& Schuster, 1995), 600; Harold Holzer, ed., *Dear Mr. Lincoln: Letters to the President* (Reading, Mass.: Addison-Wesley, 1993), 38.
2. Holzer, 71–116, 303–34, 141–70, 335–50.
3. Sally C. Petty to Abraham Lincoln, April 22, 1862, in ibid., 84.
4. William Florville to Abraham Lincoln, December 22, 1863, in ibid., 321.
5. Anonymous to Abraham Lincoln, December 30, 1861, in ibid., 155–56.
6. A. G. Frick to Abraham Lincoln, February 14, 1861, in ibid., 341.
7. Holzer printed more material in Harold Holzer, ed., *The Lincoln Mailbag: America Writes to the President, 1861–1865* (Carbondale: Southern Illinois University Press, 1998).

The Last Best Hope of Earth: Abraham Lincoln and the Promise of America

AUTHOR: Mark E. Neely Jr.
PUBLISHED: 1993
GENRE: Biography

T HIS IS not so much a biography as it is a call to arms in Lincoln scholarship. Mark E. Neely Jr. laments the focus on the private Lincoln rather than the historical implications of his presidency. As he opens the book, "The rise of psychohistory, the emphasis in women's history on the nineteenth-century family and domestic scene, and the turning inward of the 'me' generation of the late twentieth century have all played parts in directing interest more toward Lincoln's early, intimate home life." *The Last Best Hope of Earth: Abraham Lincoln and the Promise of America* focuses most of its attention on Lincoln's public policy decisions as president and ignores the "inner" Lincoln completely. It also devotes scant attention, as compared to other biographies, to Lincoln before he reached national prominence as a politician.[1]

Lincoln as commander in chief is given a full assessment in this book. Neely does find some errors in Lincoln's judgment. For example, he feels Lincoln made a poor tactical decision in 1862 in regard to Stonewall Jackson's Valley campaign. When Jackson attacked, "Lincoln behaved exactly as the Confederates had hoped he would. He began detaching troops to the Shenandoah Valley that [George B.] McClellan had assumed he would have available for his offensive." The failure of McClellan's Peninsula campaign may be due to this decision by Lincoln, though McClellan's over-cautiousness played a part as well.[2]

On the whole, though, Neely believes Lincoln was an excellent war leader. Being president during wartimes requires more than moving troops from place to place. It also requires a leader who can unite his people behind the war effort. After listing some of Confederate president Jefferson Davis's political mistakes, Neely can write, "Abraham Lincoln made no such mistakes. He may not have been, as one of his earliest admirers among British military historians put it, a 'military genius.' The term may best be reserved for General [William Tecumseh] Sherman or some other Civil War military figure who still looms large in strategic discussions at West Point. But as commander in chief, who must combine military perception with political vision and the skillful handling of personalities, Lincoln had no superior in American history."[3]

Neely makes clear Lincoln's commitment to emancipation. He relates a telling incident during the presidential campaign of 1864. During the summer of that year, it looked as though Lincoln would lose. If that happened, many of the slaves freed by the Emancipation Proclamation would be in danger. A Democratic administration elected on a platform of making slavery a nonissue in the war would hardly care about their fate. Lincoln called Frederick Douglass to the White House to devise a plan to spread the word among slaves behind Confederate lines to escape now while the proclamation was still in effect. Neely writes, "Douglass understood the import of the episode perfectly. 'I refer to this conversation,' he wrote in later years, 'because I think that, on Mr. Lincoln's part, it is evidence conclusive that the Proclamation, so far at least as he was concerned, was not effected merely as a 'necessity.'"[4] It is amazing how few writers have picked up on this startling but ultimately unnecessary plan by Lincoln.

The book devotes a chapter to the assassination because Neely sees the political aspect of it some writers have missed. Booth wrote a letter to his sister explaining that the country was for the white man and the North was losing its political liberty to a tyrant who was seeking to elevate the slaves. Neely can say truthfully, "These sentiments, expressed in a letter written probably in the summer of 1864 . . . could have been matched by many a Maryland speech or editorial. This was the state, after all, where the Lincoln administration had arrested legislators on their way to the assembly hall. The first line of the state song retained the memory of Lincoln's act: 'The despot's heel is on thy shore, Maryland, my Maryland.'"[5] Too often this is lost sight of in the writing on the assassination since so much is focused on possible conspiracies.

The book is well illustrated with three large sections of plates. These come from an exhibit at the Huntington Library that was the genesis of this book. Keeping with the theme of the book, the illustrations are for the most part political in nature. They add to the strength of the book and are not an afterthought as they are in many other books.[6]

Neely makes a good case for a return to a more public-minded approach to Lincoln. While all may not agree with his assessment, it is hard to argue that he doesn't have a case when he states, "Had Abraham Lincoln died in the spring of 1860, on the eve of his first presidential nomination, he would be a forgotten man. Whatever made Lincoln's life memorable in history occurred in the brief but eventful time between the summer of 1860 and the spring of 1865." Many books have recently been published that focus on the private side of Lincoln. However, this book attempts to redirect Lincoln studies to a different path.[7]

NOTES

1. Mark E. Neely Jr., *The Last Best Hope of Earth: Abraham Lincoln and the Promise of America* (Cambridge, Mass.: Harvard University Press, 1995), v.
2. Ibid., 65.
3. Ibid., 91, 92; see Colin R. Ballard, *The Military Genius of Abraham Lincoln* (Cleveland: World Publishing Co., 1952).
4. Neely, 118; Frederick Douglass quoted in ibid., 119.
5. Neely, 183–93, 190–91.
6. Ibid., leaf after 54, leaf after 118, leaf after 182.
7. Ibid., v.

The Shadows Rise: Abraham Lincoln and the Ann Rutledge Legend

AUTHOR: John Evangelist Walsh
PUBLISHED: 1993
GENRE: Prepresidential Years

JOHN EVANGELIST WALSH is like a present-day William Barton. Like Barton, he is at his best when looking at one famous incident in Lincoln's life and collecting all the evidence about it to reach a reasonable conclusion. He has done this with other historical figures, and *The Shadows Rise: Abraham Lincoln and the Ann Rutledge Legend* is his first entry in the Lincoln field. It makes the list because it challenges a long-held assumption head-on and completely demolishes it.[1]

This is a book that took far too long to come out. For decades the Randall orthodoxy on the Ann Rutledge story has held sway over Lincoln scholarship. In his infamous appendix to *Lincoln the President,* James Randall cast doubt on the Lincoln-Rutledge romance by unfairly attacking Lincoln's law partner, Herndon. What was even worse was the smearing of the residents of New Salem as liars or senile fools. Walsh attempts to resurrect the reputation of the legend by examining what each person actually said and determining his or her credibility.[2]

Walsh gives full credit to two scholars who first challenged the Randall view of the matter. John Y. Simon and Douglas Wilson both rebutted Randall almost simultaneously in 1990. Walsh can rightly say, "When the revolt against Randall came, it came with a bang." He praises Simon's logic as he reviews his work. "Pointing to the overlooked fact that 'no knowledgeable witness ever denied the affair,' Simon slices away at Randall's position until, in one arrowlike sentence, he hits the target dead center. Randall, he states, impermissibly 'reclassified the romance as an accusation needing proof, something of which Lincoln would be held innocent until proven guilty.' Rather, it should be taken as a normal biographical incident, 'about which a preponderance of reliable evidence should prevail.'" He also shows how Douglas Wilson used quantitative methods to show the overwhelming agreement of those in New Salem about the reality of the Lincoln-Rutledge romance.[3]

The most important witness is Isaac Cogdal. He visited Lincoln in 1860, right before Lincoln left for Washington. Cogdal asked Lincoln if he "ran a little wild" after Ann died. Lincoln supposedly said, "I did really—I ran off the track: it was my first. I loved the woman dearly and sacredly. She was a handsome girl—would have made a good loving wife—was natural and quite intellectual, though not highly educated—I did honestly and truly love the girl and think often— often of her now." This is crucial evidence, and Walsh shows why it is trustworthy. Cogdal was a close friend with Lincoln and had discussed intimate topics like religion before. Walsh also shows that Lincoln was in a sentimental mood; he would soon visit his stepmother for the last time and would be in tears delivering his farewell speech to Springfield. It would be natural for the two men to discuss old times in New Salem and Ann Rutledge.[4]

In the chapter "A Parade of Witnesses," Walsh looks at each individual who was asked about or mentioned the Lincoln-Rutledge romance. He shows many of these people were substantial citizens who did not deserve to be dismissed so easily by Randall. No other author has ever put all of these accounts together. Reading them underlines what Douglas Wilson had shown quantitatively: There is almost unanimous agreement about the reality of the romance and even of the engagement of Ann and Lincoln.[5]

Walsh makes a good argument for the overall importance of the romance: "When Ann died in all her youth and loveliness, surely some portion of Lincoln's sorely grieving heart, as he said, descended with her fever-wasted body into the grave. . . . Here is no radical or startling admission, no cause for controversy. It only repeats what everyone with any experience of life knows all too well, that such tragedies happen. . . . Invariably they leave their mark, serious or shallow, according to circumstances and to the personal temperament of the unfortunate sufferer."[6] Ann was one more in a parade of deaths in Lincoln's early life. It is not absurd to conclude this contributed to his melancholy.

It is a testament to the strength of the reputation of James Randall that he was able to hoist his unhistorical appendix on Lincoln scholarship without a dissenting voice for almost fifty years. As Walsh writes, "Not the least surprising aspect of the Lincoln-Rutledge question, as it has existed up to now, is the absence of any sustained investigation . . . it can still be said with perfect justice that the Rutledge legend in its full extent today stands largely unanalyzed, and very nearly unapproached." This state of affairs was helped along by the defenders of Mary Todd Lincoln, but there is no real reason scholars didn't make at least a cursory review of the matter. As the evidence shows, the Ann Rutledge romance is one of the best-attested episodes in Lincoln's life. Thankfully, due to Walsh and others, Ann is no longer being erased in the Lincoln story.[7]

NOTES

1. For another example of Walsh and a legendary incident in Lincoln's life, see John Evangelist Walsh, *Moonlight: Abraham Lincoln and the Almanac Trial* (New York: St. Martin's, 2000).
2. James G. Randall, *Lincoln the President: Springfield to Gettysburg*, 2 vols. (New York: Dodd, Mead & Co., 1945), 2:321–42.
3. John Evangelist Walsh, *The Shadows Rise: Abraham Lincoln and the Ann Rutledge Legend* (Urbana: University of Illinois Press, 1993), 55, 55, 56.
4. Isaac Cogdal as quoted in ibid., 84; Abraham Lincoln as quoted in ibid., 85; ibid., 82–83.
5. Walsh, 99–110.
6. Ibid., 139.
7. Ibid., 5. For a summary of how scholars have viewed the story, see Michael Burkhimer, "On the Ann Rutledge Merry-Go-Round," *Lincoln Herald* 104, no. 4 (Winter 2002): 151–58.

The Inner World of
Abraham Lincoln

AUTHOR: Michael Burlingame
PUBLISHED: 1994
GENRE: Psychology and Religion

FEW LINCOLN books have been as original and daring as Michael Burlingame's *The Inner World of Abraham Lincoln*. Using the tools of a psychobiographer, he sheds new light on how Lincoln's psyche and subconscious contributed to his actions. Early on he succinctly lays out the case of why this type of study is invaluable: "Because Lincoln's leadership played such a vital role in preserving the Union and abolishing slavery, his personality deserves the fullest analysis."[1]

The book is topical rather than chronological. Each chapter is an intense study on one facet of Lincoln's life. Burlingame includes chapters on Lincoln's hatred of slavery, his anger and sometimes cruelty, his ambition, and his marriage. This book is no idle guessing on Burlingame's part. He offers a virtual avalanche of sources and notes throughout the book.[2]

The most convincing chapter is "I Used to Be a Slave: The Origins of Abraham Lincoln's Hatred of Slavery." Burlingame points out how much Lincoln hated slavery from an early age. This might be the best and most moving writing ever done on Lincoln and slavery. He also shows Lincoln could be quite radical in his hatred. Others have argued this point before, but Burlingame has a novel reason for Lincoln's hatred. He writes, "As a youth, Lincoln was like a slave to his father, who insisted that his son not only labor on the family farm but also that he work for the neighbors and turn over every penny he earned." At another point he concludes, "Because his father treated him like a slave, Lincoln empathized with the bondsmen and felt a special urgency about freeing them."[3] The connection of Lincoln's unhappy youth to his hatred of slavery is an interesting path of study and should be perused further.

The chapter titled "Lincoln's Anger and Cruelty" is certainly original. Most people would not associate those two traits with Lincoln, but Burlingame shows that they existed, particularly early in Lincoln's career. As a young man, Lincoln was apt to use political ridicule to best his opponents. This faded over the years, but Lincoln could still show flashes of anger. Burlingame does not see anger as controlling Lincoln though. He writes, "The remarkable thing about Lincoln's temper is not how often it erupted, but how seldom it did, considering how frequently he encountered the insolence of epaulets, the abuse of friends and opponents alike, and the egomaniacal selfishness of editors, senators, representatives, governors, cabinet members, generals, and flocks of others who pestered him unmercifully with petty concerns."[4] The instances of Lincoln's compassion far outweigh the anger and cruelty he sometimes showed, but Burlingame is right to show they were part of Lincoln's makeup too.

In "The Most Ambitious Man in the World," Burlingame sees Lincoln's ambition as compensation for lack of parental love as a youngster. For this he again blames Lincoln's father. "His father, utterly different from Abraham, offered little nurturance. Perhaps the best thing Thomas Lincoln ever did for his son was to marry Sarah Bush Johnson, who cherished the lad. But by the time she arrived on the scene, the boy's psyche had endured much. Lincoln thus seems to have suffered from emotional malnutrition. To compensate for the damage to his self-esteem, he sought in political life a surrogate form of love and acceptance he had not found at home."[5] While this assessment of Thomas Lincoln may be too harsh for many, Burlingame does offer strong arguments for it.

Burlingame's attitude toward the Lincoln marriage can be surmised from the title of the chapter "The Lincolns' Marriage: 'A Fountain of Misery, of a Quality Absolutely Infernal.'" Never has so much negative material on Mary Todd Lincoln been presented in one place. It is this chapter that has drawn the most fire from critics. However, as much as they might want to, the apologists for Mary cannot simply make this material go away. One can quibble with some of the evidence Burlingame presents, yet one can't dismiss it all. Burlingame offers strong evidence Mary was involved in fraud and theft as first lady. He also offers evidence that Mary often resorted to violence with her husband and servants. Mary threw potatoes, books, and chased Lincoln with a broom. She also apparently threw hot coffee in his face. Echoing Herndon, Burlingame suggests this unhappiness helped Lincoln reach the presidency by seeking an escape.[6]

This book is very controversial, and some would disagree with Burlingame's conclusions. However, what they cannot say is that he hasn't done his homework. The amount of new and overlooked material Burlingame has unearthed in this book is staggering. Even if one doesn't agree with much of this book, it is still an essential read. *The Inner World of Abraham Lincoln* will be one of those books on which scholars have to take a position; it simply can't be ignored.

NOTES

1. Michael Burlingame, *The Inner World of Abraham Lincoln* (Urbana: University of Illinois Press, 1994), xiii.
2. Ibid., vii.
3. Ibid., 20–56, 37, xv; for another example of Lincoln's attitude, see LaWanda Cox, *Lincoln and Black Freedom: A Study of Presidential Leadership* (Columbia: University of South Carolina Press, 1981).
4. Burlingame, 147–23, 150–55, 208.
5. Ibid., 236–67, 257.
6. Ibid., 268–362, 304–7, 277, 325–26.

The Jewel of Liberty: Abraham Lincoln's Re-Election and the End of Slavery

AUTHOR: David E. Long
PUBLISHED: 1994
GENRE: Presidency

OF ALL the books written on Lincoln's reelection, this is the best. David E. Long's *The Jewel of Liberty: Abraham Lincoln's Re-Election and the End of Slavery* combines solid interpretation and an easy writing style. The revisionist school had focused on the divisions in Lincoln's Republican Party during the campaign. This book takes a broader view of the long-term effects of the election on the country. Revisionists have long tried to downplay the difference between the contestants. Long shows how profoundly Lincoln and George B. McClellan differed in political philosophy. He also shows that because the ramifications of their respective political platforms were so different, the 1864 election can rightfully be said to have been a watershed event in American history.[1]

Long follows the events of the campaign in a quick-paced narrative style. He puts special emphasis on the race issue. The Democratic Party sought to paint the Republicans as the radical party on race. Long points out that "a number of Democratic publications during the campaign sought to excite common racial prejudices. The Society for the Diffusion of Political Knowledge, which became a primary Democratic propaganda producer, turned out a number of circulars that criticized the Emancipation Proclamation and supported slavery while arguing the natural inferiority of blacks." It even produced a forged pamphlet that made it seem the Republican Party was calling for "miscegenation," or the intermarriage of whites and blacks. This was anathema to an overwhelming majority of Americans in 1864. The fraud was exposed, but many Democratic voters felt it represented the views of the Lincoln administration anyway.[2]

According to Long, historians need to focus on the two major questions about the election: "Two questions were of surpassing importance in 1864, and both were resolved by Lincoln's re-election. First, would the Union have been restored if McClellan won? . . . Second, would emancipation have survived Lincoln's defeat?"[3]

Long makes a strong case that the answer to the first question would have been a resounding no. McClellan's platform called for a negotiated peace leading to reunion. It also implicitly abandoned emancipation and conscription. It is true McClellan had disavowed the "peace plank" in the platform and called for the war to continue. Long points out, however, his plan would have destroyed the war effort. "It would have been difficult for McClellan to have withdrawn the Emancipation Proclamation without also discharging all black soldiers. By November 1864, nearly one-fifth of all Union soldiers and sailors were black. . . . Even if he had discharged only the former slaves, more than 100,000 men in uniform would have been lost. At a time when Lincoln had to issue draft calls for a half-million men each, first in July and again in December, the loss of 100,000 men would probably have dealt a fatal blow to McClellan's prospects of battlefield victory." In addition, he wouldn't have been able to call for conscription of Northern whites, since the regular Democratic Party would desert him. McClellan was running on a platform that was out of date and could never have been implemented successfully.[4]

In regard to the second question, a McClellan victory would have doomed emancipation. As Long states, "He probably could not have preserved the Union under any circumstances, but if he could have, it would have been at the expense of emancipation. The minimum result of a McClellan victory would have been the continuation of slavery in some form for some time. Thus the most important and benevolent act performed by a president would have been voided." It is a moot question, anyway, because as Long showed earlier, emancipation and victory were inseparable.[5]

Ultimately, Long feels it was the battlefield victories of the North that paved the way for Lincoln's victory. William Tecumseh Sherman's capture of Atlanta in early September was crucial. The Democratic Party was confident in the summer as the war dragged on and casualties mounted. Lincoln himself despaired of victory. The turnaround in September was complete. Long ironically states, "The Democratic convention concluded on August 31. Delegates celebrated in the streets of Chicago, confident that in November they would gain control not only of the White House and Congress but of most statehouses in November. Unknown to them, as they were adopting a platform calling for a cease-fire and nominating a war supporter to run on it, dramatic events had transpired in Georgia."[6]

The title *The Jewel of Liberty* comes from a letter Lincoln wrote to the new governor of reconstructed Louisiana. Lincoln had asked Governor Michael Hahn to grant the vote to some of the freed slaves. He wrote, "This will probably help, in some trying time to come, to keep the jewel of liberty within the family of freedom." While Lincoln's death prevented his getting all he wanted in that case, Long shows how his reelection ensured that the "jewel of liberty" would at least have a chance to survive—a chance a McClellan victory would have doomed.[7]

NOTES

1. For a revisionist view of the election, see William Frank Zornow, *Lincoln and the Party Divided* (Norman: University of Oklahoma Press, 1954); for a more journalistic view of the election, see John C. Waugh, *Reelecting Lincoln: The Battle for the 1864 Presidency* (New York: Crown Publishers, 1997).
2. David E. Long, *The Jewel of Liberty: Abraham Lincoln's Re-Election and the End of Slavery* (New York: Da Capo, 1997), 174, 154–56.
3. Ibid., 265.
4. "McClellan's Acceptance Letter" in ibid., 275–77; Long, 265–66, 266.
5. Long, 269.
6. Ibid., 211, 210–11, 189.
7. Abraham Lincoln to Michael Hahn, March 13, 1864, as quoted in ibid., vii.

The Presidency of Abraham Lincoln

AUTHOR: Philip Shaw Paludan
PUBLISHED: 1994
GENRE: Presidency

*T*HE PRESIDENCY OF ABRAHAM LINCOLN is the best single-volume treatment of Lincoln as president. Following the lead of Mark Neely's *The Last Best Hope of Earth,* Philip Shaw Paludan eschews all attempts at finding the inner Lincoln. Instead, he emphasizes Lincoln's actions as president as well as his political thought. He spells out his thesis in a bibliographic essay: "The major argument of this book is that Lincoln respected equally the nation's institutions, manifested in the political-constitutional system, and its ideals, revealed in the Declaration of Independence. He saw those institutions as providing the process necessary to realize those ideals." The reaction against revisionism has led many to downplay the importance of the Constitution to Lincoln in favor of the declaration. Paludan shows they were of equal value in Lincoln's thought.[1]

The major area where this is evident is Reconstruction. Paludan praises Lincoln's efforts in Louisiana: "Lincoln had wanted to achieve the ideal of equal liberty under law by expanding freedom within the context of existing traditions. He tried to demonstrate that the existing polity could be rescued from slavery, not by waging a war of ideals against institutions, Union against liberty, but by proving liberty and equality were linked to self-government and that government could act to expand as well as to ensure both." Lincoln's use of the provision in the Constitution ensuring a republican government in each state was very useful to him in this regard. Had he insisted on immediate equality, without working through the legal channels, he would not have had that tool.[2]

Paludan covers the major areas of conflict and decision throughout the book. Lincoln's decision to reinforce Fort Sumter is evaluated. Paludan praises Lincoln's maneuvering of Jefferson Davis into the position of firing the first shot. He writes, "Lincoln's actions handed the decision to fire to Jefferson Davis. The rebel president, who had been claiming that his nation stood for traditional and conservative ideals, would have to calculate the cost of beginning the war."[3] This topic has been covered before, but Paludan distills it to where one can clearly see the wisdom of Lincoln's decision.

Another major crisis Lincoln faced was the possible breakup of his cabinet at the end of 1862. Paludan handles this episode well and shows the level of political skill Lincoln used to diffuse the matter. A congressional delegation of Radicals came to Lincoln demanding he reorganize his cabinet by dropping the conservative secretary of state, William H. Seward. This delegation was backed by the secretary of the treasury, Samuel P. Chase. Lincoln got both men to resign, so he could not accept either resignation. As Paludan writes, "Lincoln's strategy worked, and it also taught valuable lessons to the principals. Both factions believed their side had won a victory and would now be more influential than before."[4] Sending a message to both sides that their voice would be heard was the best possible result of this unfortunate event.

Paludan gives Lincoln high marks on his handling of the economy, something most historians ignore. He paints a rosy picture: "Across the whole economy wealth grew so enormously that, despite the loss of the Confederate states, the Gross National Product (GNP) grew from $3.804 billion in 1860 to $4.019 billion by 1864." Paludan credits Lincoln's Whiggish economic views, which stressed governmental intervention in the economy, for this. "He was urging congressional support for economic growth that would enrich the domestic economy and add strength for war, knowing those resources would overwhelm the south." Without a strong economy, the Union could not win, and Lincoln succeeded in ensuring the North was wealthy enough to support the war.[5]

Like Gary Wills, Paludan stresses the importance of the Gettysburg Address in changing America. He sees Lincoln's speech as redefining the very of idea of government: "A new vision of liberty and government was emerging in the crucible of war. An older idea of liberty from government was being transformed into a vision of liberty because of government. The government's new responsibility was to assist, to enable, to provide an environment for liberty." Paludan rightly states, "At Gettysburg Lincoln had shown Americans how to think of their government and themselves in a way that affirmed their finest possibilities." The "new birth of freedom" Lincoln promised was that government would be an active force in ensuring equality for all.[6]

Lincoln is generally considered to be America's greatest president, and this book goes a long way toward explaining why. *The Presidency of Abraham Lincoln* deserves to have a wider influence in Lincoln literature. It presents a credible account of Lincoln during his presidency. Lincoln as a man aiming for the ideal of equality, but using the existing forms of government to do so, is a description of him that makes a lot of sense. Anyone wanting a better understanding of the decisions Lincoln made those fateful years would do well to remember this book.

NOTES

1. Philip Shaw Paludan, *The Presidency of Abraham Lincoln* (Lawrence: University of Kansas Press, 1994), 363; see Mark E. Neely Jr., *The Last Best Hope of Earth: Abraham Lincoln and the Promise of America* (Cambridge, Mass.: Harvard University Press, 1995).
2. Paludan, 311.
3. Ibid., 66.
4. Ibid., 172–75, 177.
5. Ibid., 211, 211.
6. See Gary Wills, *Lincoln at Gettysburg: The Words That Remade America* (New York: Touchstone, 1992); Paludan, 230, 230.

Lincoln in
American Memory

AUTHOR: Merrill D. Peterson
PUBLISHED: 1994
GENRE: Historiography

THE SUBJECT of Lincoln historiography is deep and complicated. Different generations have interpreted the man in ways that reflect their time. What Lincoln meant to America in 1920 is not the same as what he meant to America in 1970. Merrill D. Peterson's *Lincoln in American Memory* is the best study of how Lincoln has been viewed since his assassination until the present day. It is an encyclopedic account that covers everything from sculpture to advertisements.

The book begins with an account of how America and the rest of the world reacted to the news of the assassination. The effect was almost a personal calamity to most Americans. As Peterson shows, that impression carried over into the lives of their children. "Lincoln's death sank into the hearts and captivated the minds of the generation that grew to maturity after the Civil War. Many of them could say, with Elbert Hubbard, 'The story of Lincoln's life had been ingrained into me long before I could read a book.' So, too, the portrait image of Lincoln. It hung from a million walls like a family icon."[1]

Peterson includes many humorous illustrations throughout the book. Lincoln's image was used to sell things like insurance. He was also used as a political symbol for such causes as child labor and socialism. The most creative use of Lincoln was by the anti-Prohibitionists. They circulated a copy of the liquor license that his store in New Salem had to have in order to sell individual drinks. The Lincoln image has been so powerful that it makes good sense to use it, whether he would have agreed with the cause or not.[2]

One of the major areas of Lincoln iconography is statues. Peterson makes clear that even this was sometimes a battleground. Cincinnati erected a statue of Lincoln in 1917. It was a rough, unkempt, and disheveled figure. When a copy of the statue was going to be placed in London, Robert Todd Lincoln objected vigorously. "Robert Lincoln learned of this plan at the time of the Cincinnati dedication. He penned an indignant protest to President [William Howard] Taft, asking his good offices to put a stop to what he considered an abomination. The statue, he said, 'is a monstrous figure . . . grotesque as a likeness of President Lincoln . . . defamatory as an effigy.'" This controversy shows the duality of Lincoln's image in the American mind. The sculptor wished to emphasize the Western frontier aspect of Lincoln, while Robert wished to highlight Lincoln as the presidential statesman. This tension is a theme running throughout the book.[3]

A major actor in this conflict was Lincoln's law partner, William Herndon. Peterson gives a great deal of space in the book to this influential figure and finds some fault in Herndon's philosophy. Herndon always stressed he was presenting the "real" Lincoln in his lectures. To him, Lincoln's pioneer roots and inner thoughts were the only genuine areas of study, but as Peterson states, "He had set up a false dichotomy between an *ideal* Lincoln and a *real* Lincoln, and supposed that in representing the latter he would foil the enemies of the man he loved and revered." It is obvious that the "real" Lincoln is the man Herndon spoke about and the statesman as well. Calling either one the "real" Lincoln is unhistorical.[4]

The painful disillusionment felt by many blacks with Lincoln during the civil rights era is documented by Peterson. He describes how Malcolm X had questioned Lincoln's importance in emancipation, yet he was not the only one. "Other blacks seemed anxious to smash the old idol altogether. They expressed anger for Lincoln. 'How come it took him two whole years to free the slaves?' one asked. 'His pen was sitting on his desk the whole time. All he had to do was get up one morning and say, 'Doggonit! I think I'm gon' free the slaves today.'" This view of Lincoln's possible actions is hopelessly naive, yet, unfortunately, it is still popular among many today.[5]

Peterson makes clear that recent scholarship has acquitted Lincoln of many of these supposed sins: "If the war was fundamentally about slavery and freedom, as historians from Allan Nevins to James McPherson maintained, then it was fundamentally about emancipation. That was not to say that the President placed emancipation ahead of saving the Union, for he clearly did not. . . . He hated slavery from the depths of his being, but he had a high official duty to the Union." However, the newer scholarship has shown Lincoln saw emancipation as being possible only through the Constitution and Union.[6]

Peterson's is the definitive book on Lincoln historiography. It contains insights into not only Lincoln but also American history. Lincoln has, in some ways, become a blank slate on which successive generations write their own story. The only problem with this area of Lincoln study is that there is no ending. Peterson's book at some point will have to be updated, but for now, Peterson's stands out above all others.

NOTES

1. Quoted in Merrill D. Peterson, *Lincoln in American Memory* (New York: Oxford University Press, 1994), 6.
2. Ibid., 364, 159, 248.
3. Ibid., 209, 210.
4. Ibid., 79.
5. Ibid., 357.
6. Ibid., 383; see James M. McPherson, *Abraham Lincoln and the Second American Revolution* (New York: Oxford University Press, 1991).

Lincoln

AUTHOR: David Herbert Donald
PUBLISHED: 1995
GENRE: Biography

THIS BIOGRAPHY represents a lifetime of Lincoln scholarship. David Herbert Donald is one of the giants in the field. This book was published almost fifty years after *Lincoln's Herndon*, Donald's first book on Lincoln.[1] His long-awaited *Lincoln* lives up to the high expectations many set for it, and it is an essential Lincoln book.

In the beginning of his book, Donald points out some ways his biography is different from others. He doesn't engage in what he sees as peripheral issues. He sticks to Lincoln. By doing this, he states, "I have, I think, produced a portrait rather different from that in other biographies. It is perhaps a bit more grainy than most, with more attention to his unquenchable ambition, to his brain-numbing labor in his law practice, to his tempestuous married life, and to his repeated defeats."[2] This is not to say Donald's view of Lincoln is negative. It is on the whole admiring, but it is not a eulogy.

The book does focus on the above-mentioned aspects of the Lincoln story more than most biographies do. Donald includes a whole chapter on Lincoln's law practice that is thorough and well written. He mentions all the major cases Lincoln was involved in and stresses the large amount of time Lincoln spent on his law practice; it was more time than he spent on politics.[3]

As far as the Lincoln marriage, Donald does mention some "tempestuous" events, but he stresses the positive. He writes, "For all their quarrels they were devoted to each other. In the long years of their marriage Abraham Lincoln was never suspected of being unfaithful to his wife. She, in turn, was immensely proud of him and was his most loyal supporter and admirer." Donald doesn't discount the negative material Herndon collected about Mary Todd Lincoln. When discussing the sources he used to analyze the marriage, he admits Ruth Painter Randall's apologetic *Mary Lincoln: Biography of a Marriage* must be "balanced" with *Herndon's Lincoln*.[4]

Both Lincoln's ambition and his defeats are told in detail. After his defeat when running for the Senate in 1858, he was devastated. Donald relates, "Though Lincoln was not surprised by the outcome of the election, he was bitterly disappointed. Once again, he saw victory escape from his grasp. With one more defeat added to his record, he had received yet another lesson in how little his fate was determined by his personal exertions. At times he felt very blue, and on the day the legislature elected Douglas, he was sure that his political career was ended." Lincoln's ambition made him jealous of Douglas's success. When Lincoln's career was at a low ebb, he showed particular anger toward his rival. Donald explains, "The edge to Lincoln's remarks went beyond campaign banter and suggested his disappointment that his old rival Douglas, now the most powerful member of the United States Senate, was 'a giant,' while Lincoln remained one of the 'common mortals.'"[5]

Donald believes Lincoln was essentially a passive man. This may have been an unfortunate choice of words. Passivity does not equal sloth or laziness. Donald means Lincoln had a fatalism that led him to believe events were foreordained by God or necessity. Donald explains, "From Lincoln's fatalism derived some of his most lovable traits: his compassion, his tolerance, his willingness to overlook mistakes. That belief did not, of course, lead him to lethargy or dissipation. Like thousands of Calvinists who believed in predestination, he worked indefatigably for a better world—for himself, for his family, and for his nation." Whether Lincoln was passive or not is debatable, but Donald does have quotes from Lincoln and those who knew him best who remarked on this aspect of his personality. He places much importance on a quote Lincoln made to a Kentuckian about slavery: "I Claim not to have controlled events, but confess plainly that events have controlled me."⁶ It is, in fact, the frontispiece to the book

Donald sees the reinforcement of Fort Sumter as an example of Lincoln's passivity affecting his presidential decisions. Commenting on the various controversies historians have debated, he states, "None of these able scholars has, in my opinion, given enough attention to Lincoln's newness to Washington, his inexperience as an administrator, and his fatigue after his exhausting journey and inauguration. Nor has Lincoln's essential passivity, his preference to react to events rather than to take the initiative, been sufficiently stressed."⁷

Lincoln is sure to remain the biography most scholars refer to for some time. It has, in large part, replaced Benjamin Thomas's *Abraham Lincoln: A Biography* as the standard life of Lincoln.⁸ What makes this Pulitzer Prize–winning book such a good read is the depth of knowledge Donald brings to the subject as well as his great storytelling ability. The Lincoln community was lucky to have had such a distinguished figure as Donald, and *Lincoln* is his greatest gift to that community.

NOTES

1. See David Herbert Donald, *Lincoln's Herndon* (New York: Da Capo, 1989).
2. David Herbert Donald, *Lincoln* (New York: Simon & Schuster, 1995), 14.
3. Ibid., 142–61, 149.
4. Ibid., 108, 108, 613; see Ruth Painter Randall, *Mary Lincoln: Biography of a Marriage* (Boston: Little, Brown & Co., 1953); and William H. Herndon and Jesse W. Weik, *Herndon's Life of Lincoln* (New York: Da Capo, 1983).
5. Donald, *Lincoln,* 228, 163.
6. Ibid., 15; Abraham Lincoln to Albert Hodges, April 4, 1864, as quoted in ibid., 11.
7. Donald, *Lincoln,* 645.
8. See Benjamin P. Thomas, *Abraham Lincoln: A Biography* (New York: Modern Library, 1968).

Abraham Lincoln: From Skeptic to Prophet

AUTHOR: Wayne C. Temple
PUBLISHED: 1995
GENRE: Psychology and Religion

A LINCOLN book that has new information and primary sources is a valuable find. For one to be full of this type of material is remarkable. Wayne C. Temple's *Abraham Lincoln: From Skeptic to Prophet* combines illustrations, photographs, and the actual religious material Lincoln read and heard in his lifetime with sober analysis. The result is a one-of-a-kind Lincoln study.

The book is an attractive one. It has many wonderful drawings from Lloyd Ostendorf. These include a drawing discussing religion with a minister and the charming cover of the Lincoln family at church. The book also includes photographs of obscure Lincoln sites, like the grave of Lincoln's grandmother Bersheba and the church where Lincoln's son Willie's funeral service was held. These photographs are simply not available in other sources. The book is laid out in chapters with names from books of the Bible. For example, Lincoln's early life is "Genesis," and his funeral is "Lamentations." This novel way of organizing the book adds to its warmth and originality.[1]

As the title makes clear, Temple sees the young Lincoln as skeptical in religious matters. But Temple finds nothing unusual in this: "Countless thousands of developing striplings have gone through the same period of doubting. For example, at the age of fifteen summers, Robert Browning—who later won wide renown as a famous poet—militantly challenged, publicly, the whole basis of Christianity. And yet, in due time, he regained his belief in God and later presented his own son for baptism."[2] Lincoln's questioning of belief, while in his twenties in New Salem, might have shocked the pious but was not unheard-of.

Temple gives a large amount of the credit for Lincoln's move away from skepticism to Rev. James Smith, the minister of the First Presbyterian Church in Springfield. Smith, a native of Scotland, wrote an apologetic tome for Christianity called *The Christian's Defense*. Like Lincoln, Smith as a youth had turned away from religion. Hearing a moving sermon one day, Smith converted to Christianity. His book was an answer to all his old doubts. Lincoln encountered the book while visiting his in-laws in Kentucky in the 1840s. Temple writes, "Lincoln supposedly declared that the author's argument had forced 'him to change his views about the Christian religion.'" He was so impressed with it that he brought it back to Springfield and arranged a meeting with Smith through a mutual friend, Thomas Lewis.[3]

The death of Edward, Lincoln's second son, brought Lincoln closer to Smith. According to Temple, "In the 'seasons of sorrow' which followed this soul-searching event, Dr. Smith moved even closer to the distraught Lincolns and 'administered to them those consolations which the Gospel of the Son of God can alone communicate.'" Lincoln and Mary soon became regular attendants at Smith's church. Did Smith convert Lincoln to orthodox Christianity? Probably not, but because he shared a similar skeptical background, he made Lincoln see religion could be gained on reason.[4]

There are a number of religious rituals printed throughout the book. One can read what exactly was said at Lincoln's Episcopal wedding and at Mary Todd Lincoln's funeral. Temple reprinted what most books simply mentioned. One gets a better feel for the sadness at the funeral in his account because the entire eulogy of Mary is there for the reader. The most moving part is reading of how the Reverend James Armstrong Reed compared Lincoln and Mary to two trees he had seen in the mountains. They had grown entwined with each other over the years. Lightning struck the taller one, and it died. Reed goes on to say, "The other apparently uninjured had survived for some years but it was evident from the appearance of its leaves that it too was now quite dead. It had lingered in fellowship with its dead companion, but the shock was too much for it. In their sympathetic fellowship and union, both trees suffered from the same calamity."[5] A more sympathetic and poetic appraisal of Mary after the assassination has never been given.

In the final analysis, Temple comes to see Lincoln as a "monotheist." He concludes, "As we have seen, rarely did he mention Jesus Christ except as a historical figure. It would seem the Trinity meant little to Lincoln. God was the one to whom he prayed; He was the one true God that revealed things to him." Temple compares Lincoln to Thomas Jefferson and Benjamin Franklin. His beliefs were similar to theirs, but Lincoln went further. He believed God controlled events on earth directly, while Jefferson and Franklin deistically believed God did not interfere in the affairs of men.[6]

Temple has spent a lifetime researching Lincoln, and this book shows his efforts have paid off. Temple's assessment of Lincoln's religious views is compelling. Lincoln was no atheist, but Temple believes whether he was a Christian or not is unknowable. In some ways, it depends on one's definition of *Christian*. Either way, Lincoln was a religious man who took God and spirituality seriously.

NOTES

1. Wayne C. Temple, *Abraham Lincoln: From Skeptic to Prophet* (Mahomet, Ill.: Mayhaven Publishing, 1995), 158, cover, 8, 173, xi.
2. Ibid., 15.
3. Ibid., 38–40, 40.
4. Ibid., 41, 38.
5. Ibid., 29–32, 400–408; Reverend Reed as quoted in ibid., 401.
6. Temple, 371, 371.

An Oral History of Abraham Lincoln: John G. Nicolay's Interviews and Essays

AUTHOR: Michael Burlingame, editor
PUBLISHED: 1996
GENRE: Reminiscences

I T WOULD be difficult to think of anyone more loyal to Lincoln than his secretary, John Nicolay. Nicolay and his assistant, John Hay, set out to write the "official" biography of their boss. They had the blessing of Robert Todd Lincoln, who allowed them sole access to his father's papers. To supplement this source, Nicolay conducted interviews in both Springfield and Washington with those who knew Lincoln. When it came time to write the biography, the interviews were hardly used. It may have been because the material might have embarrassed Lincoln's memory or angered Robert Todd Lincoln, who controlled the papers Nicolay so needed. He may also have had an innate distrust of the faulty memories of people interviewed.[1]

This material has been rescued from obscurity by Lincoln scholar Michael Burlingame, who has made a habit of making valuable material like this available to the public. In *An Oral History of Abraham Lincoln: John G. Nicolay's Interviews and Essays*, he organizes the interviews as taking place in either Washington or Springfield. To round out the book, he also includes some other interviews and short essays Nicolay wrote. Like any Burlingame book, he provides a wealth of information and sources in his notes, which, taken by themselves alone, would make this book valuable.[2]

The first interview in the book is one Nicolay had with former Illinois senator O. H. Browning. Browning drops a bombshell about the Lincoln-Todd courtship that challenges the accepted story. He introduces a third person into the troubled courtship, Matilda Edwards, who was a cousin of Lincoln's eventual in-laws. He recalls, "Mr. Lincoln became very much attached to her (Miss Matilda Edwards), and finally fell desperately in love with her, and proposed to her, but she rejected him. Douglas also fell in love with and proposed to her, and she rejected him also." The standard view of the courtship was that either Lincoln was unsure he could support Mary or her family objected. Browning's interview shows this might not be the case at all. One might be tempted to easily dismiss Browning's statements as idle gossip, but he appears to have first-hand knowledge. He states, "In those times I was at Mr. Edwards' a great deal, and Miss Todd used to sit down with me, and talk to me sometimes till midnight, about this affair of hers with Mr. Lincoln. In these conversations I think it came out, that Mr. Lincoln had perhaps on one occasion told Miss Todd that he loved Matilda Edwards, and no doubt his conscience was greatly worked up by the supposed pain and injury which this avowal had inflicted upon her."[3] One may still reject Browning's version, but he is a serious person not given to lying.

Robert Todd Lincoln provides an anecdote showing the extent Lincoln was willing to take personal responsibility to end the war. After the battle of Gettysburg, Robert E. Lee was fortified on the Potomac, waiting for his engineers to rebuild the bridge across the river so he could escape to Virginia. George G. Meade was drawn up to attack Lee. Robert recalls, "My father then said that he at once sent an attack order to Gen. Meade (I do not recollect that he told me whether the order was telegraphic or by messenger) directing him to attack Lee's army with all his force immediately, and that if he was successful in the attack he might destroy the order, but if he was unsuccessful he might preserve it for his vindication." Much is made of Lincoln's ambition, but here he was selflessly willing to allow the blame to fall on his shoulders if the attack was a failure because he saw the chance to end the bloodshed.[4]

John Hay relates some of the memorable events in Lincoln's journey to Washington as president-elect in an essay included in the book. The most humorous incident is when Lincoln gave his inaugural speech to Robert in a carpetbag. Robert had carelessly given it to a hotel clerk. Nicolay states, "A look of stupefaction passed over the countenance of Mr. Lincoln, and visions of that Inaugural in all the next morning's newspapers floated through his imagination. Without a word he opened the door of his room, forced the way through the crowded corridor down to the office, where, with a single stride of his long legs, he swung himself across the clerk's counter, behind which a small mountain of carpetbags of all colors had accumulated." Nicolay remembers how Lincoln picked each one up until he found one that his key fit. Luckily, his inaugural had not been touched, but he didn't leave the responsibility to Robert to carry it again.[5]

The material Burlingame presents is of the highest quality because Nicolay interviewed many substantial Lincoln friends and associates. His unquestionable loyalty to Lincoln gave him access others would not have had. Some of the interviews question long-held assumptions, such as the Lincoln-Todd courtship. This book is also proof new Lincoln material can be found if one looks hard enough, and Burlingame has never shied away from doing that.

NOTES

1. See John G. Nicolay and John Hay, *Abraham Lincoln: A History,* 10 vols. (New York: Century, 1890). This biography is wholly eulogistic and spends a lot of time on the history of the period rather than Lincoln. Michael Burlingame, ed., *An Oral History of Abraham Lincoln: John G. Nicolay's Interviews and Essays* (Carbondale: Southern Illinois University Press, 1996), xiv, xvi.
2. Burlingame, vii–viii, 123–58.
3. O. H. Browning, June 17, 1875, in ibid., 1, 2.
4. Robert Todd Lincoln, January 5, 1885, in ibid., 88–89.
5. John G. Nicolay, "Some Incidents in Lincoln's Journey from Springfield to Washington" in ibid., 109–10.

With Charity for All: Lincoln and the Restoration of the Union

AUTHOR: William C. Harris
PUBLISHED: 1997
GENRE: Presidency

ONE OF the great mysteries of the Civil War is what would have happened with the Reconstruction of the South had Lincoln lived. The revisionist view held that Lincoln would have acted exactly like Andrew Johnson, while the newer view is that Lincoln would have aligned himself with the Radical Republicans and initiated a vigorous Reconstruction policy. William C. Harris's *With Charity for All: Lincoln and the Restoration of the Union* argues for a middle ground.[1]

In Harris's view, Lincoln's actions would have been dictated by events. He writes, "According to the president, the pace of reconstruction would vary with the military and political circumstances in each state; he did not believe that a rigid rule should or could be applied for the South as a whole, a point Lincoln made both in his Proclamation of Amnesty and Reconstruction and in his April 11, 1865, address on reconstruction, delivered three days before his assassination." Lincoln had to keep his wartime coalition together, and being rigid or ideological could have jeopardized it.[2]

Harris believes that faint outlines of what Lincoln's philosophy of Reconstruction was are discernible. He concludes, "Lincoln favored a large measure of self-reconstruction, a position that owed a great deal to the nineteenth-century American commitment to local self-government as the cornerstone of republicanism and the nation's federal system of government." Lincoln also assumed that such a policy would serve the practical purpose of luring the Southerners back to the Union by assuring them Washington would not be dictating to them. Lincoln was very loyal to any Southerners who did return to the Union. He supported them wholeheartedly and did not quibble too much with what they were doing in their reconstructed governments as long as they embraced union and emancipation. Harris feels had Lincoln not done so it would have seemed a betrayal to him.[3]

Each area occupied by advancing Federal troops is covered, and Harris does an excellent job of documenting the twists and turns of local politics in each state. Lincoln's experience with North Carolina is instructive and probably did much to shape his views on Reconstruction. The Outer Banks of North Carolina were occupied early in the war, but the interior of the state remained in Confederate hands. Lincoln appointed conservative Edward Stanley as military governor. Lincoln hoped he could get an early start in the state's reconstruction. Stanley was a poor choice and managed to alienate many potential Unionists by his attempts to stifle any antislaveryism. Many boycotted the elections he held, and Lincoln eventually suspended him as governor. Lincoln had learned a valuable lesson. Harris thinks, "The president's unhappy experience with Stanley and the unwanted conflict with Radical Republicans over the quasi-civil regime in North Carolina contributed to his failure to send another military governor to the state. Lincoln preferred to wait for more substantial evidence of returning loyalty, coupled with emancipation sentiment, before encouraging a new reconstruction effort in North Carolina." In other words, Lincoln realized any new government could not be imposed by Washington; in order to succeed it must have some public support.[4]

Would Lincoln have continued a "hands-off" policy after the war? Harris feels it is doubtful: "It is inconceivable that Abraham Lincoln, despite his wartime reluctance to dictate to loyal Southern governments, would have permitted events to take the calamitous course that followed under Johnson. This war president's confidence in the returning loyalty of Southerners would have been sorely tested after the war by reports of defiance coming from the South and repeated by many Northern Democrats." A Lincoln who worked hard to have the ballot given to black soldiers would not have stood idly by while the Southern states enacted "black codes," and a president who made emancipation and union equal goals of the war would not have allowed a quasi-slavery to be introduced. Harris is right when he concludes, "Though Southern Unionists had demonstrated no important support for black rights, particularly political equality, they could hardly have failed to follow Lincoln's entreaties on fundamental rights for blacks. The consequence of losing the president's support would have been too great for Southern loyalists to risk defying his wishes."[5]

This book is the most comprehensive treatment of Lincoln and Reconstruction. Other books have usually focused on specific cases such as Louisiana. Each state had different circumstances, and Lincoln acted accordingly. The picture that emerges is a more nuanced view of Lincoln's role in Reconstruction. It is not simply a question of whether Lincoln was a conservative or a Radical; he doesn't fit neatly into either category. He held some beliefs sacred, including union and emancipation, but he saw there were different ways to ensure both. Lincoln's pragmatism was one of his strongest assets, and it is a tragedy the country never got to see him apply it to the riddle of Reconstruction.

NOTES

1. For the best representation of the respective views, see James G. Randall, *Lincoln the Liberal Statesman* (New York: Dodd, Mead & Co., 1947); and LaWanda Cox, *Lincoln and Black Freedom: A Study of Presidential Leadership* (Columbia: University of South Carolina Press, 1981).
2. William C. Harris, *With Charity for All: Lincoln and the Restoration of the Union* (Lexington: University Press of Kentucky, 1997), 2.
3. Ibid., 9, 9.
4. Ibid., 61, 71.
5. Ibid., 274, 275.

Lincoln's Photographs: A Complete Album

AUTHOR: Lloyd Ostendorf
PUBLISHED: 1998
GENRE: The Lincoln Image

L LOYD OSTENDORF was one of the foremost authorities on Lincoln photographs. Throughout his life he collected, cataloged, and classified photographs. He also made many beautiful drawings of Lincoln and his family in various scenes. He even drew a composite picture of what Lincoln's mother, Nancy Hanks, may have looked like. The Lincoln image was something that obviously fascinated him. One can sense his enthusiasm as he writes, "His is a fascinating face, one that attracts people, whether he appears homely to some, or handsome to others, a face singularly unique; and a face interesting from every angle. His features were coarse and angular—toughened by frontier life and the set-backs and tragedies he experienced. . . . His photos show a wonderful face—a good and manly face to study. It shows so much power and sheer magnetism—one can almost, but not quite, know the man behind it."[1]

In 1963 he published *Lincoln in Photographs: An Album of Every Known Pose*.[2] After the publication of that book, he found more Lincoln photographs. In 1998 Ostendorf published a similar book and expanded it to include many of Lincoln's family and associates. Though the books are similar, *Lincoln's Photographs: A Complete Album* is different in scope and can be considered a new work.

In order for the reader to have ready access to photographs, Ostendorf classifies them with an *O* and a corresponding number, so the first photograph taken of Lincoln is O-1. He copied this technique from the pioneer of Lincoln photographic studies, Fredrick Hill Meserve, who labeled his photographs with an M. The photographs are usually arranged in chronological order, but because new photographs were found and others redated, the numbers do not always match the order in which they were taken. At the end of the book, he reprints the photographs in numerical order to the total of 130.[3]

Many of the photographs of Lincoln are familiar images. Ostendorf brings new life to them by putting them in the context of their time and technology. Lincoln had his first photograph taken in 1846 when he was elected to Congress. Surprisingly, the next one was not taken for eleven years. Almost all of the photographs are from the last seven years of his life when he gained national prominence. Ostendorf labels the images taken with multiple lenses with letters. These photographs were used for stereoscopes, which would give the viewer a three-dimensional effect. The stereoscope was popular in the day, and many wanted to have a card of Lincoln in their collection.[4]

A couple of points stand out when viewing these images. Many of the Lincoln photographs are very similar. This is not surprising, since one sitting produced many poses. Sometimes it is merely a matter of Lincoln moving his arm slightly. Also, some of the newly discovered photographs were taken from such a distance that Lincoln is barely visible. It is little wonder they escaped detection.[5]

O-130 deserves special mention. It is supposedly a long-lost photograph of Lincoln in death. Only one photograph of Lincoln in death has been thought to be in existence (O-119). It was taken from a balcony, so Lincoln's corpse is hard to see. Ostendorf claims O-130 is a close-up of Lincoln taken clandestinely on April 16, 1865. The photograph shows a peaceful Lincoln with his eyes closed. If true, this is an astounding find. Unfortunately, O-130 is too good to be true. Lincoln iconography expert Harold Holzer has shown it to be just a retouched image of another Lincoln photograph. It may have been a case of Ostendorf's enthusiasm getting the better of him.[6]

There are many photographs of Lincoln's family. Mary is well documented, as are her sons. The most tantalizing photograph is one purported to be Edward Lincoln, the Lincolns' second child, who died at age three. It shows a "sweet-faced" boy staring earnestly at the camera. No image of the boy was thought to be in existence. Supposedly, the photograph had lain forgotten in a drawer of one of the custodians of the Lincoln tomb for decades. Is this Eddie Lincoln or another find too good to be true? Time will tell.[7]

Ostendorf adds some photographs that had been thought to be Lincoln but are now known to be otherwise. The most famous is the "Hanover Junction Lincoln." This is a photograph of a bearded man with a top hat at a station Lincoln passed on his way to Gettysburg. By blowing up the image of the man, Ostendorf shows it could not be Lincoln because the facial features and body type do not match. It is one of many examples of people "finding" Lincoln in photographs where the image is unclear.[8]

The completeness of this volume makes it the essential tool of reference for Lincoln photographs. Ostendorf's legacy is his dedication to the preservation and interpretation of the Lincoln image. This book and his wonderful art will be treasured for as long as Lincoln is studied.

NOTES

1. For the Nancy Hanks image, see cover of H. Donald Winkler, *The Women in Lincoln's Life* (Nashville: Rutledge Hill Press, 2001); Lloyd Ostendorf, *Lincoln's Photographs: A Complete Album* (Dayton: Rockywood Press, 1998), 3.
2. Lloyd Ostendorf, *Lincoln in Photographs: An Album of Every Known Pose* (Dayton: Morningside: 1963).
3. Ostendorf, *Lincoln's Photographs*, ix–x, 381–417.
4. Ibid., 4–5, 6–7, 83.
5. See, e.g., ibid., 132–35 (O-71 and O-72); see, e.g., ibid., 372 (O-129).
6. Ibid., 374; Harold Holzer in speech delivered at Lincoln Forum V in Gettysburg, November 2000.
7. Ostendorf, 298–301, 364–65.
8. Ibid., 292–93; see ibid., 289–91 for other examples.

Herndon's Informants: Letters, Interviews, and Statements About Abraham Lincoln

AUTHORS: Douglas L. Wilson and
Rodney O. Davis, editors
PUBLISHED: 1998
GENRE: Reminiscences

L INCOLN SCHOLARS owe an enormous debt of gratitude to William Herndon. His efforts in collecting information about Lincoln's life before he became president have made much of Lincoln biography possible. Without him, we would know next to nothing about Lincoln's first thirty years. Where Herndon has been controversial is in his interpretation of this information. His views have been questioned by scholars such as Ruth Randall and Jean Baker, primarily because of his negative view of Mary Todd Lincoln. In order to rebut what he has said, they have attacked his credibility. The unfortunate result of all this was the valuable material he collected lay unused and unanalyzed for decades.[1]

Thankfully, Douglas L. Wilson and Rodney O. Davis have given us all this material, unfiltered, in *Herndon's Informants: Letters, Interviews, and Statements About Abraham Lincoln*. One can now make up one's own mind. Before this book, Herndon's notes and interviews were available in the Library of Congress on microfilm. Certain copies were also available in some libraries. The general reader had access to them only through the sometimes selective quoting of Lincoln scholars. Wilson and Davis have completed the painstaking effort of interpreting this sometimes illegible material and putting it in an easily digestible form. They wisely do not attempt to correct grammar or spelling; they leave the material exactly as Herndon wrote it.[2]

Reading this large tome cover to cover is well worth the effort. The people most intimate with Lincoln recall his life and character. Lincoln's stepmother gives a touching remembrance of him shortly after the assassination. She recalled to Herndon in an interview, "I saw him Every year or two—He was here—after he was elected President of the US. (Here the old lady stopped—turned around & cried—wiped her eyes and proceeded). . . . He was dutiful to me always—he loved me truly I think. I had a son John who was raised with Abe Both were good boys, but I must say—both now being dead that Abe was the best boy I Ever saw or Ever Expect to see. . . . Abe and his father are in Heaven I have no doubt, and I want to go there—go where they are—God bless Abe."[3]

There is a lot of valuable material about Lincoln's days in New Salem. James Short recalls the first time he ever saw Lincoln: "Mr. L at this time was about 22 years of age; appeared to be as tall as he ever became, and slimmer than of late years. He had on at the time a blue cotton round about coat, stoga shoes, and pale blue casinet pantaloons which failed to make the connection with either coat or socks, coming about three inches below the former and an inch or two above the latter." Short remembers a virile yet prudent man during those days: "Mr. L was very fond of out door recreations & sports, and excelled in them. He lifted 1000 pounds of shot by main strength. He never played cards, nor drank, Nor hunted."[4]

It is clear from reading this book, Lincoln was skilled and interested in politics from an early age. His close relative John Hanks offers evidence Lincoln was interested in politics as a teenager: "He often for amusement for his play fellows—neighbors and friends made quite good stump speeches when between the ages of 15 & 20." Barely literate J. Rowan Herndon, who knew Lincoln as a young man in New Salem, wrote a letter to Herndon recounting his memories of a twenty-five-year-old Lincoln campaigning: "During harvest there was some 20 men in the field he got his Diner and went out to the field where the men ware at wort i gave him & entroduction and the Boys said that they Could not vote for a man unless he Could make a hand well Said he Boys if that is all i am sure of your votes he took hold of the Cradle Led the way all the Round with Perfect ease the Boys was satisfide and I dont think he Lost a vote in the Croud."[5]

It is also clear that Lincoln was an enigma even to those who knew him well. Fellow lawyer and friend Leonard Swett wrote to Herndon, "I would like to have you write me what the skeleton was with Lincoln. What gave him that peculiar melancholy? What cancer had he inside? You may send it by express and as soon as I read it, I will express it back to you. I always thought there was something but never knew what." One of Lincoln's most important political associates, David Davis, could truthfully write, "He was the most reticent—Secretive man I Ever Saw."[6]

Herndon's Informants has been a godsend to scholars. Wilson and Davis contributed significantly to the rise in quantity and quality of Lincoln scholarship. This book will take its place with *The Collected Works of Abraham Lincoln* as an essential tool for any Lincoln biographer.[7]

NOTES

1. See Ruth Painter Randall, *Mary Lincoln: Biography of a Marriage* (Boston: Little, Brown & Co., 1953), and Jean H. Baker, *Mary Todd Lincoln: A Biography* (New York: W. W. Norton, 1987).
2. Douglas L. Wilson and Rodney O. Davis, eds., *Herndon's Informants: Letters, Interviews, and Statements About Abraham Lincoln* (Urbana: University of Illinois Press, 1998), xxiv, xxv.
3. Sarah Bush Lincoln to William Herndon, September 8, 1865, in ibid., 108.
4. James Short to William Herndon, July 7, 1865, in ibid., 72, 73.
5. John Hanks to William Herndon, June 13, 1865, in ibid., 43; J. Rowan Herndon to William Herndon, May 28, 1865, in ibid., 8.
6. Leonard Swett to William Herndon, February, 14, 1866, in ibid., 214; David Davis to William Herndon, September 20, 1866, in ibid., 348.
7. See Roy P. Basler, ed., *The Collected Works of Abraham Lincoln,* 8 vols. and index (New Brunswick: Rutgers University Press, 1953).

Honor's Voice: The Transformation of Abraham Lincoln

AUTHOR: Douglas L. Wilson
PUBLISHED: 1998
GENRE: Prepresidential Years

S OME WOULD call Douglas L. Wilson a neo-Herndonian. He probably would not disagree with this assessment. Nobody has done more to resurrect the reputation of Lincoln's third law partner. Wilson's work on Herndon is impressive. Both he and Rodney Davis published an authoritative version of the interviews and letters Herndon collected over the years concerning Lincoln's early life. It was this work that led Wilson to write *Honor's Voice: The Transformation of Abraham Lincoln,* a book that seeks to reinterpret Lincoln's life as a young man. The book covers the period from when he left home at age twenty-one until he married Mary Todd at age thirty-three.[1]

Wilson opens the book with an exhaustive appraisal of Lincoln's famed wrestling match with Jack Armstrong at New Salem. He recounts how various biographers both added and subtracted from the story. By going back to the actual accounts by eyewitnesses, he comes to a decision of what is the most likely series of events. Wilson sees the betting done by the supporters of each to be the decisive factor. It seems Lincoln wrestled Armstrong in a scientific match that was more a test of strength than anything. Lincoln was winning, so Armstrong fouled him by quickly yanking his leg, causing him to fall. Lincoln took this in good humor, but something else quickly got his ire. Wilson writes, "Lincoln's reported anger and defiance would seem to have been directed not so much toward Armstrong as toward those who would construe his being illegally thrown as a defeat, a matter of some consequence since it entailed the forfeiture of the bets placed on him."[2] Lincoln's standing up for those who bet on him to the point of willingness to fight for them is what gained the admiration of those who watched.

Some might object that too much time is spent on an unimportant wrestling match. Wilson admits it was not a "turning point" in Lincoln's life, but it was important in the short run because he gained valuable friends who would support him in his stay at New Salem. Wilson is more interested in using the match as an example of how Lincoln biography works. Many simply copy what goes before without looking at the original sources.[3]

The two chapters on Lincoln's courtship with Mary Todd are nothing less than a wholesale rewriting of the event. Wilson rejects the notion Lincoln broke off his engagement with Mary Todd on the "fatal first" of January 1841. The traditional view is that Lincoln doubted his ability to support Mary and thus ended their courtship. Wilson sees it much differently. In his view, Lincoln was involved with Mary only superficially and toward the end of 1840 realized he did not love her. Matilda Edwards's arrival on the scene convinced him of it. He quickly fell in love with the beautiful and kind Matilda. Mary grew furious and told Lincoln he was honor-bound to marry her. Lincoln felt horrible about treating a woman so poorly. On top of this, his best friend, Joshua Speed, was interested in Matilda as well. All of this led to Lincoln's emotional breakdown.[4]

It is hard to abandon the long-held view of the matter and embrace Wilson's. There is a temptation to dismiss his account as being too fantastic, yet he offers a good deal of evidence for it. He is absolutely right; historians have ignored the many references to Matilda Edwards in the matter. The standard reason used is that Mary's sister quoted Matilda as saying Lincoln never tried to court her. That may be accurate, but they leave out this important passage in the very same interview: "In his lunacy he declared he hated Mary and loved Miss Edwds. This is true, yet it was not his real feelings. A crazy man hates those he loves when at himself."[5] Even if one rejects much of Wilson's re-creation of the events, it is no longer possible to simply sweep Matilda under the rug.

Biographers usually assume that it was the near duel between Lincoln and James Shields that brought Lincoln and Mary together again. Once again Wilson shows this assumption is not supported by the facts. He feels the reunion happened after the duel through the intervention of friends, and what ultimately caused Lincoln to finally wed Mary was his sense of honor. Wilson writes, "To judge from his letters and his behavior during this period, Lincoln had been suffering from a loss of confidence and the consequent 'gem' of his character, his ability to keep his mind made up." This view is not the majority, but it is a plausible scenario.[6]

Wilson's Lincoln is one who undergoes much anguish, but he emerges at the end of the book as one who is ready for the great tasks ahead of him. Wilson concludes, "The world found out about Lincoln's hard-won resolution, for his rock-solid ability to keep his resolves once they were made would undergird his performance as president. And that would make all the difference."[7]

NOTES

1. See Douglas L. Wilson and Rodney O. Davis, eds., *Herndon's Informants: Letters, Interviews, and Statements About Abraham Lincoln* (Urbana: University of Illinois Press, 1998).
2. Douglas L. Wilson, *Honor's Voice: The Transformation of Abraham Lincoln* (New York: Knopf, 1998), 19–52, 36, 37; the title of this book comes from a line in Thomas Gray's "Elegy Written in a Country Churchyard" (1751).
3. Wilson, *Honor's Voice,* 49.
4. Ibid., 195–264; the term *fatal first* comes from a letter Lincoln wrote his friend Joshua Speed in 1842, quoted in ibid., 257.
5. Elizabeth Todd Edwards to William Herndon in Wilson and Davis, 444; Matilda Edwards as quoted in Wilson, *Honor's Voice,* 225–26.
6. Wilson, *Honor's Voice,* 265–92, 290.
7. Ibid., 323.

Lincoln's Men: How President Lincoln Became a Father to an Army and a Nation

AUTHOR: William C. Davis
PUBLISHED: 1999
GENRE: Presidency

FROM TIME to time a Lincoln book appears that reminds us of the enormous personal appeal he had to so many. A book like this reminds one of why studying Lincoln is so rewarding. William C. Davis, a prolific Civil War author, was the perfect choice to write a book about the president's relationship with the rank and file of the Union army. Lincoln created an army from across the North that combined people from all sides of the political spectrum, but Davis shows in *Lincoln's Men: How President Lincoln Became a Father to an Army and a Nation* that in the end they became his army. Davis retells anecdote after anecdote highlighting the president's overwhelmingly positive interactions with his soldiers.

Lincoln had scant military service to his credit, a few months in the Black Hawk War in 1832, so he was not an experienced leader when it came to leading an army. A professional soldier might be expected to do better, but Lincoln had what many officers did not have. He had an uncanny ability to connect with people from all walks of life and a personal magnetism that inspired loyalty.[1]

The president needed to make that personal connection to the army. Davis writes, "From the very first, Lincoln never forgot the importance of showing himself to his volunteers, or of granting them as much access to him as the mounting pressure of the crisis allowed. He needed them, and he needed to have them behind him, and with them the uncountable men at home who might be required before the business was finished." Lincoln knew if the public thought he sympathized with the soldiers, they would be much more willing to volunteer and fight.[2]

The president had to keep an open-door policy. He once said, "This ready means of access is, I may say, under our form of government, the only link or cord which connects the people with the governing power." Davis sees Lincoln's access as having many benefits: "What Lincoln did not say was that every soldier who called, whether he left entirely satisfied or not, went away with an experience he would relive and retell for the rest of his life. More immediately, every soldier who felt that at least he had been given a fair hearing went back to his regiment a living ambassador for Lincoln." Word could be quickly spread that Lincoln was a man who listened to what the soldiers had to say.[3]

The election of 1864 shows the extent Lincoln was able to win over the soldiers. Davis analyzes the results: "In the armies he carried nearly eight votes out of ten, even though almost half of the soldiers had been Democrats before the war. In [William Tecumseh] Sherman's armies, where Lincoln was especially popular, he took 86 percent of the vote, and only one regiment, the Seventeenth Wisconsin, returned a Little Mac majority. In the Army of the Potomac, Lincoln wound up with seven out of ten votes." It is surprising Lincoln was able to do so well with the soldiers when he was running against a soldier himself. George B. McClellan was at one time extremely popular with the Army of the Potomac, an army he had done much to create, yet Lincoln was still able to soundly beat him even here.[4]

Davis does a particularly good job describing the feelings of anger and sadness many veterans felt about the assassination. He writes, "However they interpreted the loss, they all felt it deeply. 'No man, not even Grant himself, possesses the entire love of the army as did President Lincoln,' said a Wisconsin soldier. 'We mourn him not only as a President but as a man, for we had learned to love him.'" Many soldiers felt the need for vengeance against the South as a whole. Davis relates one frightening but telling quote from a soldier: "I have heard only one sentiment expressed, & it seems to be universal throughout the army. Woe to the South if this Army is compelled to pass through it again." Luckily, cooler heads prevailed and acts of vengeance were rare, but the soldiers' feelings for Lincoln made the potential for them quite real.[5]

As the veterans got older they cherished the memory of their fallen hero. Davis writes, "For generations after the war, until they themselves passed from the scene, the aging veterans carried with them their attachment to Father Abraham, often twisted, increasingly romanticized, and sometimes reduced to nothing more than senile fable. The important thing is not *what* they remembered accurately, but that they wanted to remember and the fact they clung so tenaciously to any recollection at all."[6] The Union soldiers would go on with their lives and become productive citizens, but Father Abraham was just too powerful an image to forget.

NOTES

1. William C. Davis, *Lincoln's Men: How President Lincoln Became a Father to an Army and a Nation* (New York: Free Press, 1999), 7–12.
2. Ibid., 31.
3. Abraham Lincoln as quoted in ibid., 130; Davis, 130.
4. Davis, 223.
5. Ibid., 243; Union soldier quoted in ibid., 242.
6. Davis, 251.

Abraham Lincoln: Redeemer President

AUTHOR: Allen C. Guelzo
PUBLISHED: 1999
GENRE: Biography

THIS BOOK is not so much a traditional biography as it is an intellectual biography. Allen C. Guelzo's *Abraham Lincoln: Redeemer President* is the first biography to focus on Lincoln as a man of ideas. After listing many of the intellectual currents that lay behind Lincoln's thought, Guelzo states, "Taking these as the principal guideposts for understanding Abraham Lincoln asks that we do something which virtually no modern biographer has managed to do, which is to read Lincoln seriously as a man of ideas. As Mark Neely has complained, Lincoln biography tends to travel either the road of personality-history . . . in which Lincoln's achievements are explained in terms of temperament or genealogy; or else the road of public-history."[1]

The first current of thought Guelzo analyzes is the Calvinism of Lincoln's parents and its possible effects on him. The central tenet of Calvinist thought was predestination. Predestination believed God had determined all events beforehand, and those who would be saved and would go to heaven were chosen by God before they were even born. While Lincoln rejected his parents' Calvinistic Baptist religion and never formally joined any church, Guelzo maintains the idea of predestination still permeated Lincoln's thoughts. He saw God or "necessity" shaping events.[2]

According to Guelzo, it was Lincoln's trouble with the implications of predestination that led him to his early religious skepticism.

"Predestination set the threshold of acceptability with God excep-
tionally high, and for those who could get over it, and be somehow
certain they were of the elect for whom Christ died, it gave 'the most
exulted ideas.' . . . But for those lacking the spiritual athleticism to
vault over that bar, it could trigger killing despair, 'gloomy apprehen-
sions . . . that they would ultimately be lost after all their fond hopes
to the contrary,' and a deep-seated and persistent melancholy." Lincoln could not reconcile eternal punishment with mankind lacking a
free will.[3]

Lincoln never rejected religion outright. As Guelzo writes, "And
yet Lincoln still believed that religion if not certain religious leaders
needed to play a public role in the formation of a Whiggish national
culture. The 'moral training' of evangelical religion and the 'hopes
and consolation of the Christian faith,' Lincoln wrote in 1863, were
the best cultural mechanisms for promoting 'elevated and sanctifying
influences.'" Lincoln's belief in the importance of morality to a society goes back to his Whig roots.[4]

Guelzo stresses Lincoln's attachment to the principles of the Whig
Party. The Whig Party was influenced heavily by the Protestant theology of the nineteenth century, which looked to the improvement of
men through government and morality. Guelzo states, "Every issue
Lincoln spoke for as a legislator—the railroads, land grants, tariffs—
and every rhetorical gesture, from his abusive early political journal-
ism to the refinement of the Gettysburg Address, was ungirded by his
unwavering allegiance to Whig ideology."[5]

Even as a Republican, Lincoln kept these ideas at the forefront of
his politics. In the Lincoln-Douglas debates he stressed the immoral-
ity of slavery. Guelzo describes his Democratic opponent's reaction:
"Douglas was aghast at Lincoln's proposal to turn a debate on public
policy into a forum on morality. Citizens and communities, in Douglas's lexicon, were simply individuals possessing the right to do as
they pleased with what property they pleased as a matter of choice,
and questions of whether the choices were moral or not were not the
business of anyone outside those communities."[6] Other books may
stress the moral nature of Lincoln's argument against slavery, but
Guelzo is the only writer to tie it to his Whig background.

Guelzo sees Thomas Jefferson as Lincoln's intellectual foil. While the assertion of equality in the Declaration of Independence was one of Lincoln's core beliefs, he parted ways with Jefferson on almost everything else. The difference was that "Lincoln glorified progress, middle-class individualism, and the opportunity for economic self-improvement which the new capitalist networks of the nineteenth century were opening up across the Atlantic world." Jefferson instead viewed a nation of self-sufficient farmers as the ideal. He once said, "Those who labour in the earth are the chosen people of God, if ever he had a chosen people, whose breasts he made his peculiar deposit of substantial and genuine virtue." The difference was, Lincoln had lived the life of a farmer as a young man, so he consequently had no romantic notions of the life. Jefferson, on the other hand, never actually toiled in the field himself. The hard labor was left to slaves. Ultimately, Lincoln's vision has won out and made America a world power.[7]

There is something to be said for Guelzo's approach to Lincoln biography. It is a breakaway from the traditional dichotomy of Lincoln the man versus Lincoln the public figure. The actual ideas that influenced Lincoln have been given scant attention. By delving into them, Guelzo has trailblazed a new area in Lincoln scholarship.

NOTES

1. Allen C. Guelzo, *Abraham Lincoln: Redeemer President* (Grand Rapids: Eerdmans, 1999), 19.
2. Ibid., 102–42.
3. Ibid., 37.
4. Ibid., 322, 154.
5. Ibid., 458.
6. Ibid., 225; see Henry V. Jaffa, *Crisis of the House Divided: An Interpretation of the Lincoln-Douglas Debates* (Chicago: University of Chicago Press, 1982).
7. Guelzo, 6; Thomas Jefferson as quoted in ibid., 6.

Don't Shoot That Boy! Abraham Lincoln and Military Justice

AUTHOR: Thomas P. Lowry
PUBLISHED: 1999
GENRE: Presidency

A FACET of the Lincoln story that has had enormous appeal over the years is his compassion and mercy for Union soldiers facing execution. The granting of clemency to these men is part of the Lincoln legend. Thomas P. Lowry takes a close look at the legend in *Don't Shoot That Boy! Abraham Lincoln and Military Justice*. To do this, he looks at more than five hundred previously neglected court-martial records. Employing quantitative analysis, he presents a highly original book about this aspect of Lincoln's presidency. Once again a Lincoln scholar has shown it is possible to find "new" Lincoln material.[1]

Lowry devotes chapters to the different types of offenders. He starts with officers and moves down to enlisted men. He also looks at the types of offensives, ranging in severity from murder to sleeping sentinels. In each chapter Lowry gives a brief summation of every case and what actions Lincoln took. He gives context to the decisions by telling the reader what was going on in the war at the time these cases reached Lincoln's desk, so the reader can understand Lincoln was not making decisions in a vacuum. The decisions Lincoln made could affect the war effort.[2]

There were competing forces affecting Lincoln. On one hand, he had to maintain discipline in the army; on the other, he had to please family members and politicians who demanded clemency for their constituents. Lowry sees Lincoln as torn between the two. "Whether Lincoln's inner moral compass was actuated more by genuine compassion, a wish to please his constituents, or by a natural reluctance to spill more blood than that already soaking in the ground of America, it was inevitable that he, in the dual role of Supreme Civilian and Commander in Chief, would find himself torn between stern duty and the hopes of redemption through clemency."[3]

The most common misdeed was desertion. During the Civil War, Union army desertions totaled over 250,000. The penalty for desertion was death by firing squad, but that figure shows this was not much of a deterrent. Lowry shows, too, that the Union high command was apt to recommend clemency. Often they would sentence a man to death and then recommend the president commute the sentence. "In 93 percent (93%) of the cases, the President overturned the original sentence of the court—but his actions did not fly in the face of the system. . . . Lincoln was in agreement with the general convening the court-martial 86 percent (86%) of the time." It may seem a strange system, but Lincoln was often following the advice of his officers when offering clemency. The difference between the two percentages represents the cases where Lincoln offered clemency on his own.[4]

When it came to murder or rape, Lincoln's penchant for mercy was severely tested. The percentages drop significantly in these areas. Of the sixteen murder cases to come before him, Lincoln commuted the death penalty in only eight, or 50 percent of them. Lowry sees a sterner Lincoln in this area. "What we learn about Lincoln in this study of murder cases is that his legendary 'compassion' was tempered by the need for justice. He hated intentional meanness and cruelty. In most (but not all) murder cases with those traits, he was quite willing that the defendant swing from a rope or face a firing squad."[5]

There is a certain egalitarianism to Lincoln's decisions. When speaking of high-ranking officers, Lowry finds, "Lincoln endorsed the sentences rendered against forty-one percent (41%) of them, while for crimes committed by lower-ranking officers, such as lieutenants, the figure is only twenty-four percent (24%). In the cases where enlisted men insulted or attacked their officers, Lincoln agreed with only eight (8%) of the sentences—a compelling difference! In brief, the higher the rank, the less the chance that Lincoln would extend clemency. If Lincoln had a bias it was against rank." These differences show Lincoln understood the difficulty of expecting a civilian army to act as a professional force, so he made allowances for the lower ranks.[6]

Lowry believes at the end of his study the Lincoln legend of mercy is well deserved. He concludes, "Lincoln looked for a chance to spare the nonviolent offender. He did not like crimes of meanness or cruelty, nor did he look kindly upon crimes against women, and, most vividly of all, he did not tolerate men who came into the Union seeking candidates for the job of killing Union men. But in nearly every other category, the legend of his compassion is not a legend at all, but truth." Lincoln did indeed distinguish between types of crimes, but Lowry thinks the numbers show "every man should have his chance. Lincoln's urge to remit was very real, but it was selective, not universal. Through these numbers, we can further comprehend the moral and political values which guided Lincoln through our nation's most terrible calamity."[7]

NOTES

1. Thomas P. Lowry, *Don't Shoot That Boy! Abraham Lincoln and Military Justice* (Mason City, Iowa: Savas Publishing, 1999), x.
2. Ibid., contents.
3. Ibid., 52.
4. John Y. Simon, foreword to ibid., iii; Lowry, 141–42.
5. Lowry, 181.
6. Ibid., 262.
7. Ibid., 263, 263.

On Hallowed Ground: Abraham Lincoln and the Foundations of American History

AUTHOR: John Patrick Diggins
PUBLISHED: 2000
GENRE: Historiography

J OHN PATRICK DIGGINS takes on some of the great "isms" of American intellectual history in *On Hallowed Ground: Abraham Lincoln and the Foundations of American History*. Marxism, republicanism, and pragmatism are the main alternatives America might have perused instead of the liberalism that has guided it since its inception. Diggins sees Lincoln as embodying the liberal tradition as well as being its greatest spokesman. The book's emphasis is not so much on Lincoln but rather on the intellectual tradition he advocated so forcibly.

Liberalism should not be confused with current-day Democratic politics. Diggins is quite clear on what *liberalism* means. "By the phrase 'Lockean liberalism,' I mean a body of ideas that regards matter and property, comprehended by a mind and conscience, as elementary and irreducible realities and views liberty and natural rights as the means by which happiness is pursued and freedom protected." This type of liberalism is the bedrock of Lincoln's political thought.[1]

Diggins also takes on a newer "ism." Multiculturalism believes that America cannot have a common creed or belief system because the nation is made up of too many diverse cultures and ethnic groups. The belief also carries the notion that the dominant European male viewpoint does not speak to oppressed groups within the nation. Diggins writes sadly, "Today we seem to have lost our capacity to be astonished when we are told that America is too radically diverse and multicultural to have its own defining principles."[2]

Since the African-American population has been the most marginalized in America, it would seem multiculturalism would speak to it. In the final chapter of the book, Diggins shows the liberal tradition has been embraced de facto by most black leaders. "For all the contemporary clamor over multiculturalism and diversity, it is remarkable to find black intellectual history steeped in liberalism that many of today's radical scholars refuse to acknowledge." He mentions Booker T. Washington, Frederick Douglass, Martin Luther King Jr., and others. These men often differed in the tactics to be used, but they based their ideas on the liberal tradition of America and did not look to a different culture for the answer. They simply wanted full participation in America's tradition.[3]

Marxism is the major alternative the book examines. Diggins finds a startling similarity between the antebellum South and the former Soviet Union. "Both the South and the Soviet Union denied the liberal principle that an individual exists for his or her own sake and not for the good of the 'organic society' or social 'solidarity.'" The slave was simply a means to an end. Marxism has not proved to be an attractive alternative to most Americans. Lincoln's emphasis on the Declaration of Independence, and his support of economic improvement by the individual, places him squarely against the Marxist tradition.[4]

Just as Marxism is the alternative of the Left, republicanism is the Right's alternative to the liberal tradition. This school of thought believes that before liberalism there was a philosophy that emphasized civic virtue over the individual's benefit. Some scholars have attempted to portray the American Revolution as a radical effort to go back to a simpler republican past. Diggins disagrees: "Had the Revolution been inspired by the principles of republicanism, one would expect the Declaration of Independence to have demanded a right to participate in politics in the name of public virtue—a subject upon which the document remained silent. Lincoln correctly interpreted the declaration as granting Americans the right to pursue a life of labor and industry." This is a failure to understand that the liberal tradition was present at the very founding of America. There was no time when republicanism reigned supreme, save in the wishful minds of some academics.[5]

The last of the great alternatives Diggins takes on is pragmatism. Pragmatism is the thought that we must experiment to find what works for the most people, and whatever that might be is therefore right. Diggins dismisses pragmatism as not a true political philosophy. Speaking of pragmatism he writes, "I concluded that America's one original contribution to the world of philosophy, pragmatism, taught us how to think and act, not what to think and believe; it rejected authority for methodology, logicality for experimentation, truth for technique. Pragmatism rested all knowledge on experience, on the premise that nothing could be known unless we engage the world and learn to cope." This was the path of Stephen A. Douglas, not of Lincoln.[6]

Diggins's book is a rich intellectual history of America. He ably defends the position that the ideals of Lincoln made America a great country. He demonstrates that while the alternatives have been fashionable at times, they've never had the staying power of liberalism. Diggins does an excellent job of showing Lincoln's thought as far from outdated; his ideas offer the best route any country could take, regardless of its ethnic or historical background.

NOTES

1. John Patrick Diggins, *On Hallowed Ground: Abraham Lincoln and the Foundations of American History* (New Haven: Yale University Press, 2000), xiv.
2. Ibid., xx.
3. Ibid., 275, 275.
4. Ibid., 200.
5. Ibid., 58.
6. Ibid., xiii.

A New Birth of Freedom: Abraham Lincoln and the Coming of the Civil War

AUTHOR: Henry V. Jaffa
PUBLISHED: 2000
GENRE: Presidency

WHEN *A New Birth of Freedom: Abraham Lincoln and the Coming of the Civil War* was published, it had been forty years since Henry V. Jaffa had written a Lincoln book. His 1959 *Crisis of the House Divided* is an acknowledged classic that challenged the then prevailing notion that Lincoln and Douglas were very similar in their political views. Jaffa's newer book may have been a long time coming, but his efforts have paid off in producing another essential Lincoln book. In his first book, he used the Lincoln-Douglas debates to probe Lincoln's thoughts on the nature of slavery and freedom. In the sequel, he uses Lincoln's First Inaugural Address as his skeleton key to understand Lincoln's thoughts about the nature of the American Union on the eve of the Civil War.[1]

The bulk of the First Inaugural Address is rarely quoted. It does lack the moving rhetoric of the Gettysburg Address, but Jaffa shows why it should not be dismissed so lightly. He argues throughout this book that it is one of the best speeches on the nature of the Union ever given. It effectively rebuts the views expressed in many of the more famous documents concerning the Union such as the Kentucky and Virginia Resolutions, which argue for a Union that must have as its first priority states' rather than individual rights.[2]

Lincoln's chief intellectual adversary in the book is John C. Calhoun, the great antebellum proponent of states' rights and nullification. This is an important contest, since so much of Confederate thought on secession was guided by Calhoun. Jaffa shows how Lincoln picked away at Calhoun's theories until there was nothing left. Lincoln could see they were based on faulty premises and logic.

Calhoun was guided by the notion that Jefferson had made a mistake by claiming "all men are created equal." Jaffa quotes an 1848 speech by Calhoun: "We now begin to experience the danger of admitting so great an error to have a place in our declaration of independence. For a long time it lay dormant; but in the process of time it began to germinate, and produce its poisonous fruits. It had strong hold on the mind of Mr. Jefferson, the author of that document, which caused him to take an utterly false view of the subordinate relation of the black to white race in the South." In Calhoun's mind, it wasn't the individual who was important but rather group interests.[3]

To deal with the fact the South was losing its preeminence from the growing power of the North, Calhoun formulated his notion of the concurrent majority. The idea would be that any minority group that was powerful enough could have a veto over the majority. This way the majority would have to respect the will of the minority, and the "tyranny of the majority" would be avoided. The idea was, if the majority could not function without the minority, its viewpoints would have to be respected. Calhoun saw the slave interest in the South becoming a minority over time, and this doctrine could act as a check against what he perceived as Northern aggression.

There are a number of flaws in this doctrine. Jaffa points out, "By the logic of his own theory, Calhoun would be required to grant each individual a veto upon every action of the government. . . . This absurdity is avoided only by restricting the concurrent majority to those groups or groupings that have the ability to endanger the self-preservation of the numerical majority so as not to compel it to grant the veto power." The Southern system has already taken away the slave's status as an individual, so Jaffa can say, "Thus it is not the natural right to self-preservation of every human individual that counts but only the rights of those groups . . . that have the power to control their own destinies. Hence the slave states constituted a minority, but the slaves did not."[4]

Echoing his earlier book, Jaffa points to the Declaration of Independence as the place from which Lincoln's rebuttal will come. "For Lincoln and the Founders, there was only one answer to the question of who ought to be counted among those whose consent was required for the just powers of government. That answer was given by the 'laws of nature and of nature's Gods,' whose premise was that 'all men are created equal.'" In Lincoln's mind, interests were not something that could be given rights. Only the individual had any claim to intrinsic rights, so any attempt to place the "rights" of a particular state over those of a person was a subversion of the intent of the Founders.[5]

A New Birth of Freedom is not a light read. It is a weighty book, but the effort pays off. Jaffa is undoubtedly one of the greatest thinkers to ever tackle the Lincoln theme. He gives so much to ponder and digest that his book will stay with the reader for some time to come.

NOTES

1. See Henry V. Jaffa, *Crisis of the House Divided: An Interpretation of the Issues in the Lincoln-Douglas Debates* (Chicago: University of Chicago Press, 1982).
2. Henry V. Jaffa, *A New Birth of Freedom: Abraham Lincoln and the Coming of the Civil War* (Lanham, Md.: Rowan & Littlefield, 2000), 37–57.
3. John C. Calhoun, 1848, as quoted in ibid., 212.
4. Jaffa, 438, 439.
5. Ibid., 439.

The Young Eagle: The Rise of Abraham Lincoln

AUTHOR: Kenneth J. Winkle
PUBLISHED: 2000
GENRE: Prepresidential Years

L INCOLN'S CLOSEST friend, Joshua Speed, once compared Lincoln's rise from humble beginnings to the White House to an eagle taking flight. Kenneth J. Winkle's *The Young Eagle: The Rise of Abraham Lincoln* takes a critical look at this rise and seeks to analyze it in the context of the social currents of the time. Winkle finds the usual retelling of the story too simplistic and wrong in many respects. "This 'log cabin myth' served Lincoln well in life but has forever haunted his posthumous reputation. Following his lead, biographers have reiterated the self-made myth, vastly overstating Lincoln's humble beginnings, denigrating his ancestry, impugning his parents' character, and questioning their legitimacy and even his own." By using the modern tools of social science, Winkle goes beyond the anecdotes and stories to the actual measurable conditions of Lincoln's life.[1]

This book bucks the neo-Herndonian trend of taking a harsh view of Lincoln's father and presents the most sympathetic picture of Thomas Lincoln since Louis Warren's in the 1920s. Winkle even writes glowingly of the hard years spent in Indiana. "Surrounded by relatives, neighbors, and friends, the Lincoln family felt economically secure. Their farm flourished, and they engaged in the kind of neighborly reciprocity that characterized the advancing frontier. A decade after arriving in Indiana, the Lincolns were farming about forty acres of land." Winkle might be understating the effect the many deaths of Lincoln's loved ones had on him during this time when he says, "From a perspective, however, his experience was unexceptional, even commonplace." This might be true, but for a nine-year-old that is small comfort.[2]

Winkle offers reasons why Thomas Lincoln's reputation for shift-lessness is unfairly earned. He writes that the changing economy of the time left the pioneer in a transitional state. Winkle writes, "As a transitional figure, therefore, Thomas could hardly help but seem unsure, even confused. After all, he inhabited the shifting zone between the two economic worlds, a pioneer of sorts on the fringe of both worlds but at home in neither. Part-time farmer and part-time craftsman, Thomas succeeded fully in neither world and therefore has been judged a failure in both."[3] In short, Thomas was a victim of circumstances beyond his control.

This changing economy may have been reflected in the friction between Lincoln and his father. Lincoln was coming of age in a time when he had more options than his father. The rise of the city, and the new range of choices in professions offered to sons of farmers, left their fathers with little power over them, since ownership of the land was not something they necessarily desired. Thomas may have been confused that Abe would not offer him obedience because he assumed Abe would want to inherit his farm.[4]

Abe's stepbrother John probably had his father's favor because he didn't partake in the newer economy and followed Thomas into farming. One of the sadder facts of Abe's life is there never was a reconciliation with his father. When Thomas was close to death, his stepson wrote Abe a message from his father: "he wonts me to tell your wife that he Loves hure & wants hur to prepare to meet him at ower Savours feet." The sad fact is, Thomas had never met Mary. Abe did go to visit his sick father, but it was a false alarm. When Thomas was really dying shortly after, Abe did not go. Winkle relates the pathetic end: "According to Johnston, Thomas Lincoln believed that God 'has a Crown of glory, prepared for him.' Five days later, Thomas died at age seventy-three. His son did not attend his funeral."[5]

By looking at Springfield's demographics, Winkle feels he can better explain the dynamics of Lincoln's courtship of Mary Todd. Not only was the economy in a period of transition, but so was the family. "With the decline in both parental authority and economic motivations for marrying, couples expected to cultivate an emotional intimacy during an extended period of betrothal." Lincoln's long courtship with Mary and its on-again, off-again quality was not all that unusual.[6]

These changes may also help to explain the tempestuous marriage of the two. "Above all, Abraham and Mary Lincoln approached their middle-class marriage from two opposing perspectives. When he married, Abraham Lincoln was just leaving the traditional folk economy in which he had been raised." Conversely, Winkle sees Mary as marrying down, since she was from the upper class. This is probably the weakest argument in the book because it fails to explain all of their problems and leaves out the factor of mental illness in favor of a purely sociological explanation.[7]

Winkle's book is the most thorough on the rise of Abraham Lincoln. The statistical analysis of the economics and demographics of Illinois in the first half of the nineteenth century helps the reader have a better understanding of the environment in which Lincoln was living. This does not, however, explain Lincoln's rise in and of itself but does give the most detailed description of its background.

NOTES

1. Kenneth J. Winkle, *The Young Eagle: The Rise of Abraham Lincoln* (Dallas: Taylor, 2000), ix, x.
2. See Louis A. Warren, *Lincoln's Parentage and Childhood: A History of the Kentucky Lincolns Supported by Documentary Evidence* (New York: Century, 1926); Winkle, 19, 14.
3. Winkle, 72.
4. Ibid., 72–73.
5. John D. Johnston to Abraham Lincoln, May 1849, as quoted in ibid., 144; Winkle, 145.
6. Winkle, 207.
7. Ibid., 223.

The Lincoln Enigma: The Changing Faces of an American Icon

AUTHOR: Gabor S. Boritt, editor
PUBLISHED: 2001
GENRE: Historiography

A S THE Lincoln theme entered a new century, there wasn't a better choice to collect and edit the latest scholarship than Gabor S. Boritt. The reason Boritt has so many books on this list is that he allows the different writers in his collections of essays to do what they do best. In many of the essays in *The Lincoln Enigma: The Changing Faces of an American Icon,* he has picked some of the top scholars in the field to showcase their area of expertise. Douglas Wilson writes on the young Lincoln. Jean Baker writes on the marriage of Lincoln and Mary Todd. Harold Holzer presents new Lincoln images. Some of the other scholars contributing essays include big names like David Herbert Donald, Robert V. Bruce, and Boritt himself.[1]

The most thoughtful essay in the book is by Robert Bruce. His "The Riddle of Death" takes a close look at Lincoln's ambition and finds a deeper reason to it than many would guess. Bruce concludes Lincoln did not believe in the traditional Christian doctrine of the afterlife, so he sought a different kind of immortality. "Lincoln's antidote for despair was the concept of immortality through remembrance, eternal consciousness by proxy in the mind of posterity. His desperate will to achieve this was a powerful force in his uncommonly absorbing ambition." Bruce does not see Lincoln as doing anything immoral to achieve this fame. What made Lincoln such a successful leader was his ambition tinged with genuine humanity toward others.[2]

The weakest essay is Jean Baker's "Mary and Abraham: A Marriage." Baker is a skilled apologist of Mary Todd Lincoln and provides much in the way of the social currents relating to courtship and marriage of the time. What she does not do is convincingly tie these currents to Mary, who as first lady did not live the typical nineteenth-century life. Baker sees as her chief adversaries writers such as Michael Burlingame and Douglas Wilson, who have shown rather convincingly in their own works that Mary's problems were very real and do not allow themselves to be explained away easily. She unfortunately follows the pattern of many of Mary's apologists by labeling all who are critical of Mary a priori haters of her and thus not to be trusted. She writes, "My response is that we have too many historians deciding that they don't like Mary Lincoln and with the extraordinary vehemence extrapolating their personal judgments onto the marriage." These two men are serious scholars, and their work deserves careful rebuttal, not personal psychoanalysis. Baker would have been better served to use her considerable talents to focus on Mary herself and try to connect her more firmly with the social currents of the time. Boritt was correct to include this essay, though, because it shows how wide the gulf has become in the interpretation of Mary.[3]

Douglas Wilson solidifies his reputation as the foremost authority on Lincoln's youth in "Young Man Lincoln." Here he presents a man unsure of himself in many ways. "We frequently hear that true champions are people who never doubt the eventuality of their own success. . . . In this light, it seems important to recognize that Abraham Lincoln, our greatest national hero, was apparently not such a person. He believed in himself, and that to an extraordinary degree, but his belief was balanced by a fearful conviction that even the noblest human aspirations and the worthiest efforts are subject to inscrutable contingencies and limitations." Wilson is right to often point out that it is assumed Lincoln's innate greatness made his election to the presidency inevitable, while the fact is, Lincoln himself had strong doubts.[4]

Harold Holzer uses his knowledge of Lincoln iconography to present a wide range of Lincoln images. They range from postal stamps to book jackets to kitschy lawn ornaments of Lincoln. Holzer calls the most unusual statue of Lincoln "Dying Colossus." It is a sixty-two-foot-high steel-and-fiberglass statue. It was dedicated in 1969 but never found a home and wandered across the country. A campground bought the enormous statue but has since closed down. The statue is not accessible to the public and is falling apart. It must even serve as target practice for someone because it is full of bullet holes.[5]

The turn of the century seems a good time to stop and survey Lincoln scholarship. Boritt gives some reasons why this is necessary: "The story stays alive, and though some would stuff and mount him, he won't let us. It is a cliché by now yet still true that history is a never-ending conversation between the past and the present, and among Lincoln scholars the goal still is—some will call it anachronistic—to find the truth. So it is good that our cab stops and we are forced to get out and take stock." Only Boritt could put together a book that would "take stock" so well.[6]

NOTES

1. Gabor S. Boritt, ed., *The Lincoln Enigma: The Changing Faces of an American Icon* (New York: Oxford University Press, 2001), ix–x.
2. Robert V. Bruce, "The Riddle of Death" in ibid., 130–45, 144.
3. Jean H. Baker, "Mary and Abraham: A Marriage" in ibid., 36–55, 37; see Michael Burlingame, *The Inner World of Abraham Lincoln* (Urbana: University of Illinois Press, 1994), and Douglas L. Wilson, *Honor's Voice: The Transformation of Abraham Lincoln* (New York: Knopf, 1998).
4. Douglas L. Wilson, "Young Man Lincoln" in Boritt, 20–35, 35.
5. Harold Holzer and Gabor Boritt, "Epilogue: Lincoln in 'Modern' Art" in ibid., 146–277, 214–15, 208–9, 218–19, 252–53.
6. Boritt, xvii.

Blood on the Moon: The Assassination of Abraham Lincoln

AUTHOR: Edward Steers Jr.
PUBLISHED: 2001
GENRE: Assassination

With the publication of William A. Tidwell's *Come Retribution* in 1988, the study of the assassination underwent a paradigm shift. This book argued the Confederate government was involved with Booth and his conspirators. In 1995 the author pushed this argument to the limit in *April '65* by arguing Confederate partisan leader John Mosby was on his way to meet John Wilkes Booth after the assassination. While these works were not convincing to all, they did raise a number of questions. Nobody could deny the amount of Tidwell's original research, and his theory became the major competitor of the notion that Booth and his cohorts had acted alone.[1]

What was needed was a synthesis of the best of Tidwell's material and the assassination itself in a single volume. Edward Steers Jr. has taken this research and his own to create the most convincing account of the assassination ever produced in *Blood on the Moon: The Assassination of Abraham Lincoln*. He argues convincingly that Booth could not have succeeded putting together his conspiracy without the help of Confederate agents in Canada. He also takes on some of the persistent myths of the assassination, like the "innocence" of Samuel Mudd and the illegality of the trials of the conspirators.

The roots of the assassination most likely go back to the establishment of Confederate spies in Canada. In 1864 Jefferson Davis decided to establish agents there to interfere in the presidential election. He also wanted them to cause as much harm to the Northern

297

war effort as possible using any means, fair or foul. In a stunning chapter titled "The Black Flag Is Raised," Steers shows even biological warfare was attempted by trying to infect the North with yellow fever from contaminated clothing. This may not jibe with the romantic image of the Confederate leadership, but this romanticism is something Steers feels is long overdue for a reevaluation.[2]

At some point Booth came to these men with his plan to capture President Lincoln. These men had connections to the spy system in southern Maryland, an area Booth would have to navigate if he wanted to bring Lincoln from Washington to Richmond. As Steers writes, "The key to any effort to reach Richmond lay in southern Maryland and her people. Here one could travel as safely as could be expected. Occupied by Federal troops, the area was also home to forces friendly to the Confederate cause. . . . The people of southern Maryland were as staunchly Confederate as the people of Richmond." The Confederates in Canada gave Booth a letter of introduction to one of the chief spies in this area, John Surratt. Surratt introduced Booth to Dr. Mudd and others who would help him in his plot of capturing Lincoln. The letter is of supreme importance. If Booth did not have it, he would not have had the connections and the help he needed to plan his escape route.[3]

At some point the plan turned to assassination. Some of the conspirators were able to escape the noose by claiming they knew about only the kidnapping plot and not the assassination. Whether Booth decided to change the plan on his own or at the behest of others cannot be proved either way. Steers hints of a possible connection with a plot to blow up the White House with explosives but does not state he can prove it.[4]

The Mudd family has argued for decades that Dr. Samuel Mudd was innocent. He was simply doing his duty as a doctor in helping an injured man on the night of the assassination. However, according to Steers, "There are too many fingers pointing in the direction of Mudd's guilt." The chapter on Mudd shows how he lied throughout his ordeal and how absurd the story he told investigators was. The truth is, there is not much room to argue the doctor's innocence without obscuring the facts.[5]

The military trials of the accused have long been assumed to be illegal and a gross injustice. Steers ably comes to their defense. When examining the law and the situation then existing, he finds nothing unusual in the proceedings. In fact, they were the best course the government could have taken. "No matter how one compares a military trial with a civilian trial, the real difference between the two forms in July of 1865 was the belief by the government that a civil trial would result in jury nullification due to strong Southern sympathies in the civil population of the District of Columbia." The government did not have much of a choice with a bitter Civil War just ending and a potential jury pool from the losers of that war.[6]

Steers is quite right when he states, "When Booth entered the presidential box at Ford's Theatre on the night of April 14, 1865, he held a small derringer in his hand. While it was Booth's hand that held the gun, there were many fingers on the trigger." After reading this book, it would be hard to argue with that conclusion. *Blood on the Moon* will take its place as the "classic" study of the assassination for this generation.[7]

NOTES

1. See William A. Tidwell, James O. Hall, and David Winfred Gaddy, *Come Retribution: The Confederate Secret Service and the Assassination of Lincoln* (Jackson: University of Mississippi Press, 1988); and William Tidwell, *April '65: Confederate Covert Action in the American Civil War* (Kent, Ohio: Kent State University Press, 1995).
2. Edward Steers Jr., *Blood on the Moon: The Assassination of Abraham Lincoln* (Lexington: University Press of Kentucky, 2001), 46, 39–59.
3. Ibid., 64, 73.
4. Ibid., 90–91.
5. Ibid., 145, 144–54; for a definitive case for Mudd's guilt, see Edward Steers Jr., *His Name Is Still Mudd: The Case Against Dr. Samuel Alexander Mudd* (Gettysburg: Thomas, 1997).
6. Steers, *Blood on the Moon*, 223.
7. Ibid., 7.

Lincoln's Virtues: An Ethical Biography

AUTHOR: William Lee Miller
PUBLISHED: 2002
GENRE: Biography

A N HONEST politician is thought to be an oxymoron. Lincoln was a successful professional politician his entire adult life. Was he able to do it ethically? The last book considered here attempts to answer this question. William Lee Miller's *Lincoln's Virtues: An Ethical Biography* views Lincoln through the lens of morality. Miller feels it is possible to do so because "Abraham Lincoln turns out to have been a man who thought more, and expressed himself more often, on right and wrong, on the better and the worse, in human conduct, than one might have anticipated." It is true that honesty is part of the Lincoln legend, but Miller shows the real picture is not that of a simple do-gooder. The real Lincoln was a deep thinker on the nature of both morality and ethics.[1]

Often writers will get around the political aspect of Lincoln's life by stating he was a politician before he became president, but once in Washington he became a "statesman." Miller believes this is a fallacy. "But although, to be sure, Lincoln changed, as we all do, and kept learning, as some do—I believe Lincoln learned a great deal—I suggest, nevertheless, that there was on this point no radical discontinuity in his life. Having the awareness and doing the deeds that are encompassed by the term 'politician' would be essential to his achievement." Miller points out that even when Lincoln was supposedly a "statesman," he was at the height of his political powers. Lin-

300

coln was the same man his whole life, and inventing some amazing transformation upon his election to the presidency is unhistorical.[2]

Miller deftly scorns those who believe Lincoln had complete freedom of action as president. He writes, "Weighing goods and evils against each other is an appropriate method in a wide range of social and political questions—more so than a popular moralism with its premature absolutes and 'principles' may grant. In a giant social collaboration like national life, compromise is necessary and usually worthy." Critics who often assert Lincoln should have acted on slavery sooner and was a reluctant emancipator conveniently forget that issuing an Emancipation Proclamation before the country was ready would have ended all hope of freedom in the foreseeable future.[3]

There were times Lincoln realized that compromise was no longer an option. Miller compares Lincoln to Martin Luther at these times. Luther once said to the Catholic Church, "Here I stand: I can do no other." Lincoln could be just as inflexible. Miller points out, "Lincoln, the prudent and responsible calculator, reached a moment like that more than once in the years 1860–1865. In 1864 he would write of the promise of freedom to black Union soldiers, 'and the promise being made, must be kept.' In his last Annual Message he would insist that he would return no one to slavery, and that 'if the people should make it an executive duty to reenslave such persons, another, and not I, must be the instrument to perform it.'"[4]

Lincoln's ambition is so often highlighted, it has become a given. In one of the funniest quotes from a Lincoln book, Miller writes, "There is, in fact, a quotation from Herndon that has become a cliché, about Lincoln's ambition being 'a little engine that knew no rest.' When you read a steady diet of Lincoln interpretations and you see on the page the word 'ambition,' you say to yourself, Here comes that engine again, and sure enough, the quotation from Herndon comes chugging along hereafter." The quote from Herndon is so pithy that biographers just cannot resist it.[5]

Miller judges Lincoln's ambition a necessary attribute. "Had Lincoln been simply an honest, kindly, modest, 'humble' person . . . who always told the truth and took great trouble to return your pennies and helped you home when you were drunk in the snow, but who out of his humility never put himself forward or sought preference or argued against you or tried to organize to get votes to beat you . . . the moral loss to the world would have been immense." *Ambition* is a morally ambiguous term. Saying Lincoln was ambitious is not akin to saying he was immoral. In fact, Miller is arguing that Lincoln's ambition was inherently moral because it allowed him to leave the world a better place.[6]

Miller's book is one of the more enjoyable reads in Lincoln literature. His dry wit permeates the book. *Lincoln's Virtues* is a welcome antidote to the newer books purporting to show the "real" Lincoln by highlighting his politician status. Miller concedes Lincoln was a politician but refuses to believe this prevented him from being the truly moral and ethical man he was. "There would never come a time when Abraham Lincoln abandoned the role of politician, or rose above it to some allegedly higher moral realm. What he did instead as a lifelong politician was to realize that role's fullest moral possibilities."[7]

NOTES

1. William Lee Miller, *Lincoln's Virtues: An Ethical Biography* (New York: Knopf, 2002), xvi.
2. Ibid., 115, 115.
3. Ibid., 438.
4. Martin Luther as quoted in ibid., 438; Miller, 438–39.
5. Miller, 64–65.
6. Ibid., 65.
7. Ibid., 115.

INDEX OF AUTHORS

INDEX OF GENRES

Printed in the USA
CPSIA information can be obtained
at www.ICGtesting.com
JSHW022209140824
68134JS00018B/950